TURNING CONFLICT
INTO PROFIT

A ROADMAP FOR RESOLVING
PERSONAL AND ORGANIZATIONAL DISPUTES

TURNING CONFLICT INTO PROFIT

A ROADMAP FOR RESOLVING PERSONAL AND ORGANIZATIONAL DISPUTES

Larry Axelrod and Rowland (Roy) Johnson

The University of Alberta Press

Published by

The University of Alberta Press
Ring House 2
Edmonton, Alberta, Canada
T6G 2E1

**Library and Archives Canada
Cataloguing in Publication**

Axlerod, Larry, 1959-
    Turning conflict into profit :
    a roadmap for resolving
personal and organizational differences /
Larry Axelrod and
Rowland (Roy) Johnson.

        Includes bibliographical references
        and index.
        ISBN 0-88864-440-X

    1. Conflict management.
2. Interpersonal relations.
I. Johnson, Rowland, 1967- II. Title.
    HD42.A96 2005   303.6'9
    C2005-901128-9

The University of Alberta Press is
committed to protecting our natural
environment. As part of our efforts,
this book is printed on Enviro Paper:
it contains 100% post-consumer recycled
fibres and is acid- and chlorine-free.

The University of Alberta Press gratefully
acknowledges the support received for
its publishing program from The Canada
Council for the Arts. The University of
Alberta Press also gratefully acknowledges
the financial support of the Government
of Canada through the Book Publishing
Industry Development Program (BPIDP)
and from the Alberta Foundation for the
Arts for its publishing activities.

All rights reserved.
First edition, first printing, 2005.
Printed and bound in Canada by AGMV
Marquis Printing Inc., Monmagy, Quebec.
Copyediting by Brendan Wild.
Indexing by Judy Dunlop.
Interior design by Nine Point Design.

Canada Council   Conseil des Arts
for the Arts   du Canada

Canada

Contents

Preface

GOT CONFLICT? Has conflict with co-workers, colleagues, managers, employees, or others undermined your productivity, blocked your success, or even made you ill? If so, you share this experience with many others who experience conflict as volatile and harmful—as an obstacle to success and profit.

For our purposes, *profit* represents the goals and aspirations we pursue in our professional endeavours. These pursuits include the more explicit financial concept of profit in terms of "revenue less expenditures," but they also include outcomes such as social contribution, professional growth, and personal satisfaction and achievement.

Conflict tends to make us want to either *lean away* from the threat or *charge into* it with all the force we can muster. However, drawing on principles of psychology and sociology, and years of practical experience as conflict resolution consultants, we demonstrate that the best path through conflict to profit is to take a surprising third approach: *leaning into* conflict. Consider the following non-work situation familiar to most of us:

> A six-year old boy went out to dinner with his family for a special occasion. He was a challenging and, at times, defiant youngster. When he arrived at the fancy restaurant, he proceeded to lie down on the floor in a high-traffic aisle and wouldn't get up. A classic struggle ensued. At first, the family tried to ignore him and avoid the whole situation. When he did not move, and as others started to become annoyed, his parents attempted to coax, persuade, command, and eventually threaten him so he would get up and

"act properly." They said, "If you don't get up you'll have to sit in the car during dinner!" In response, the boy became even more resistant and obstinate. Now what to do?

Certainly it was wrong for the boy to lie on the floor. However, using power and coercion to resolve the conflict and to overcome his resistance was clearly not working. The boy had figured out that his parents would never leave him alone in the car for hours. Their use of physical force in the past had only reinforced the child's defiance today, and clearly it could not be used when he grew older.

Observing the interaction, a relative approached the boy and, instead of commanding him or chastising him, simply asked him why he was lying on the floor. The boy said, "I'm tired, hungry, and have no energy." The relative rubbed his chin thoughtfully and asked him if he wanted something to eat so that he'd be less hungry and could get some energy. The boy nodded and the relative gave him some bread. After the boy swallowed, the relative pointed out to him that he should now have some energy and that he could now get up and move to his chair. The boy thought for a moment, got up, and took his seat.

This case demonstrates the inclination we have to either lean away from or charge into conflict and resistance. If we can avoid conflict, we usually do. If we cannot avoid or do not want to avoid conflict, we fight. Yet, by approaching conflicts with neither a flight nor fight impulse, but with curiosity, mutually satisfying solutions can often be found. In the above scenario, only after the boy's resistance was overcome would the door be effectively opened to discuss the problems associated with lying on the floor in a restaurant, such as safety risks, denying his family a good time, and postponing his getting a meal. At this point the child could be instructed that he cannot do it again, not simply because the authority figure says so, but also because his conduct created real risks to himself and others and kept him from his own goal of enjoying a good meal with his family. In the final analysis, the relative's approach to this struggle resulted in greater understanding of and for the boy, improved relationships, and a fun evening out.

In doing mediation, coaching, consulting, and training, we frequently hear about and observe this type of struggle in professional situations and relationships. We see the strong tendency of those in power, as well as those with little power, to avoid conflict and hope it will go away. We observe parties who simply ignore each other while they allow a conflict to fester and grow. Alternatively, we see people use coercion and threats to "motivate" behaviour while their targets use resistance and passive-aggression in response. In one case, two workers had not spoken to each other for eight years. They had, however, spoken consistently and explicitly *about* each other to their co-workers over that time period, eroding morale and driving valuable people out of the division and organization. We have seen the productivity and health of people and groups slowly erode due to conflict, as well as bring about crises that lead to devastating consequences.

There is a better way! We can prevent conflict from leaving a legacy of harm to ourselves, to others, and to the organizations with which we work. We can use conflict to inspire us to achieve new learning, innovation, and growth. To profit from conflict, this book will advance your understanding of conflict, explore how you and others react to conflict, and identify how you may unwittingly be sabotaging your own success, achievement, and happiness.

In this book, we offer insights into these critical dynamics. We discuss the nature of conflict and describe how we can effectively approach conflict by *leaning into* it to create profit for our organizations and ourselves. We translate research, theory, and cases into practical steps for resolving conflict. In addition, we ground our examination of conflict by referring to real conflict situations that we have encountered in the various organizations with which we have worked. In some cases we have altered the characteristics of the involved parties or their setting in order to maintain our commitment to confidentiality. In other instances, we have amalgamated two or more cases into a single case study to enhance the relevance of the situation for the topic being discussed. In all cases, the situations we describe have actually happened and these real-life experiences have greatly informed the thinking and perspectives presented in the book.

To visually represent the complete conflict-to-profit transformation, we have developed a model based on the image of an hourglass. This image is used as a metaphor for the narrow path one must take to move from the trap of conflict, on one side, to the profit track on the other. An hourglass symbolizes important aspects of this flow, including the roles of timing, balance, and the constricted nature of the transition. In the final chapter we use the hourglass model to portray the interrelationships among those concepts relevant to turning conflict into profit.

This book guides you in inverting the hourglass, breaking free of the Conflict Trap, and travelling through the narrow aperture to professional achievement and profit.

FIGURE P.1

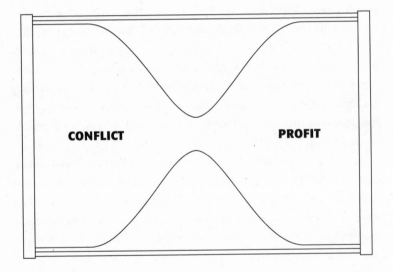

Acknowledgements

THE ORIGINAL INSPIRATION FOR THIS BOOK came from frequent requests we received from workshop participants and clients for a resource that described the ideas and approaches that we apply in our consulting work. We thank all the engaging and spirited people who asked for this resource. Our thanks also go to the many colleagues of ours (too many to name) who have shared their wisdom, energy, and knowledge with us over the recent years.

More specifically, we want to recognize the efforts of several close colleagues who willingly invested their time and energy to help this book become a reality. Our thanks go to Leah Benner for her time researching concepts, organizing references, and offering valued input on the emerging manuscript; to Robert Laing, Karen Rolston, Marilee Sigal, and Duncan Wilson for their time, enthusiasm, and sage guidance reviewing initial drafts of the manuscript; to the copyeditor, Brendan Wild, for preparing the final manuscript; to the reviewers for their advice and enthusiastic support for this project; and to all those affiliated with the University of Alberta Press for their professionalism, support, and assistance in turning our manuscript into this book.

In addition, we want to thank our spouses, families, and friends for being there for us as we spent many days and nights thinking, planning, writing, re-writing, and editing the manuscript. Your positive and unwavering support through this process helped ensure its completion.

Finally, we want to acknowledge the thousands of people with whom we have had the good fortune to teach, coach, advise, counsel, and confront. Your stories and challenges have revealed to us the complexity of human interaction and the nature of the conflicts we all face in our personal and work lives. You have also demonstrated time and again the power we each have to have to learn, grow, and change—to move from conflict to healthier relationships and greater achievements. We appreciate the opportunity to have been part of your lives.

Larry Axelrod and Rowland (Roy) Johnson

PART
1

THE FOUNDATIONS AND FALLACIES OF CONFLICT

1

Conflict Defined

Steve and Eleanor are work partners at a small engineering firm. Eleanor is frustrated with Steve because he never puts in his fair share of overtime, leaving her with the responsibility of trying to keep their project on schedule. Steve is becoming upset with Eleanor because she has become very critical of his work lately. They used to be the up-and-coming stars of the company, but they now feel trapped in an unproductive and strained partnership and have not come up with a new idea in months.

David and Sarah, two assembly line workers, got into an argument over the person David has started dating. Sarah keeps criticizing David's choice of women, and jokes with him that he can do better. David wishes Sarah would just shut up.

Margaret, a nurse manager, has been offered a promotion to Unit Director. She would like the added responsibility and compensation of the role, but she also has been told she will need to work more hours. She is concerned about the impact on her family life.

Kenneth, a financial analyst, wants a promotion to handle more challenging business ventures. His boss likes him, but he does not think that Kenneth is quite ready for the promotion. He does not want to give him more responsibility than he can handle for fear that Kenneth will lose his self-confidence and might cause some damage by making a bad decision.

Lois, the principal of a private school, has to decide who will teach what courses in the next term. She feels the energy in the school has dipped over the last few terms and wants to shake things up. She knows certain teachers will resist the changes and, as a change management strategy, she is keeping them in the dark as long as possible to avoid conflict. She has told the more receptive teachers of her plans and of their new assignments and mandated that they keep the information confidential.

DO THESE SITUATIONS INVOLVE CONFLICT? If so, what aspects of these situations define the conflict, and what effects might each conflict have on the workplace and the efficiency of the organization? We begin our exploration of *Turning Conflict into Profit* by defining what *conflict* is and considering its cultural meanings in our society. To know how to tap the potential for growth, discovery, and achievement that exists in conflict, we need first to understand what it is and how it has come to be viewed in western culture.

According to the *Oxford Dictionary*, conflict is defined as a "clashing" of opposed principles or interests. "Interests," in this concise but ambiguous definition, represent the needs, desires, or goals of an individual or collection of individuals (e.g., a work team, organization, or nation). Hocker and Wilmot, in their book *Interpersonal Conflict*, define conflict more thoroughly as "an expressed struggle, between at least two interdependent parties who perceive incompatible goals, scarce resources, and interference from the other party in achieving their goals."[1] Forsyth defined conflict as a striking together with force and described it as it applies to groups when the actions or beliefs of one or more members of a group are unacceptable to—and hence are resisted by—one or more of the other group members.[2] From our view, each of these definitions includes important elements of the conflict experience, but they either lack specificity or overstate some aspects. We need to apply the conceptual understanding to the reality of conflict in workplaces if we are to better understand the full cultural meaning of conflict in our individual and organizational lives.

Based on our involvement in thousands of conflict situations, we contend that conflict involves two central characteristics:

(a) A perceived contradiction of interests in which one or more needs, goals, or desires are perceived to be threatened

(b) A situation of interdependence in which the attainment of one's interests is dependent to some extent on the choices or behaviour of others

Thus the central concepts involved in creating conflict include *contradiction of interests, perception of threat or loss, mutuality, and interdependency*. In addition, conflict involves a certain energy or force and a dose of resistance. Conflict is not simple disagreement. For example, two people arguing about who will win the Stanley Cup or the Super Bowl are not necessarily in conflict. Nor are two people who have an intellectual debate about the merits of capital punishment, or which candidate should win the next election. In each of these cases, there may be a clash of opinions, and this clash may become quite volatile; however, there may not be any real "interests" at stake other than the psychological desire, perhaps, to be right. If parties do not have an investment in the outcome, if the outcome does not threaten their interests, and if the achievement of a particular outcome is not to some extent dependent on the other party, the debate may simply be an intellectual exploration of possibilities. On the other hand, if either party has bet money on the Super Bowl, has established part of their identity as a Canadiens' fan, or is ideologically committed to the electoral party leader, they may very well experience themselves in conflict with the other person.

Conflict is not simply about competition, although competition can contribute to conflict. Consider two people vying for the same job. Although they are clearly in competition with each other, and only one of them can win the competition (i.e., get the job), they are not really in conflict with each other. They are not interdependent: neither one has direct control over the pending decision and cannot therefore be considered to be in a position to block, threaten, or put at risk the other person's needs or goals.

To illustrate these points, consider a case in which a surgeon and an anaesthesiologist were reportedly in conflict. The surgeon was upset with the length of time it took the anaesthesiologist to anaesthetize patients, thereby limiting the number of surgeries the surgeon could complete in a day. The conflict materialized when the surgeon began to publicly criticize the anaesthesiologist's competence and skill. Key interests at stake were financial achievement, for the surgeon, and professional reputation and job security, for the anaesthesiologist. Also at stake were emotional interests, such as maintenance of self-esteem, feelings of respect, and financial security. The individuals also shared certain interests (although they lost focus of these while in the midst of the conflict) such as ensuring safe and effective surgical outcomes for their patients.

This situation involved a contradiction of interests as perceived by both parties. As well, each party had a certain level of control over the attainment of the other's interests. The anaesthesiologist could try to work faster; the surgeon could stop denigrating the anaesthesiologist. As with many conflicts, an external factor contributed to the conflict—in this case the compensation method. The surgeon was remunerated according to how many patients he operated on. The anaesthesiologist was paid a salary by the hospital based on time worked, not number of procedures. This interdependent clash of interests had turned into vitriolic attacks on each other's professionalism, and had significantly disrupted the efficiency and the working relationships among all the staff in the operating room.

Two Types of Interests in Conflict: Practical and Psychological

This situation highlights the types of interests that may be at stake in conflict. From our view, the concept of interests can be divided into two basic categories: the *practical* and the *psychological*. Practical interests include such tangible needs as physical safety and comfort, relief from hunger and thirst, health and well-being, and accrual of financial security. Practical interests can involve one's individual needs (e.g., money, safety, credibility) or the interests of individuals or groups that one has a mandate to serve or protect (e.g., nurses for patients, teachers for students, managers for an organization, board members for stakeholders or shareholders, politicians for the electorate). Practical interests can be viewed as those that parallel the first two levels of Maslow's Hierarchy of Needs, a psychological theory that suggests that all human needs manifest in five tiers and that we can only focus on more advanced needs when the more basic needs in our lives have been satisfied.[3]

Psychological interests involve the range of social, esteem, and personal growth needs that are more consistent with levels 3, 4, and 5 of Maslow's hierarchy. They involve the affective, emotional, and principles-based parts of the self (e.g., the need to be needed, the need to be respected, the need for healthy relationships, and the importance of values). Although we can separate the practical from the psychological, in reality they are closely linked and all conflicts involve the perception of interests in both categories as being in jeopardy.

To demonstrate this confluence of interests we can refer to another type of conflict that arises in health care but which also parallels the functioning of teams in many workplaces. This situation involves a group of health care professionals who are expected to function as a team (e.g., doctors, nurses, social workers, physical and occupational therapists, hospital managers); they come together to decide when a patient is ready for discharge. In terms of practical interests, all parties in this decision share at some level the interest of serving the health and well-being of the patient. However, it is notable how often these teams cannot agree on a decision, and how volatile and personal the ensuing discussions can become. When conflict arises due to disagreement, team members start to characterize each other, generally behind the others' backs, as "unethical," "cruel," "incompetent," "ruthless," "uncaring," and so forth. This symptomatic response to conflict parallels decision-making processes in other industries, such as deciding on the readiness of a new product for distribution, or whether or not to implement a new product line, merger, or computer system.

On the surface this disagreement is seen in terms of different opinions about the readiness of the patient for discharge. In reality, though, this type of conflict has its roots in differing interests, the perception of interests, and expectations about how decisions should be made (which we will discuss later). Interests include both the practical and the psychological, many of which are not identified openly but which nevertheless affect the perspective of each individual. For example, the doctor may lose billing opportunities if the patient stays in the hospital, since he cannot operate on another patient until the bed is free. Alternatively, he may be concerned about malpractice if the patient leaves too early. The nurse may feel a personal obligation to make sure each patient is completely well before discharge. He or she may also just want to be seen as an equal member of the team and not as subservient to the doctor, and hence disagrees as a means of asserting individuality. The manager may feel budgetary pressures, or may have her salary linked with achieving fiscal targets and therefore needs to move patients out of the hospital as quickly as possible. All involved individuals want to be respected for their differing professional experience, expertise, and positions. All have reputations to protect. All of their interests will influence their opinions about the patient's readiness for discharge, the appropriateness of the discharge, and their approach to the team decision-making process. In addition, team members' historic relationships with and views about each other will affect their approaches to the team discussion and will shape their views, positively or negatively, about each other's perspectives. They all share one common interest, and yet their other, more contradictory interests are a common cause of conflict among health care teams.

Thus, in each conflict situation many interests may be at stake. Using the hierarchy of needs structure organized, by Maslow, the following table outlines the range of interests some of our clients describe as being at risk in professional or business conflicts.

FIGURE 1.1
Organizational Hierarchy of Interests

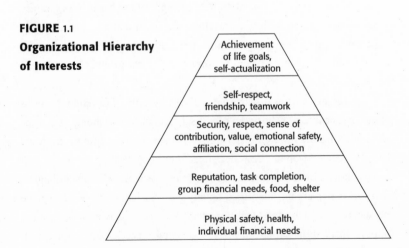

Achievement of life goals, self-actualization

Self-respect, friendship, teamwork

Security, respect, sense of contribution, value, emotional safety, affiliation, social connection

Reputation, task completion, group financial needs, food, shelter

Physical safety, health, individual financial needs

Ultimately, if we perceive that any of these interests are threatened for us or for those we have a mandate to protect, we will resist the opposing force that has control over that interest. We become motivated to have the interest satisfied.

Conflict Is a Natural Part of Life

From the moment of birth we encounter conflict in our lives. We consistently find ourselves in situations where our needs and desires diverge from those of the people in our lives—our parents, our relatives, our teachers, our neighbours, our friends, our enemies, our children—the list goes on and on, depending on the range of people who may have some relation to our lives. It is not surprising, then, that conflict arises as a natural part of work life, where interdependence between workers is often critical to success but choices about who we work for and with are often beyond our control.

Yet conflict itself is not the problem! It is how we respond to conflict that is the real issue. Most people report to us that they view conflict as unpleasant and negative. As many of our workshop participants and clients have stated, "I'll do anything to avoid conflict." They perceive conflict solely as a threat rather than as a natural and unavoidable part of life. When we want to avoid conflict, or when it takes us by surprise, its occurrence results in our feeling disoriented and in crisis, dismayed that our daily lives have been involuntarily altered.

However, it is helpful to acknowledge that we will inevitably encounter situations where our interests appear to be at odds with others', and when we have competing internal needs. Consider the following examples:

- A manufacturer wants to keep costs at a minimum while its employees want to earn as much as they can.
- The CEO wants a manager to work overtime to complete a project while the manager has promised his child he would attend the school play.
- The surgeon wants to work faster to make more money while the anaesthesiologist wants to work more slowly to ensure patient safety.
- Many of us want to lose weight, but we also want to eat foods that we enjoy and that sustain us emotionally, not just physically.

- Leaders want to be fair to employees, but they also want to exercise personal discretion as they make employment-related decisions.

Life is, after all, a constant negotiation that aims to meet needs and achieve goals. The only point at which we no longer encounter barriers to meeting our needs is that point at which we no longer have needs: the point at which we die. We pursue the self-assigned but impossible task of meeting our needs armed with the assumption that we should be able to do so unfettered by the needs of our co-workers, colleagues, or competitors. When we ignore their needs, and consequently encounter their resistance to our own, we experience that conflict as a threat. When conflict is interpreted as a threat, the result is that we seek to avoid it (the *leaning away* predisposition) or defeat it (the *charging into* predisposition). Experiencing conflict as threat, rather than as an opportunity, roots us in the conflict and perpetuates the impression that conflict is negative.

Author and philosopher Karl Jaspers articulated his observation of conflict's inevitability in this way:

> But we cannot avoid conflict, conflict with society, other individuals and with oneself. Conflicts may be the sources of defeat, lost life and a limitation of our potentiality but they may also lead to greater depth of living and the birth of more far-reaching unities, which flourish in the tensions that engender them.[4]

Ultimately, it is the emotional response (e.g., fear, anger, loss, resentment) that results from a need being threatened or denied that is experienced as problematic and negative. It is the often-subconscious choice made about how to respond to a conflict that is crucial in determining whether or not we get trapped in the conflict, or if we profit by using the conflict as a means to discover growth and achievement.

We want to stress that although we encounter many people in conflict who ardently deny any emotional investment in the conflict, we have learned from direct experience that it is the emotional, psychological elements of a conflict that fuel what we call the *Conflict Trap*. This trap is characterized by the conflict responses of denial, detachment, and despair. In well over 90 percent of the nearly two thousand conflict situations we have dealt with, it was the psychological interests and emotional aspects of the conflicts that created the strongest barriers to achieving resolutions. This was true for men as well as women, CEOs as well as front-line workers, professionals and labourers, financial experts and artists, and so on. The importance of individuals' psychological reactions to conflict has been neglected in much of the literature that deals with conflict. However, it is crucial that we appreciate and understand the psychological elements that contribute to conflict if we are to find solutions that maximize outcomes and minimize harmful impacts.

Two Sources of Conflict

Many academics and authors have classified the sources of conflict into dichotomies. Some describe conflict as a tension between the priority of maintaining a cordial and cooperative relationship between individuals and the priority of getting the task done. Others distinguish between personal aspects and substantive aspects of conflict. Although these distinctions are helpful, from our view all conflicts are about relationships and tasks. All conflicts are personal—at least to the people involved—and they are about substance. Consider an employee who was just told he is about to be laid off. The employer will often add the clarifying statement, "It isn't personal, you know," intending to help the employee feel better. The employee's likely response may be, "What do you mean it isn't personal?" in light of the fact that his personal life is about to be dramatically altered. The conflict builds from there.

Based on our experience, we propose here a more descriptive dichotomy to clarify the distinction between *process* conflict and *outcome* conflict. We offer this categorization as a means to shift the focus away from interpreting all conflict as deeply personal and emotional events to a more objective assessment of the practical issues and interests at stake.

To illustrate, try the following exercise: Sit next to a partner. Place a blank sheet of paper in front of you and prepare for both of you to use a single writing utensil (i.e., place one of each of your hands on one pencil or pen). Without any talking, draw a house.

We usually set aside several minutes to complete the exercise. Typically what happens is that each person waits a moment to see what his or her drawing partner will do. Soon, one person starts the drawing process and the other follows along until the first person stops, signalling that it is time for the other person to take control. The drawing process continues, with each person adding new elements to the house. The houses often end up with a similar look (a square frame, an A-shaped roof) and with similar features (windows, a chimney with curly smoke, a door, a sidewalk, trees).

In the exercise, tension arises because two interdependent people seek to create a shared *outcome* and *process*. The outcome source is what the house should look like. If the parties disagree about what the house should look like—which occurs more frequently when this exercise is done with multinational groups—the writing utensil will carry a degree of pressure or tension as different views are pursued, as will the parties, typically in terms of confusion and frustration.

Metaphorically, the house represents the outcome of any project, decision, or task. In the discharge–planning example, the outcome is the decision to discharge the patient or not.

The process in the exercise is how the house gets drawn. In other words: who draws what, when, and in what way. In the discharge–planning example, the process involves who should be involved in the decision, perceptions of authority and expertise, and other factors that contribute to how the involved parties go about making the decision.

All conflicts can be broken down into differences about process or differences about outcomes, or both. Many complainants we have worked with have been far more upset about the *process* or about "not being consulted" than they were about the *outcome* or the decision that was made. Conflicts remained volatile, however, because the focus remained on the outcome differences while the key interests connected to process issues were neglected.

To illustrate this distinction using an international situation, the conflict between the Israeli and Palestinian leadership involves outcome differences, such as beliefs regarding historic rights to a piece of land, the right of a nation to exist, questions about how to divide up the land base, and how to ensure security and stability for all parties. It also involves process differences about who should be involved in negotiations, what format should be used for negotiations, and what interim steps should occur during negotiations. Each source of conflict has played a role in impairing the achievement of a mutually acceptable outcome.

In business-related situations, we regularly experience both process conflicts, often perceived as issues of inclusion, and outcome conflicts, often perceived in terms of fairness. The following table presents common psychological and practical interests as they manifest themselves in terms of the two sources of conflict, as well as the key emotional response to conflict that can arise if one's interests are not met.

FIGURE 1.2

Key Interests at Stake for Different Sources of Conflict, and the Primary Emotional Impacts if Interests Are Not Met

SOURCE OF CONFLICT

		Process	Outcome
TYPE OF INTEREST	**Psychological**	Reduction of Anxiety	Happiness
		Self-respect	Sense of Accomplishment
		Self-esteem	Job Satisfaction
		FEAR if not met	RESENTMENT if not met
	Practical	Sense of Fairness	Financial Reward
		Own Interests Considered	Reputation
		Other's Interests Known	Relationships
		if not met, ANGER	if not met, LOSS

In terms of "process conflicts," key psychological interests include avoidance of anxiety, and enhanced self-respect and self-esteem that derive from being included in a decision process. If you are not included in the process, you will experience some level of fear and paranoia prompted by the uncertainty created by this exclusion. Key practical interests at stake in process conflicts include a sense of confidence in the fairness of the process, knowledge that your own interests and ideas are being heard and considered, and the opportunity to hear other parties' interests and ideas. If process conflict undermines the achievement of these interests, you tend to get angry at the injustice of the process.

In terms of "outcome conflicts," key psychological interests at stake include a sense of accomplishment, job satisfaction, and an overall sense of happiness with one's work situation. If psychological interests are not met, you tend to become resentful of the other parties who appear to be satisfied with their outcomes. Key practical interests at stake include financial rewards, professional reputation, and stable and well-functioning relationships. If the outcome of a conflict results in your practical interests not being met, a primary initial response will be a strong sense of loss. We observe this sense of loss in individuals when organizations downsize, when promotions are given to others, and when unwelcome transfers occur—that is, when any change process results in an individual's practical interests not being met. This sense of loss leads to its own emotional grief cycle.

When the key interests at stake for conflicted parties are met, the Conflict Trap is opened and profit is far more achievable. We refer to this process as *convergence* because the disparate interests of involved parties converge toward mutually acceptable resolutions. When key interests are not met, the conflict will rev up and the parties and their organizations may find themselves trapped in a situation dominated by fear, anger, resentment, and a perpetual sense of loss. We refer to this dynamic as *divergence* because the Conflict Trap leads people to dig in their heals, ignore common interests, and focus on battling over perceived divergent needs and goals.

Responses to Conflict are Learned

How people respond to situations of conflict is learned, both in terms of which interests are viewed as priorities and which approaches they employ while pursuing those interests. Much research has focused on outlining the manner in which people respond to conflict, often called conflict styles.[5] Many other resources are available that offer a comprehensive review of conflict styles. For our purposes, suffice it to say that people develop a pattern of response with regard to conflict during their years of upbringing and socialization. The patterns adopted by most people in response to conflict, such as avoidance, accommodation, compromise (leaning away from), or competition (charging into), contribute to keeping them trapped in conflict.

For example, the old saying "spare the rod, spoil the child" suggests that the best way to teach a child to conform, obey, avoid mistakes, or act properly is by charging in with punishment, and the threat and use of physical pain. It suggests that to do otherwise—lean away by accommodating, placating, or avoiding—is to promote an unhealthy sense of power and control in the child over the parent. Those who use aggressive methods to control children refer to this proverb as a justification for the use of physical force. In contrast, the alternative viewpoint, which can be expressed as "swing the rod, suppress the child," suggests that the use of violence and punishment can stifle a child's thinking and expression and thereby create a compliant—albeit anxious and fearful—child.

Either approach shapes a child's response to conflict. Of course, neither statement reveals a complete truth. Neither sparing nor swinging the proverbial rod will necessarily improve behaviour in the long run. Notably, such shaping processes do not stop at puberty; they continue throughout adulthood in organizations, as suggested by the cartoon below.

FIGURE 1.3

"So, does anyone else feel that their needs aren't being met?"

Ultimately, individuals' perceptions of and responses to conflict are shaped by their socialization, in combination with their personalities, as well as the organizational climates in which they work. In the cartoon, the clear goal of the supervisor, the one holding the rod, is to tell the workers that their needs do not matter. As we point out in chapter 3, this approach has harmful, often devastating consequences on people and organizations. Yet, this domineering approach remains in use when compliance is valued more than critical thinking, control more than contribution, and competition more than collaboration. Such tactics continue to be employed even though research clearly indicates that a coercive approach to conflict and leadership leads to compromised insight, inspiration, or investment, and produces diminished profit and achievement. An oppressive and fear-provoking organizational culture can suppress the most well-meaning, confident, and highly placed employee.

Beliefs that Accelerate Conflict in Workplaces

Imagine a society whose residents hold no preconceptions about each other, no expectations of privilege, and no desire to compete in win–lose terms. This imaginary place would be devoid of several key elements that stir conflict into harmful and debilitating outcomes: preconceptions about others, beliefs about one's sense of entitlement, and an overly competitive ideology. These three elements underlie what people expect to find in their workplaces and professional relationships; they directly contribute to the initiation and escalation of most workplace conflict. Similar to certain chemicals and their use to accelerate the speed and intensity of a fire, these belief systems serve as accelerants to naturally occurring individual and organizational conflict.

Consider the following examples:

- A leader believes that members of certain ethnic groups do not possess the qualities necessary to succeed in leadership roles and therefore does not offer serious consideration to members of those ethnicities for available positions. That leader will create more negative conflict than a leader who respects diverse backgrounds and remains open to all potential candidates. Quite often, these prejudicial leaders are not even aware of their own prejudices and typically rationalize their choices to themselves and others on the basis that "those candidates simply do not have the right 'personality' or 'style' for the job."

- The nurse who feels she is entitled to, and therefore expects, respectful communication from physicians at all times, but who then experiences rude and arrogant treatment, will reasonably feel a higher degree of psychological conflict than will her colleague who believes that physicians have more stressful jobs than nurses and therefore expects them to be disrespectful.

- The employee who feels entitled to and therefore expects job security from his company, in exchange for his loyalty, will feel a heightened sense of conflict with the employer if he is "downsized" than will the employee who does not expect to work for the same company all his life.

- The company president who expects her staff to simply follow directives will experience and create more conflict when orders are not simply followed than will a company president who expects her staff to raise concerns, or object to and question directives if they disagree.

In an organizational setting, we refer to the "us versus them" dynamic, or preconceptions about others, as *otherness*. *Otherness* contributes two contrasting accelerants to conflict. The first accelerant involves preconceptions that others are the same as you. If you believe your co-worker thinks the way you do (e.g., values direct communication), and you then find out otherwise (e.g., the person values venting to others), the unexpected clash becomes hotter and more personal. The second accelerant involves preconceptions more commonly understood as prejudice—but in a much broader sense. By *prejudice* we mean preconceived beliefs that one's way of looking, acting, being, and thinking is the "right" way, and that those who look, act, or think differently are fundamentally inferior to oneself. Whether in the form of sexism, racism, ageism, heterosexism, or anti-Semitism, or in other biases and prejudices against particular behaviours (e.g., promiscuity, drinking, cigarette-smoking), prejudice and stereotyping lead people to act in a manner that exacerbates naturally occurring conflicts that arise with others. These beliefs inhibit relationships, create resentment, and diminish the dignity—not to mention the productivity—of the target of these beliefs, and of the organization.

A sense of entitlement leads one to think he deserves, rightly or wrongly, whatever it is that he wants, and this causes one to feel even more conflicted with those who stand in his way. Alexi Yashin, a professional hockey player, sat out an entire season rather than accept a smaller salary than that which he thought he deserved, hurting himself, his team, and his fans. In contrast, baseball player Ken Griffey Jr. accepted less than he was worth on the open market in order to play in his hometown. Our sense of entitlement or self-righteousness clearly contributes to the emergence and escalation of conflict situations and impedes turning conflict into growth. In a survey we conducted with a major hospital in Vancouver, staff reported that wealthy patients constitute one of the most challenging patient groups to work with. Staff explained wealthy individuals tend to be more demanding and convey a sense that they are entitled to quicker and more attentive service than are other patients. Staff reported that these expectations of entitlement could cause a great deal of conflict between themselves and these patients.

A competitive belief system leads people to argue, advocate, and fight for their needs and their needs alone, because, after all, that is how progress and truth are achieved. Social research has demonstrated that competitive people who pursue win–lose outcomes see interdependence in terms of power and that they view co-operation as weak and unintelligent.[6] For them, the experience of conflict produces a kind of "rigid" or "black and white thinking" that restricts judgement and results in an inability to consider alternatives. Writer and philosopher Derrick Jensen makes this observation:

> If you believe the fundamental organizing principle of the world is competition (or if the fundamental organizing principle of your society is competition) you will perceive the world as full of ruthless competitors, all of whom will victimize you if they get the chance. The world as you perceive it will begin to devolve into consisting entirely or almost entirely of victims and perpetrators: those who do, and those who get done to…. Your society will

devolve—not in perception but in all truth—into these roles you have projected onto the world at large. You will begin to believe that everyone is out to get you. And why not? After all, you are certainly out to get them.[7]

This mindset shapes one's understanding of how to act and expectations of how others will act, leading one to always be ready to fight, not just compete, for one's share—whether fair or not. This narcissistic view of the world is illustrated by the following image of a balloon on guard:

FIGURE 1.4

A Narcissist's View of the World

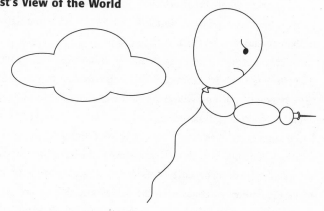

Such belief systems, and the expectations they create, serve as lightening rods that transform naturally occurring clashes of individual or group interests into conflicts that damage the health and achievements of individuals and organizations. Research in psychology has shown that expectations exert a powerful influence on reactions to new events and stimuli.[8] The person who expects certain outcomes is far more likely to experience and cause conflict than is the person who has hopes, dreams, and goals, but does not have preconceived expectations and biases about others, or who holds to blind dogma about win–lose competition as the path to achievement and profit. We will review later how managing expectations is a key strategy in the prevention of negative conflict and for turning natural conflict into profitable outcomes.

Conflict Is about People:
Perspectives, Choices, and Behaviour

Finally, although we agree with the many authors who attribute workplace conflict to systems, group cultures, policies, and other organizational dimensions, we observe that conflict, at its core, is about people—our needs, choices, and behaviour. As suggested by Slaikeu and Hasson, "Conflict itself is not the problem. Unresolved conflict is."[9] However, Slaikeu and Hasson place much of the responsibility for unresolved conflict on the existence of "weak systems." Systems certainly play a role, particularly by supporting the effective resolution of conflict. Yet, whether it is the anaesthesiologist working too deliberately, the leader needing to be right, the co-worker taking credit for the work of others, or the boss suppressing dissent, people must be accountable, and be held accountable, for their individual choices and behaviour.

Far too often we hear people say, "I didn't do anything wrong; everybody does it," or, "It's not my fault; things are just too stressful here," or, "It's hopeless, nothing will change." People at all levels of organizations damage others and themselves because they do not understand what is happening to them or how they can think differently about their conflict situation. The misattribution of the causes of conflict to the systems, policies, and culture of organizations downplays the reality that individuals made the choices or engaged in the behaviours that caused the conflict to emerge. We believe that understanding conflict in terms of individual responses and choices is critical to learning how to adopt new, more constructive approaches to conflict when it arises. Therefore, in this book we focus on the individual forces that bring people into conflict—with themselves and with others—in order to shed insight onto how to change from "fight and flight" responses to approaches that support individual and organizational health and success. We also explore organizational and cultural dimensions of conflict in order to understand the relationship between individuals and organizations and to identify organizational approaches that will support effective conflict prevention and resolution.

Conflict at a Glance

- Conflict is a clash of opposing interests.
- The central concepts involved in creating conflict include *contradiction of interests, perception of threat or loss, mutuality and interdependency.*
- Conflict can be about practical and, or, psychological interests. It is difficult to address higher psychological interests without addressing practical considerations first, as described by psychologist Abraham Maslow.
- Conflict is inevitable, ubiquitous, and natural.
- Conflict sources can be rooted in processes—that is, how interests are addressed or not—or rooted in outcomes—that is, whether or not interests are addressed.
- Our responses to conflict are nurtured and learned responses more than they are part of our instinctive nature. What is not yet learned can be trained, and what has been learned can be re-trained.
- A sense of entitlement, a competitive ideology, and prejudicial beliefs and values influence how we view and respond to conflict, either successfully or unsuccessfully.
- Conflict is driven by the individual experiences that shape our subjective perceptions of others, our working environments, and ourselves—sometimes with little regard for objective truth. Perception is reality.
- Conflict causes and is caused by our natural urge to either *lean away from* (flight) or *charge into* (fight) conflict. The most effective response is neither of these, but is, instead, to *lean into* conflict.

2

The Conflict Trap
DENIAL, DESPAIR, AND DETACHMENT

FIGURE 2.1
The Conflict Trap

THE
CONFLICT
TRAP

The Conflict Trap

SO, WHAT HAPPENS to most of us when we get into conflict? Appreciating that conflict is closely tied to perceptions of threat and loss, we have observed a common pattern of emotional reaction to conflict that parallels the experience of bereavement as described by psychologist Elizabeth Kubler-Ross and funeral specialist William Lamers.[10] Grief psychology describes general stages that most people move through as they work to accept loss. Complicated grief is the condition that arises when a grieving person gets "stuck" in a grief stage, which leads to a number of significant negative impacts on the individual and those around him. This experience of "being stuck" is what we mean when we describe individuals or groups who are in the Conflict Trap.

Applying this concept to workplace conflict, we observe that people, in response to conflict, grieve the loss of relationships, opportunities, security, and other valued psychological and practical interests that are related to their working lives. People also experience a type of anticipatory grief in response to perceived threats to their interests. In this state of anticipatory grief, people are motivated to prevent that grief from occurring by becoming more aggressive in the pursuit of their interests (charging into) or by minimizing the importance of the interests under threat (leaning away from). Although people tend not to perceive their emotional response to threat in terms of grief, we find that they end up going through a parallel process.

Thus, the stages of the Conflict Trap include Denial, Despair, and Detachment. Although we will discuss the three stages in a linear sequence, not all individuals experience them in this order.

FIGURE 2.2
Denial in the Conflict Trap

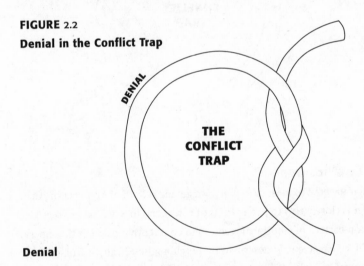

Denial

Karen, the CEO of a large organization, picked up the reference letter for the CFO candidate. The last line of his reference letter read, "He is efficient in the extreme. He does not suffer fools, and to Mr. Bentley, everyone's a fool." What did that mean? With abundant references about his dedication to his work and his ability to turn around the sinking profits of corporations, Karen felt he was right for the job.

That was nine years ago. Shortly after Jim was hired as the CFO, the cracks began to show. Though he surpassed all expectations of his efficiency, expertise, and dedication, the management team was concerned. His direct reports had frequently complained to management in the beginning about his demanding and autocratic leadership style, but Karen wondered if this was not just an adjustment to a new style in the workplace. "Besides," Karen had thought, "maybe I've been holding their hands too much. It will be good to have someone toughen them up a bit." That is when communication completely broke down and people started to lose interest in the work. Some were out of the office more frequently, while others simply quit. New people were hired but did not seem to have the spark of creativity. Then, allegations of unprofessional conduct arose. Karen listened to the complaints but it seemed like the staff were contributing to the problem with Jim. Now, morale is down, absenteeism is up, and though the balance sheet has less red on it, there are no new ideas for the future and the financial outlook is bleak. Karen has just received a letter from a past employee's lawyer stating that the company is being sued for their lack of response in curtailing Jim's "harassment."

Denial is typically the first stage of the Conflict Trap. Characterized by simply failing to acknowledge that a problem is lurking or exists, denial can be both intra-personal and interpersonal. Denial manifests intra-personally as the classic "lying to yourself." In our case example, Karen simply did not want to believe that Jim's downside might be a problem. Even with clear signs, she chose to ignore the potential for interpersonal concerns to arise and to interpret seemingly negative observations and reports in their most positive light.

Denial functions as a defence mechanism. We need to deny certain problems to protect against despair and depression. In many circumstances, denial is a perfectly healthy response. Denying the possibility that I will get run over by a car when I leave my house today allows me to function normally in the world and to prevent myself from obsessing about all the many, awful things that could happen to me. Some mental health issues, however, such as agoraphobia (the fear of being out in public) and obsessive-compulsive disorders, actually pose problems because people are not able protect themselves psychologically through the use of denial.

Any strength, when it is overused, becomes a weakness.

On the other hand, denial in other circumstances can be very destructive. When I see that the mole on my cheek has grown and darkened, I can deny the potential risk of cancer by assuming that it is not worrisome and that doctors do not really help anyway. Many patients risk their health and ultimately lose their lives because they deny that the early symptoms of illness could be indicative of something more serious. In conflict, our first response is to minimize the problem or avoid it all together. In denial, we essentially lean away from the conflict by avoiding confronting the reality of a situation and the implications of the conflict. Some statements that characterize intra-personal denial include these:

- "Everything's fine."
- "It's not a problem."
- "But I'm right."
- "It's no big deal."
- "That's just the way things are."
- "I thrive on abuse."

Of course, if a conflict is relatively minor and manageable, it is not a matter of denial to trust your ability to handle the situation or detach by assessing that you have little invested in the outcome. A person who thinks to herself, "I can handle it"—in a manner that is rooted in self-knowledge and the comfort of working with the conflict—is not necessarily in denial. However, in our experience, many people misinterpret the nature of the conflict and its impact on them. They delude themselves with self-effacing comments like "I can handle it" when they actually mean that they do not want to have to deal with the conflict, or they hope it will simply go away on its own.

The intra-personal impacts of denial can involve anxiety, confusion, frustration, emotional numbness, stress, a false sense of well-being, and even euphoria. When we are in denial, things can look pretty good because we refuse to look at what conflicts might exist, what problems need solving. Individuals in denial, at a surface level, cannot see anything that needs to be solved!

FIGURE 2.3

Denial and self-deception can endure for a long time. Denial can be like putting the proverbial rose-tinted glasses on. Things look fine, if not rosy, if we spend our energy focusing straight ahead on what we want to look at. However, we also experience a haunting sensation of the grey and disturbing images that exist on the periphery, outside the view of the lenses.

Over time, denial starts to require more energy than would acknowledging the conflict as a problem. In fact, as we pointed out previously, to other parties involved in the conflict denial will actually appear to provide support for the conduct or decisions that cause the conflict. To Karen and Jim's staff, Karen's denial will be viewed as support of Jim's intolerant and harmful behaviour. As well, Jim's thinking that his behaviour is working will be reinforced because he will perceive his interests as being met. At some point, the costs of denial become larger than the risks of dealing with the problem. At this stage of denial, people often focus solely on the perceived risks (e.g., making things worse, losing one's job, being labelled a "complainer") associated with confronting the conflict. However, when prompted to weigh the risks of leaning into the conflict against the costs of ignoring it, the choice becomes much more clear.

Interpersonally, denial manifests as avoidance, preternatural cheerfulness, and significant inconsistencies between what is said and what is done. I am in denial when I say to myself, "There's no problem," when really there is one. We are in denial when either one or both of us *perceive* "there is no problem" when really there is.

Most commonly, we see situations in which one party perceives a problem and the other person, often recognized as the more powerful of the two, denies that there is any concern. For example, a client of a community-based not-for-profit agency we worked with had a conflict with the executive director who ignored her complaints and refused to meet with her, saying, "I don't see any problem." In her frustration, the client characterized the director as being "so far behind, he thinks he's first!"

Sample statements that characterize denial in terms of interpersonal conflict include these:

- "We haven't got time for this."
- "We haven't got the resources for this."
- "They'll work it out."
- "It's just a personality conflict."
- "Every business has its problem people."

We say we have not got the time or the resources to deal with a given conflict, but we somehow manage to find more time and resources, many times over, to deal with the negative impacts of that conflict!

As in intra-personal denial, interpersonal denial can be healthy. Choosing not to respond to a conflict on an interpersonal level may be the optimal strategy if the cost required to address it (financial or otherwise) is worth more than the gain that will be achieved by addressing it. However, as with intra-personal denial, interpersonal denial is counter-productive when there are legitimate issues that require attention; such is the case when we need to continue to work with the person or persons with whom we are in conflict.

Denial amplifies negative impacts, increases divergence, postpones resolutions, and allows misperceptions and misunderstandings to solidify unchecked.

It has been our experience that most employees and organizational leaders, when in conflict, err on the side of denial rather than response. In other words, the modus operandi for many of us is to "leave it alone" and hope conflict will dissolve. For example, one senior human resource leader once told us, "If employees can't work out conflicts on their own, then we don't want them working here anyway." She presumed that they could do away with conflict simply by hiring the right kind of people. Although we support the notion that employees should be able to work out their conflicts, we know that most of us simply do not have the training, skills, opportunities, or the institutional safety to do so.

One such case involved a high degree of conflict and negative feelings among three separate but interdependent groups of senior professional staff. The vice-president, who initially sponsored a process to facilitate the resolution of these concerns, imposed the caveat that we, as facilitators, were not to do anything that might evoke or address people's emotions. This vice-president was so uncomfortable with the emotional component of people that she preferred to deny the problem and avoid engaging in critical aspects of the conflict. We quickly withdrew from the process with the knowledge that without the freedom to address emotional issues and psychological interests we could never achieve group convergence, nor find resolution for the myriad conflicts facing the groups. This sort of denial is one of the reasons that keep individuals and organizations stuck in the Conflict Trap.

One good indicator that you or someone else is using denial in a counterproductive way is when you use, or when you hear another use, intensifiers such as *always, never, extremely, everything, nothing, ever,* and *forever*. Often, these intensifiers surface in discussions of conflict because a person is describing a strongly negative *emotional impact*. For example, when frustration and resentment can no longer be denied, I may blurt out, "You *never* help out!" The other person hears an inaccurate description of the actual events and will be quick to counter-attack with the assertion, "That's not true! You said 'never,' and yet back in 1976...." Intensifiers deny the existence of more than one perspective. This mode of expressing denial suggests that there is only one truth.

The opposite of a shallow truth is false; the opposite of a deep truth is also true.[11]

FIGURE 2.4
Despair in the Conflict Trap

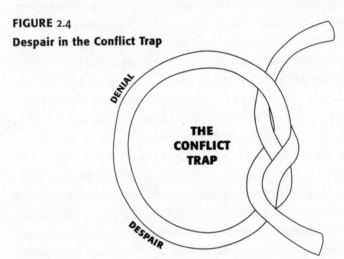

Despair

Students of undergraduate psychology may remember seeing fuzzy black and white movies on the work of B.F. Skinner in their first-year introductory psychology course. The movies portrayed examples of Skinner's research into theories of behavioural psychology. One movie focused on the principle of learned helplessness. Apparently filmed in an era before there were standards for the ethical treatment of animals, this short film depicted the effects of reward and punishment on a laboratory rat. When the rat happened to display a behaviour desired by the experimenter, such as hitting a black button, it would receive a pellet of food. The rat would then hit the button enthusiastically, reaping its rewards. When the rat happened to hit a white button, the use of which the experimenter wished to discourage, the rat would receive an electrical shock administered through the steel floor of the cage. The rat did not require much of this "negative reinforcement" to completely ignore the white button. Then the experimenter decided to get nasty. Food pellets appeared randomly, without any connection to the rat's pushing buttons. The rat responded by slowly finding them, sometimes eating them, and at other times leaving them. The rat stopped pushing buttons. Then, electrical shocks were administered at random intervals and without any connection to the buttons. At first, the rat tried everything to stop them: pushing the black button, trying to escape, and even pushing the white button. At the end of the film, the lecture theatre of keen psychology students was left with the lasting memory of a time-elapsed image of the rat after a random sequence of food and shocks had been administered for a few hours. The rat lay on its side in a corner of the cage, curled up in a ball. It ignored all food, and when a shock was given the rat no longer made any attempt to escape or fight but only kicked a rear leg slowly.

Despair is a natural response to threat or actual loss, particularly when you perceive that you have little or no control over outcomes. Despair sets in when denial breaks down. We can no longer pretend to ourselves, or others, that everything is fine. Like denial, despair can manifest both intra-personally and interpersonally.

Despair is characterized by its own small cycle of impacts. When denial first breaks down, we typically experience anxiety, resistance, frustration, fear, anger, or hostility. In addition, there may be a sense of guilt or regret. If we tend to use a more competitive style in conflict, we may regret the things we said and did. If we use a more accommodating style in conflict, we may regret all the things we did *not* say or do. We may try to negotiate or bargain with others in a last attempt to change conditions before we give up. Then the "long dark night" of sadness, futility, and depression that characterize despair sets in.

Statements that reflect despair intra-personally include these:

- "I can't believe it. Why me?"
- "This can't go on."
- "I never knew I could feel so bad."
- "It's hopeless."

Hopelessness and helplessness are feelings that occur at the nadir of despair, and they draw most people back into denial or into the next phase of detachment in the Conflict Trap.

Interpersonally, the impacts of mishandled conflict leave people feeling saturated in negativity. One woman described herself as feeling like a "sponge" in the workplace. She reported that she always accommodated the needs of everyone else: her co-workers, managers, and clients. She accepted their complaints, criticism, and abuse, believing that she was strong enough to handle it all. As a result, she described herself as so soaked in negativity and despair that she began "leaking" negativity and pessimism onto others. As she slipped further into despair, she described herself as "squirting" the unhealthy and uncooperative negativity that she had endured for so long back at colleagues, superiors, and clients, like a sponge bursting from saturation.

Despair manifests interpersonally as blaming, low morale, and chilliness; it manifests organizationally in hostile work environments, high rates of turnover, and in a negative reputation as an awful place to work. People who work in such environments might be heard to make some of the following statements:

- "Things never change."
- "It's all management's/the union's fault."
- "Welcome to my nightmare."
- "It's unfair, but what can I do?"

Or they say nothing at all.

Individual and group morale plummets to the point that staff and management, like the rat in the example mentioned above, are united by their growing sense of hopelessness and helplessness. In the end, they continue to go to work as a means of survival but nothing more. Loftier goals associated with making contributions, with personal growth and happiness, fade in the fog of despair and a sense of helplessness.

FIGURE 2.5
Detachment in the Conflict Trap

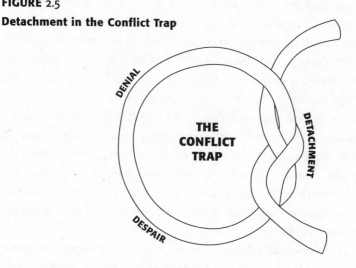

Detachment

For weeks, Fazil has been trying to find out what has been going on. As the director of a library he had heard complaints from staff in the past, but they had tapered off and he had assumed things were better. Now his managers are reporting that staff members are "working to rule." While it is difficult to pin down any one activity as inappropriate, clients are complaining about staff members' attitudes and slow service. Though managers have set expectations for positive change, staff members have not responded and have successfully challenged management, through the union, as being unsupportive. Fazil is left feeling that he is outside of the conflict and is wondering, "Who's the boss?"

As we slip into the depths of despair, the hopelessness and helplessness we feel leads to an angry explosion or fight, an implosion or flight, or an opportunity to move to profit. In the Conflict Trap, an explosion can manifest as resistance to or violence directed at oneself or others. In flight, we head back into denial, away from the situation or into detachment. Detachment, like denial, is a defence against the abyss of despair and depression. Unlike the defence of denial, however, we no longer deny that there is a problem. Instead, we tell ourselves that we do not care, and we try to muddle through with our heads down in order to survive. In detachment, we release attempts to control events or improve our situation. Though there can be a sense of relief gained from detaching, it is also the most difficult stage of the Conflict Trap from which to extract and then energize ourselves and others, to bring ourselves back to productive functioning. Apathy, fear, isolation, and withdrawal all act to reinforce resistance, and this results in a dearth of opportunities to bring on positive change. We give up. We surrender. We accept feeling lost and direct our attention elsewhere in order to cope, even while we try to convince ourselves we have actually "won" by means of detaching. By detaching we come to think we have defeated the despair that emerges from within and from the individuals with whom we are in conflict.

Intra-personally, we have detached when we feel resigned, apathetic, and disinterested. We make these sorts of statements to ourselves:

- "I don't care."
- "Forget it."
- "It's hopeless."
- "Only 2,948 days left until retirement."

Interpersonally, detachment is apparent in the workplace when teamwork has broken down and people appear to have no regard or concern for the needs of others. Common statements one overhears include these:

- "Tell someone who cares."
- "Not my problem."
- "Yeah, well, if misery loves company, you're in good company."

- "Get over it."
- "Life sucks and then you retire."

Although detachment serves a protective function that allows us to divest ourselves of situations and relationships that are not under our control, detachment also keeps people, teams, families, and organizations trapped in conflict. In detachment, we are distanced from the impacts of the difficulties we encounter; however, while this may feel like a relief, we also miss out on important information about what is required to move from conflict into growth and profit.

Negative impacts, while unpleasant to witness and experience, are also messengers that carry valuable information. In every negative impact is an encoded plan to resolve problems. However, detachment discharges these messengers and enables individuals and organizations to slip back into denial that problems exist. And so the trap closes in and we enter a downward spiral of divergence and discontent.

What Traps Organizations in Conflict

When individuals suffer the negative impacts of conflict, their internal responses often manifest either actively or passively as negative interpersonal responses. As we have noted, this negativity frequently devolves from erosion to implosions, or to explosions that involve sabotage, arbitration, litigation, and even violence. In response to these destructive impacts, organizational leaders seek advice from colleagues, consultants, and books; they try to learn what it takes to move out of organizational denial, despair, and detachment to move towards organizational excellence and profit. To their dismay, they often attempt to implement their learning through the use of fairly traditional strategies (e.g., performance management and discipline, referrals to personal counselling, implementation of wellness programs, traditional leadership training); the result is that they eventually discover more resistance and unsuccessful outcomes. These failures only contribute to the trap of conflict because they erode the leader's sense of efficacy and feed a collective sense of hopelessness, helplessness, and frustration.

In chapter 1 we discussed the psychological model of Maslow's Hierarchy of Needs. Simply put, it is not enough to shoot for the lofty ideals advanced by organizational development literature. It is all well and good to "promote" a climate of collegiality, self-direction, motivation, and harmony, but if members of the organization do not feel a basic measure of security and respect, the organization cannot move to higher levels without satisfying the founding needs of the hierarchy. In other words, just as individuals cannot focus on their needs for affiliation and belonging unless their basic needs for security, food, and shelter have been met, so an organization cannot focus on maximizing its potential when its members have unmet foundational needs for security, respect, and fairness.

In summary, negative responses to conflict generally occur in three stages: Denial, Despair, and Detachment. Each stage overlaps the others, and while people frequently move back and forth between the stages, the first response of most individuals and groups to conflict that is misunderstood and mishandled, generally speaking, is to deny that the conflict exists. When the conflict cannot be denied any longer, and initial attempts to resolve it fail, people move into despair. Finally, the outward impact of despair serves to perpetuate the conflict, and in turn causes individuals to detach from the situation in order to continue to go to work. Without a conscious understanding of these dynamics, and without the curiosity and courage required to move oneself, others, and the organization beyond this Conflict Trap, individuals and organizations remain stuck in negativity and divergence, and suffer compromised growth and financial achievement.

The Conflict Trap at a Glance

- Conflict, like bereavement, is a natural process that can quickly become an unhealthy trap in which we become entrenched.
- When we are stuck in the Conflict Trap, we generally move through the stages of Denial, Despair, and Detachment. However, these stages are not necessarily sequential or linear, and some people will move through them in a different order or skip a given stage altogether. Generally speaking, individuals and organizations get trapped in one or more of the stages.
- In Denial, we attempt to defend against Despair by pretending that there is either no problem or that it is not our problem. We deny the

existence of the threat that causes the conflict or deny that the conflict's potential negative impact is meaningful.

- As Denial breaks down, we move into Despair. In Despair we develop a sense of hopelessness that things will ever improve, and a sense of helplessness about our ability to do anything positive about our situation. We may also experience Despair in the form of anger, fear, frustration, or another strong emotion.

- The more we are in Despair, the more we move towards Detachment. Detachment is the most dangerous threat to individual and group growth and profit because apathy is used as a defence against Despair. We are at the nadir of the Conflict Trap when we experience Detachment, and we are furthest from finding profitable outcomes to conflict.

- All three stages make up the Conflict Trap, in that the more we deny the more we ultimately despair. The more we despair the more we detach. The more we detach the more we deny, and so on.

- The Conflict Trap manifests personally within each of us, interpersonally between us, and cross-culturally among groups.

3

The Costs of Conflict

Mark is an administrative assistant. Shortly after joining the area, 18 months ago, he noticed that his co-worker, Tracey, a senior assistant, clearly had a strong personality. Though she was not designated as his trainer, she constantly offered unsolicited advice and criticism. With her "my way or the wrong way" approach, Mark felt bullied. Initially, Mark tried to work around her, but when this did not alter her behaviour he confronted her by saying, "You can't talk to me like that." This made things worse. Tracey then started raising her voice at Mark and gossiping about him with others. Once, she threw a pen at him. He noticed his desk was frequently rearranged and that items were missing. Mark then tried to avoid her and now the two of them do not speak. Mark complains that Tracey is hypercritical, rude, and overbearing. Tracey complains that Mark is slow and inefficient. Management now observes that Mark is calling in sick on days when he has to work with Tracey and that performance deliverables are down in their area. In performance management discussions held with each of them they each blame the other and say they cannot do their jobs without management intervening to protect them from the other person.

Personal Impacts of Conflict

When workplace conflict occurs and is misunderstood or mishandled, and we get trapped in the conflict, the impacts can range from mild annoyance, irritation, and distraction to full-blown rage, depression, and fear. By *impacts* we mean the short-term or long-term consequences of being in conflict. The impacts that result from conflict typically become entwined with the procedural or outcome issues in dispute. The emotional reactions that result significantly impair the discovery of, and movement towards, a satisfying outcome. For example, a senior executive we worked with was highly respected for his brilliant financial management and "rainmaker" interpersonal skills. As a colleague of his put it, "Things were great...as long as things were great." However, when the going got tough, the tough guy got tougher. He became insulting and belligerent to a degree that caused others to avoid him. He had gained a reputation for his inability to differentiate between having a feeling and acting on it. This was not a problem when things were going well. When he *felt* happy, passionate, motivated, and friendly he *acted* happy, passionate, motivated, and friendly. But when he *felt* fearful, angry, or upset he *acted* fearful, angry, or upset. He was a 42-year-old professional MBA who had not yet learned that simply because he had a feeling did not mean he should act on it. When conflicts arose, his negative emotional responses contributed to conflicts that remained unresolved and others became resentful of him. Initially colleagues accommodated him with a shrug of the shoulders and the resigned observation, "That's Bob!" When this form of denial no longer worked, and the negative impacts of his unprofessional outbursts continued, colleagues slipped into the leaning away response and, in their despair, tried to avoid him. When they were unable to avoid him, a few colleagues got caught up in the charging-into-conflict mode and lost their tempers with him, causing a rift of enduring and dysfunctional detachment.

The impacts of conflict on individuals can be experienced at two levels: the intra-personal and the interpersonal. When our interests or needs are not being met—when we are excluded from a decision-making process or are treated with disrespect, for example—we experience negative impacts that may include hurt, a sense of loss, a sense of injustice, anger, and so on. These are the intra-personal impacts.

When we are upset and therefore either avoid the other person with whom we are in conflict or raise our voice at them, we may feel relief, guilt, shame, or fear, while the other individual may feel attacked, hurt, angry, or shocked. The manner in which we respond to the intra-personal impacts that arise generate the interpersonal impacts.

Often, intra-personal and interpersonal impacts are intermingled and this adds to the confusion and anxiety experienced by parties in conflict. For example, our internal feelings of fear typically result in a leaning away response, of inaction. In turn, inaction on our part will likely be interpreted by others as our acceptance or accommodation of their needs and conduct, and thus serves to reinforce the continuation of that conduct. The issues in dispute become fused with the ways in which people respond to being in dispute. In other words, my anger augments the issue that made me angry in the first place, and the destructive pattern continues.

Some of the negative impacts experienced during conflict include these:

FIGURE 3.1

Personal Impacts of Conflict

Intra-personal Impacts	Interpersonal Impacts
Surprise, confusion, anxiety, worry, fear	Avoidance, silence, isolation
Hurt, sadness, depression, hopelessness	Tearfulness, sleeplessness, laziness
Anger, frustration, rage, desire for revenge	Shouting, gesturing, slamming objects
Guilt, embarrassment, shame	Apologizing, blaming, lack of genuineness
Apathy, detachment, ambivalence	Hot/cold treatment, withdrawal, disinterest

In a study that examined the impacts of conflict and stress on 85 healthcare personnel, and of how their conflict styles or responses to those conflicts shaped the outcomes of conflict and their work life, researchers concluded, "The ways in which an individual responds to the ambiguity, uncertainty, and discord that help define organizational life also shape the responses of others and, ultimately, help to create the individual experience at work."[12] In other words, our *responses* to conflict directly shape the interactions and circumstances that *cause* us conflict.

Organizational Impacts of Conflict

From the most basic perspective, organizations are institutions that bring together groups of individuals with different interests to work in a structured environment of heightened interdependence. Interdependence is created through the pursuit of overarching company goals. Typically, there are varying levels of individual commitment to those organizational goals. It is easy to see how misunderstood and mishandled conflicts can lead directly to organizational inefficiency, reduced productivity, stymied innovation, and compromised profits. Conversely, a focus on handling conflict well, to better secure employee health, cooperation, and commitment, leads to improved efficiency, creativity, and profitability.

Studies of the impacts of workplace conflict abound and have produced some of the following empirical findings.

Inefficiency and Productivity

- Employees work less, become more frustrated, and are more likely to quit after using complaint procedures they consider inadequate or unfair.[13]
- Improved worker health and safety lead to improved health status for workers, accelerated productivity, increased quality, and decreased costs.[14]
- Strong employment relationships are the key determinant of job satisfaction, which in turn is a key factor in inspiring high productivity.[15]
- Employees who perceive themselves to be bullied use 10–52 percent of their work time defending, avoiding, and venting.[16]

Stymied Innovation

- Employees who feel mistrusted withhold ideas and thus damage organizations by refusing to share information, skills, and knowledge.[17]

Compromised Profits

- Interpersonal mistreatment (i.e., rude or discourteous conduct) at work adversely affects performance and profits.[18]
- Absenteeism due to high work-life conflict costs Canadian firms 3 billion dollars a year.[19]
- Employers' financial liability has expanded for "poisoned environments."[20]

The need for employers to adopt policies and programs that recognize and support the basic needs of employees to feel respected and safe has been mounting. One recent study found that Canadian workers rated "Being treated with respect" as the most important aspect of job satisfaction (73 percent), and "Good communication among co-workers" ranked third (71 percent). In contrast, "Paying well" and "Job security" were ranked ninth (51 percent) and tenth (49 percent).[21] A coroner's jury in 2000 recommended that the broad definition of "workplace violence" include bullying behaviours; it also suggested that employers will be required to address employee interactions that cause conflict on a more formal basis than they have in the past.[22] In fact, to protect themselves from liability costs, most organizations across Canada and the U.S. have instituted policies and training programs to ensure interactions among employees comply with legal requirements. Yet even with the emergence of policies and new laws, conflict remains rampant in organizations and is a key impediment to organizational success.

Furthermore, when conflict is avoided or mishandled, the negative impacts that result can manifest in a negative corporate reputation, which generates significant barriers to the recruitment and retention of skilled employees. In terms of direct fiscal consequences, experience has demonstrated that business conflicts that are resolved by mediation efforts rather than through the courts can save organizations from 50–80 percent in legal fees and can, in some cases, preserve potentially valuable business relationships.[23] Clearly, mishandled conflict interferes with the achievement of organizational goals and the generation of profits.

Even when profit is still produced, workplace conflict inhibits organizations from achieving their full potential, just as interpersonal conflict inhibits people from achieving their full potential within personal relationships. At best, mishandled conflict creates an organization that simply muddles through in order to get by. More commonly, workplace conflict leaves organizations in a state of divergence and stagnation, or worse. In extreme circumstances, unresolved organizational conflict manifests in significant threats of litigation and the risk of violence.

Organizational Impacts and Managing Risk

The personal and organizational impacts described above represent the dark side of conflict as it manifests within organizations. However, mishandled conflict, like cancer, can and usually does present with mild symptoms at first. A few staff members appear disgruntled, absenteeism inches up, some staff members leave, others count the days to retirement, and leadership reports slumping profits or increased budgetary concerns despite attempts to reinvigorate motivation. As staff conflict heats up, a sense that something is "not quite right" pervades the organization. As with cancer, organizational ailments grow, and by the time one can no longer deny that things are not well, sickness has spread to a degree that strong medicine is required to pursue any type of recovery—medicine that is costly and generates its own negative side-effects.

The three effects we see produced by mishandled conflict, and the significant negative risk these pose to individuals and organizations, can be defined by the concepts of *erosion*, *implosion*, and *explosion*. Each of these areas is discussed below in the order of the progressive escalation of risk each represents.

Erosion

Erosion is characterized by resistance, acting-out behaviour, apathy, poor morale, and other similar dynamics that occur "just beneath the surface" in a given work area. These impacts cause the slow decay of work productivity and workplace relations and are virtually invisible at times when leaders do not want to see them or staff members choose to suffer in silence. Above-average absenteeism, disrespectful interactions, gossip, cliques in the workplace, and hostile work environments are all manifestations of unresolved workplace conflict and these erode an individual's contributions and an organization's profit-making potential.

Erosion can occur over long periods of time, even while an organization continues to be profitable on the surface. Like "sleeping" skin moles that subtly change shape and colour over time, symptoms of erosion are easy to ignore until the symptoms grow into full-fledged crises. However, by developing an organizational culture that sees conflict as opportunity, and by preparing staff to lean into conflict rather than fight or flee from each other, minor divergences can be managed and contained before they become a potentially fatal pandemic. Alternatively, the erosion caused by workplace conflict escalates over time and, if it remains unchecked, can result in implosion and ultimately explosion.

Implosion

WorldCom, Tyco International, Global Crossing, and Adelphia Communications all imploded into bankruptcy. Then, in December 2001, Enron became the largest corporate bankruptcy in the history of business. Millions of dollars, thousands of investors, hundreds of employees: all lost. Lost in an implosion of deceit, greed, and alternately leaning away and charging into conflict. Sherron Watkins, the vice-president who blew the whistle on Enron's accounting fraud, had met with Enron's founder and chairman, Kenneth Lay, prior to the exposure of the company's many difficulties. Motivated by her worry that Enron might "implode in a wave of accounting scandals," she passed on the comments of a colleague: "I know it would be devastating for all of us, but sometimes I wish we would get caught—we're such a crooked company!"[24]

Implosion manifests when the impacts of mishandled conflicts are ignored and denied so that organizations can maintain delusions of security and success. By the time conflict implodes, the organization is in crisis. Costly manifestations include decreased efficiency, an escalation in absenteeism and resignations, and mounting employee discontent that results in arbitration for contract staff and litigation for non-contract staff. These are the three Rs of implosion:

- Reputation is damaged with clients and stakeholders.
- Retention of skilled staff is low, and there is higher-than-average staff turnover.
- Recruitment presents barriers to attracting "star" employees and managers.

By the time organizations experience an implosion, they may be facing financial losses, the loss of client loyalty, and bankruptcy. Independent reviews of and research into organizational conflicts that have imploded into bankruptcy, or near-bankruptcy, reveal similar organizational characteristics with respect to their dealings with conflict:[25]

- High arrogance—distorted confidence and pride combined with practices the average person would deem unethical, abusive, or illegal but which are viewed by the organization as "very innovative," "creative," and "aggressively seeking profit."
- Low transparency—creation of a climate of secrecy wherein information becomes a means to broker power. Those with information have the power and those without it have none. One outcome of low transparency is diminished trust on the part of clients and staff.
- Values disconnect—ill-defined values guide the organization, or a void grows between how an organization defines its values and how those values are manifested in the organization's practices. For example, Enron's stated values included "Communication, respect, integrity, and excellence." No one at Enron was subsequently able to identify when those values were discussed in performance appraisals.
- Poor communication—members of the organization operate with erroneous expectations, receive unclear feedback or none at all, interdependent individuals and/or teams are unfamiliar with the activities of colleagues, and many staff members and managers encounter frustration and hopelessness.
- Narrow options—few if any means are available to address complaints fairly and in a timely manner. Imploding organizations are in crisis

mode and overemphasize "what will get us through the next hour," even as they de-emphasize strategic planning for the future.

Left unresolved, erosion can deteriorate into implosion. Likewise, implosion can further deteriorate into more dramatic and explosive incidents, such as that which occurred within NASA:

> From 1981 onward, the NASA space shuttle Columbia made dozens of astronauts' travels into space seem effortlessly accessible, even routine. That is, until February 1, 2003, when, upon re-entry into the earth's atmosphere and within minutes of its intended landing, one of the seven astronauts aboard was heard to reply to a transmission from Houston, saying, "Roger, uh...." Immediately thereafter the shuttle exploded into fragments that were scattered across the northeastern part of Texas. The image of flaming parts falling from the sky brought with it a searing déjà vu of the Challenger space shuttle's explosion less than a minute after take off on January 8, 1986. For NASA, this was yet another tragic failure that stained their long list of accomplishments, failures that included a ground-test capsule fire that killed three astronauts in 1967, and the costly and embarrassing 1990 launch of the two-billion dollar Hubble space telescope that did not work. In many cases, the causes of the tragedies were relatively minor: an O-ring, simple quality assurance testing, and the failure to designate inches instead of centimetres. In all cases, the program's funding and credibility suffered immeasurably.

Explosion

It was October 15, 2002, and it was an unseasonably warm, sunny afternoon in the western Canadian interior city of Kamloops. Dick Anderson had just returned from a difficult visit in the smaller city of Penticton, to the south. Dick hated giving layoff notices. The Ministry of Water, Land, and Air Protection was restructuring in the wake of a change in the British Columbia government. Rumours about the coming massive funding cuts had put everyone on edge. Now Dick had to let some good people go—people with families, people with mortgages. He wondered how close he was to being sacked himself. Thirteen years he had given to the Ministry. Through promotions and demotions he had seen a lot of changes. Perhaps the worst is over, he thought. It was tough to have his job taken over by Jim McCracken last spring. All the downsizing had squeezed lower middle-managers down and others up. He sensed there was good news on the horizon, though; rumours had recently surfaced that more resources were coming to help the remaining staff members who were buckling under the workload.

Dick turned the Ministry truck into the parking lot and headed into the office. He was a few minutes early for his 2 o'clock meeting and grabbed a coffee from the office kitchen on the way. Dick was known for his awkward communication style and his lack of tact with colleagues, but generally he got along all right with the office. A few staff members said their hellos as he headed to Jim's office. Jim asked him how he was doing as he closed his office door. The meeting between the two men took ten minutes. Ten minutes for Jim to tell Dick he was fired. Jim understood why Dick would want to leave the building quickly; he felt pretty awful about it himself.

Around 2:30, the Ministry truck pulled back into the parking lot. Evidentially, Dick had had second thoughts and entered the building through a back door and went back to his office. Jim was chatting with a union shop steward, Dave Mardon, when Dick re-entered his office and closed the door. A counsellor hired by the Ministry saw Dick rush in and tried to follow him but Dick blocked the door. Someone inside yelled. That is when the shooting began.

Staff quickly evacuated the building. Four hours later, when the police were finally able to enter the building, they found Jim McCracken and Dave Mardon, both family men, dead in Jim's office. Dick Anderson was found in his office, dead of a self-inflicted gunshot wound.

The explosive impacts of unresolved workplace conflict are statistically rare, but they are so catastrophic in their immediate and long-term impacts that they are feared phenomena. Explosion occurs when conflict becomes violent, physically dangerous, or life threatening. The fact that "going postal" has become a common phrase indicates widespread awareness of the potential for violence to explode out of workplace conflict.

In the year following the Kamloops Ministry shootings, several reviews and inquests were conducted to determine what happened, what caused the tragedy, and what could be done to prevent the violent manifestation of workplace conflict in the future. The recommendations of three independent committees were surprisingly consistent. Leaning into conflict was described as the most effective means to prevent workplace violence from exploding. This "leaning in" could be achieved in these ways:

- Conducting regular and fair performance appraisals
- Managing expectations clearly and consistently
- Providing complaint resolution procedures to investigate, record, and resolve staff members' concerns[26]

In the rush of organizational change and restructuring, it is a common error (and as we have seen here, sometimes a fatal one) to lean away from conflict or charge into it. When leaning away, we procrastinate. We postpone performance appraisals because we know they do not want to hear criticism. We offer "white lies" or half-truths to buy time, promising that better days and more resources are coming. We ignore staff's complaints, hoping that they will go away on their own. We ignore conflict.

When charging into conflict, we potentially ignite implosions and explosions. We skip over opportunities to support co-workers who desire to improve their behaviour; feeling hopeless that they will ever change, we move them (in humiliation) to another area, demote them, or lay them off. In an attempt to offer clear and direct information, we "tell it like it is," without tact or diplomacy. We focus on the negative aspects of their conduct and fail to include any positive feedback. We shame them. If they complain, we challenge them and direct them to take it up "with someone who cares." The embarrassment and frustration builds, in some people, into a volcano of rage that explodes violently in the workplace. This costs organizations dearly and traps some, sometimes fatally, in conflict.

The Consequences of Mishandled Conflict

Given the negative impacts of mishandled conflict we have identified above, why is it that conflict continues to trap individuals and organizations in negative and unproductive responses? How is it that conflicts continue to be mishandled and remain unresolved even when we know, intuitively, that individuals and organizations that suffer during conflicts would want them to end? What prevents us from handling conflict effectively and prevents parties from avoiding the debilitating Conflict Trap of Denial, Despair, and Detachment? What will allow parties to cultivate the sort of convergence necessary to overcome the constant clash of opposing interests and of resistance?

We have learned that when conflict is misunderstood and mishandled by the individuals directly involved, and by the organizational leaders responsible for their efforts, the Conflict Trap becomes a never-ending loop that erodes relationships and productivity and potentially escalates into implosion or explosion. Many of the individuals with whom we have worked describe their sense of a treadmill, of "here we go again" down the "well-trodden path." The negative intra-personal impacts that lead to negative interpersonal impacts become habitual, and it is not long before coming into work feels like entering a battlefield.

From our work in thousands of conflict situations, we have observed a number of psychological, interpersonal, and cultural phenomena that directly influence the initiation, escalation, and perpetuation of workplace conflict. Many of these influences function at a subconscious level and lead us to question others' motives, or to feel confused about our own needs, desires, and aspirations. To ready ourselves to lean into conflict, in order to achieve better, more profitable outcomes, we next review the range of socio-cultural influences that govern our choices and motivate our behaviour when in conflict.

The Costs of Conflict at a Glance

- Misunderstood and mishandled conflict impacts us personally and organizationally.

- On a personal level, we typically experience a range of negative impacts: frustration, anger, confusion, and sadness; the loss of motivation, self-esteem, and our sense of self-efficacy; and compromised physical health as a consequence of stress. As a result, our social network of colleagues, family, and friends will also become stressed, and our ability to achieve our peak working levels will greatly diminish.

- On an organizational level, our work teams and organizations experience negative impacts, including inefficiency, lost productivity, stymied innovation, compromised profits, and barriers to growth.

- As individuals, teams, and organizations descend into the Conflict Trap, they experience symptoms of erosion, such as low morale and inefficiency; of implosion, such as rising absenteeism, employee turnover, and failing financial health; and of explosion, like threats, violence, and even death.

4

Conflict Within

THE PSYCHOLOGY OF CONFLICT

Conflict itself is, of course, a sign of relative health, as you would know if you ever met really apathetic people, really hopeless people, people who have given up hoping, striving, and coping.[27]

ALTHOUGH CONFLICT CAN BE A SIGN OF HEALTH, in that it can invigorate people to achieve new understanding and growth, most people respond to conflict in unhealthy ways. To understand why we seem to choose illness over health, divergence over convergence, and conflict over profit, we explore the psychological, interpersonal, and cultural predispositions that impair our ability to respond to conflict productively. In this chapter, we focus on the internal, psychological mechanisms that influence our perceptions, choices, and the behaviour that has bearing on the experience of conflict.

In our work as mediators, we frequently hear people state that they cannot understand why someone else acted the way they did—their lies, their obfuscation, their hostility—all of which appear so unnecessary, so harmful. Sometimes we even have clients tell us they do not understand why they acted in the way that they did. Yet we have found that at some level:

All behaviour makes sense.

However baffling or bizarre a person's behaviour may appear, there are always explanations, from the individual's perspective, that account for the behaviour.

The problem is that most of us react to conflict in a manner that relies on instinctive judgement and self-defence and not in a way that explores the conflict and seeks to understand the situation and its effect on us. The study of psychology and perception, and our own case experience, has revealed that people's initial judgements are often clouded, misguided, or just flat-out wrong, and that their initial reactions to lean away or charge into conflict typically create further conflict and widen divergence. As a result, we impede our own ability to "make sense" of what is happening to us and to others involved in the situation. This impedes convergence and the satisfaction of immediate and long-term practical and psychological interests.

To account for these seemingly natural but counterproductive patterns, we examine in this chapter the motivational determinants that lead to the perceptions and beliefs that perpetuate conflict and the responses that trap us in a perpetual state of conflict. These determinants, drawn from a range of psychological theory and research, help us understand why we act and think in the ways we do, why others think and act as they do, and suggest pathways to avoid becoming stuck in the Conflict Trap.

Clinical Psychology and Cognition

The Seven Deadly Defences

When we feel threatened, as we do when we are in conflict, Freud and others have postulated that we have built-in psychological defence mechanisms that activate to protect us. These mechanisms are the conscious and unconscious ways in which we respond to stress. They serve to lessen negative feelings that arise from a difficult or threatening experience, and they do this most often by distorting the reality of the situation in some way. Although these instinctive mechanisms protect our psychological interests in the short-term, the distortions they create result in responses to conflict that leave us trapped in a negative mindset. In addition, excessively strong defence systems can hamper the ability of individuals to learn from new experiences, particularly experiences that involve some level of conflict.

Of the fourteen defence mechanisms originally outlined by Freud, and elaborated by others later, seven have direct implications for adults responding to conflict situations. We call these the Seven Deadly Defences. We use the word *deadly* because these defences effectively kill opportunities to achieve convergence, even as they have an initial protective effect that shields a person from unpleasant feelings or events. We review these Seven Deadly Defences below. We also consider one additional mechanism that does not have the same deadly effect but nevertheless contributes to the escalation of conflict.

1) **DENIAL**—With a role similar to that which it fulfills in the Conflict Trap, denial, as a defence mechanism, involves a person who ignores a reality that is causing unpleasantness. When in denial, we replace a realistic interpretation of potentially threatening events with a benign but inaccurate interpretation. Denial is characterized by several responses to conflict, such as "I didn't do it," "I'm not in conflict," or "It doesn't matter." In denial, feelings or actual events, or both, may be denied. For example, an employee who hears strong criticism of his work may deny having heard it, may deny that there is anything wrong with his work, or he may deny the feelings of fear and shame associated with doing a substandard job by pretending he does not care. A manager may deny having made insulting remarks about an employee—such as "You're incompetent and I'll do anything in my power to get you fired!"—and instead replace such expressions with a more benign statement, like, "I only said that you're not doing your job well and I may need to report you." In this case, a manager may replace the memory of what was actually said with a statement that more accurately reflected what she would have said had she not been so frustrated.

Consider the following illustration: we dealt with a male employee who was accused of making sexually offensive remarks about a female client. The client overheard these remarks and reported them to the employee's supervisor. The supervisor passed the complaint to us to address. We called in the employee and presented him with the allegation, making it clear we were using an informal process to help resolve the concerns. He responded by flat-out denying the allegation. In fact, he denied even being in the area where the incident took place or ever seeing the woman who made the report. Later, in the same interview, we learned from him that he believed that complaints of sexual harassment were often mishandled, leading respondents to the complaint to be treated unfairly. He described a couple of incidents that had been reported by the media that showed how unfair these processes are. He clearly felt his interests were at serious risk in this situation—both practical, in terms of his job, and psychological, in terms of his desire to see himself as an honourable and decent person. Yet his instinctive denial of the event, in spite of the evidence against him, would potentially cause him substantially more conflict with his employer and place him in further jeopardy than would his acknowledgment of the event.

We passed his response along to the supervisor and suggested to her that we needed to consider conducting a more formal investigation—a process that could lead to disciplinary outcomes for the employee. If the employer could not be confident in his willingness to interact with female clients in a respectful manner, they would need to reconsider his employment. In the meantime, the supervisor had obtained further details about the incident and had received another report of similar behaviour with another female client. We called the employee back in to try again to resolve the concerns and to address the problematic behaviour in a constructive and supportive manner. To do so, we attempted to mitigate his feelings of threat by assuring him that he was not in danger of losing his job over the statements themselves, and that we understood that at times all of us could make comments that could unintentionally cause offence and discomfort to others. Now noticeably more relaxed, he fully acknowledged his role in the second incident and partly acknowledged his role in the first complaint.

Our instinct to deny negative events and feelings is strong. Theorists have observed that denial can be effective in reducing anxiety and the physiological state of arousal that is caused by a threatening situation. Denial helps us cope on an emotional and self-protective level. Interestingly, from a cultural perspective, denial is also supported, if not encouraged, as a primary strategy for use by defendants in the western legal system.

In psychological terms, however, any long-term feelings of pain, insecurity, or guilt must be acknowledged to avoid further psychological and emotional problems. In conflict situations, denial exacerbates the original concern, necessitates the imposition of more adversarial approaches to address conflict, and leads to more damaging outcomes for the individual and the organization. For example, when we suspect that something is wrong with our health, we may feel better emotionally if we say to ourselves, "It's probably nothing." While denial reduces anxiety in the short-term, a real illness can do considerable damage if we wait in denial and do not face what is wrong.

The only successful way through negative events is to go through them.

2) **SUPPRESSION** manifests in a person who makes a conscious decision to not think about unpleasant feelings. Suppression differs from denial in that the unpleasant feelings are accessible but are deliberately ignored rather than denied. Suppression can be characterized by statements such as, "I just can't think about it." Suppression generally involves replacing unpleasant thoughts with others that do not produce stress. For example, people may suppress the feelings of humiliation they experience when someone mistreats them in public by focusing on the less stressful memory of someone else who was kind to them.

Over the years, we have found that many people who have been mistreated by others attempt to suppress or ignore their unpleasant feelings by focusing on something else. Suppression is considered a healthy defence against unpleasantness. In terms of conflict, suppressed unpleasant feelings or events typically take root in a person's subconscious—they may be ignored, but they are not forgotten. These suppressed feelings either erode a person's self-esteem over time or build into a storehouse of resentment. "The long bag we drag behind us," is how Robert Bly describes it.[28] Ultimately, the storehouse either implodes or explodes—typically in response to a minor but profound new event. It is this new event that can be the proverbial straw that breaks the camel's back.

3) **PROJECTION** involves transferring anxiety-producing feelings onto another person. For example, people who are very critical of others often believe that others are always critical of them. We have also seen a type of "reverse projection" in situations that involve interpersonal conflict. For example, we have encountered numerous people who are accused of being "intimidating" and who respond by describing themselves as being intimidated by those accusing them, or by stating how intimidated they are by an individual trying to resolve a conflict. Although the attempt to reduce anxiety through projection is understandable, it generally entrenches a conflict more deeply because it contributes to distortions and misperceptions. Now the other party not only has to deal with the initial source of conflict, the projected response adds fuel to the conflict fire.

4) **DISPLACEMENT**, which is similar to projection, functions as a defence in two ways: an impulse perceived as dangerous is redirected towards a different object, or the original impulse is replaced by a different one. In the first form, known as *object displacement*, an unpleasant emotion (e.g., anger) that is directed at an unsafe target (e.g., a client) is redirected to a target that is perceived to be safer (e.g., a co-worker, a spouse, a child). Displacement functions as a means to act on the original emotional impulse and thus enable a cathartic release of the emotion to occur. For example, an individual may feel less angry with an abusive client after he shouts at a co-worker. In the second type of displacement, referred to as *drive displacement*, the object of the emotion remains the same but the emotion itself is replaced by a less threatening one. For example, an employee's fear of her boss is reinterpreted as respect for the boss.

Displacement can produce a healthy, cathartic effect for a person, but it will also result in an unanticipated secondary harm. The following case illustrates this effect. In this particular situation, several senior employees were repeatedly frustrated with the pace of work and the limited knowledge of new staff working in an area. Rather than take their frustration out on the new staff members, they would displace their frustration on the trainers of the new staff. For example, they would approach these preceptors in a highly accusatory and hostile tone and ask them, "Did you teach them to do the job that way?" Although the instructors were identified as "safer" targets, these acts of displacement generated other rifts in the workplace and ultimately caused as much dysfunction as they would have had the supervisors vented their frustration directly onto the new staff members. Displacement provides ways to release these unpleasant feelings. However, displacement can result in damaging effects and entrench conflicted parties in the Conflict Trap.

5) **REACTION FORMATION** involves behaviour that is diametrically opposed to the impulses or feelings that one is repressing. For example, a supervisor who suppresses feelings of disappointment and frustration about an employee whom the supervisor likes as a person may compensate by appearing to be overly supportive of the employee's development and welfare. We have often encountered people in conflict who are accused of some harmful behaviour respond to the complaint by expressing considerable praise for their accuser. For example, a person might say, "I think she's great; I only have deep respect for her"—even when the person thinks that the individual in question is incompetent, or worse. This response is used to deflect or hide the negative emotion an individual experiences and it is an attempt to shield that person against the unpleasantness of an allegation. In many situations, the target of this praise can sense the underlying hostility and, confused by the inconsistency between the known and underlying messages, engages in behaviour to further frustrate the other person. At times, we have observed workplace bullies who, confronted by their managers, suddenly lavished praise on their accusers to create the perception that they could not be mean to someone they regard so highly.

6) **IDENTIFICATION** is a mechanism considered essential to human development and learning and involves taking on the characteristics of someone else in order to engage in behaviour one considers to be off limits to the self but acceptable for the other person. For example, an employee who has often been the target of her manager's critical nature may become critical of her co-workers or subordinates. In this case, the employee follows the example set by the manager as a way to

reduce her own negative feelings about being criticized constantly. This employee may also engage in this type of behaviour in order to secure the favour of the manager.

One particularly well-known variety of identification is identification with an aggressor. In such a case, someone who is victimized takes on traits of the aggressor to combat feelings of powerlessness. Nevertheless, identification is quite normal in the development process. Many leadership books stress the importance of being a role model as essential "leadership" behaviour. If managers expect staff to act respectfully and confront conflict rationally and constructively, they need to do so themselves.

7) **RATIONALIZATION** is an attempt to deny our true motives, to others or ourselves, by using a reason that appears more logical or socially acceptable than the real one. Rationalization generates different comments, such as "I didn't mean to offend," "I didn't really want the job anyway," "Everybody else does it," or "I was just too busy to finish the work." In conflict situations, rationalization enables involved parties to hide interests they seek to satisfy but that might appear selfish or improper to others; more socially acceptable interests replace these. For example, a person seeking a promotion may argue for a course of action that will better profile her skills and knowledge, even when the path is not congruent with the team's overall goals. An employee who uses the Internet to look at pornography might argue the need for a faster Internet connection so he can conduct research more efficiently, rather than identify his true motive.

Our observation is that if an unacknowledged interest plays a substantial role in influencing a decision, others will sense that something else is going on and that this deception will eventually escalate existing difficulties. To find optimal solutions to conflicts, all relevant interests need to be brought to the surface and irrelevant interests need to be effectively suppressed, or addressed elsewhere, by the person holding the interest; otherwise, the individual will corrupt the decision process and create divergence.

One healthy defence mechanism to be wary of: Sublimation

Sublimation, considered one of the healthiest defence mechanisms, involves redirecting the energy connected with an unacceptable impulse into one that is more socially acceptable. Aggressive impulses, for example, can be released by taking on challenging work, by participating in sports, or by refining creative pursuits. Humour is also a coping device that is consistent with sublimation. Although potentially beneficial to a person, sublimation can also result in harm to the self or others by creating or escalating conflicts. For example, humour is heavily predicated on relationship. While we often appreciate and enjoy humorous colleagues, those who express humour about the characteristics of others run the risk of offending those other people and creating greater conflict if they have misjudged the quality of the relationship. As another example, people who overwork themselves run the risk of alienating co-workers by creating heightened workplace competition that can cause co-workers to object by saying, "Don't work so hard, you make the rest of us look bad."

In summary, defence mechanisms enable individuals to reduce anxiety, arousal, and negative feelings caused by unpleasant or threatening events. However, as initial responses to conflict situations, defence mechanisms can often appear as defensiveness and thus widen the divide between conflicted parties. Defence mechanisms create additional barriers to the resolution of conflict in a manner that is profitable. And yet, we can retrain our minds to respond to perceived threats with thoughtfulness and curiosity rather than rigid defensiveness. We do not have to react simply from of instinct: we can control our responses and convert instinct into choice.

Deception and Shielding

Our experience points to two additional and crucial aspects of defensiveness. These deserve further exploration of their contributions to an understanding of the dynamic of conflict and the management of our own psychological responses to conflict. They are *deception* and *shielding*.

DECEPTION

An element that runs throughout most defence mechanisms is dishonesty. Most mechanisms turn on some form of deception—either deception of the self or the deception of others—and nothing seems to infuriate people more than being the target of someone else's attempt to deceive. Yet our review of defence mechanisms reveals how instinctive they are and how psychologically beneficial, in the short term, they can be. The actual motivation that underlies the activation of a defence mechanism is not to deceive—it is to reduce anxiety and to self-protect. Deception is simply the pathway used to achieve the goal. In short, lying is often used as a response to threat.

In conflict situations, however, the use of deception only serves to introduce a new and more complex factor to the conflict mix—a loss of trust. Now, interdependent parties not only have a contradiction of interests to deal with, they have little reason to trust anything said or done by the "lying" party.

In our training workshops we frequently discuss honesty as a critical factor in relationship building, effective communication, and conflict resolution. We review how all of us are, in fact, highly trained deceivers and that we often use deception in our social lives—whether in the form of lies of commission or omission. Consider the situation in which you receive a gift you do not like from someone you do like. If asked, do you tell them the truth—that you do not like the gift? Or do you lie in order to spare their feelings? How about when your spouse asks if he has become fat? Most people have a range of responses, from flat-out untruths to "tactful white lies" that dilute their true beliefs. In fact, we lie in many social situations and work encounters. If a struggling businessperson is asked by a potential client, "How's business?" this seldom prompts an honest response if the answer is "Terrible. We have no repeat customers!" For the most part, people tell lies with a positive, altruistic aim to not hurt another person or to avoid sending them the "wrong message."

People also deceive to self-protect or to protect others. These explanations for lying are reasonable on a conceptual level, and yet when we are the target or the recipient of the lie we get angry and lose trust. When we ask workshop participants to consider—if they were the gift-giver—whether they would rather be told the truth about an unpleasing gift or a lie, most say they would prefer to know the truth. While lying can be the best choice in some situations, it is important to recognize that deception creates other, often unintended impacts that may create more harmful outcomes than an initial, respectfully honest expression of feelings.

In workplace conflict situations, another consequence of lying is that an important piece of the conflict puzzle remains unmentioned, which in turn leads to further divergence. True interests remain hidden. For example, an employee who is constantly and unfairly criticized by her supervisor may hide the fact that she objects to the supervisor's behaviour, even if the supervisor asks her for feedback. The supervisor may actually interpret his own approach as beneficial because he is so *clear* about his concerns. Yet he does not appreciate the damage his tone and language do to his employee's performance and their working relationship. The employee believes that confrontation and honesty will only make things worse. Our experience is that this *leaning away* response typically makes conflicts worse. In contrast, a well-framed confrontation (i.e., *leaning into* the conflict) stands a much better chance of achieving an improved workplace for both individuals. We cannot count the number of times we have had someone say to us, "I wish she had told me sooner. I didn't realize how bad it was." The victim's deception directly contributes to the continuing conflict and causes further divergence in the future. The proverbial "tangled web we weave when at first we conspire to deceive" becomes, itself, a Conflict Trap. We have the illusion of protecting ourselves in the short-term while we actually make things worse for ourselves and others in the long-term.

More generally, when you lie about what you want, or hide what you object to, you send the message that the behaviour you object to is acceptable. The individual who engages in the offensive behaviour is reinforced for acting in that way, and this creates further divergence. We were told the story of a woman who received a ceramic frog as a gift from a friend. She told the friend she loved it, even though she actually hated it. She is now the not-so-proud owner of 15 ceramic frogs. In workplace relationships, not being honest about one's interests or feelings leads to similarly poor, and far more significant, outcomes.

Ultimately, conflict over gifts is not typically worth the risk of confronting the other person. The importance of preserving the relationship and the feelings of the other person through "tactful white lies" can outweigh the importance of the feelings about the gift. However, as described above, the avoidance of workplace conflicts by means of deception will typically come back to haunt the deceiver in far more dramatic ways. In Part 3 we will elaborate on the role of honesty and how honesty, when conveyed appropriately, fosters convergence rather than more conflict. We will describe how you can be brutally honest without being a brute.

SHIELDING

The use of defence mechanisms can also be viewed as a form of emotional shielding. We use defence mechanisms to establish a type of force field around our emotional selves to prevent further damage from occurring. This shield is similar to the medieval metal shields used by knights to defend against the weapons of their enemies. Although intended to be protective, this type of shield can have two harmful side effects. First, a shield prevents all sorts of input from getting through—not just the attacks of others. Thus, a person who daily walks through their workplace with his or her shield on will block the perception of even positive feedback and support; the individual will also be prevented from engaging in constructive measures that aim to resolve differences. Second, a shield—particularly a large one—is likely to be perceived as a weapon by other parties engaged in a conflict, not a self-protection device. Denial, displacement, projection, sublimation (in the form of humour or sarcasm), and other defence mechanisms can all sting others and result in escalating hostilities. The use of shielding is a vital response to our need to control anxiety and protect ourselves; however, when shielding is misunderstood and becomes too deep and intractable, it ends up generating a paradoxical effect: it escalates conflict and increases the attacks made on the person busy shielding himself. To move toward convergence and profit, the shields must at some point be lowered, and new experiences must be engaged.

Social Psychology and Emotion

Emotion, Cognition, and Action

FIGURE 4.1
The Anxiety Curve

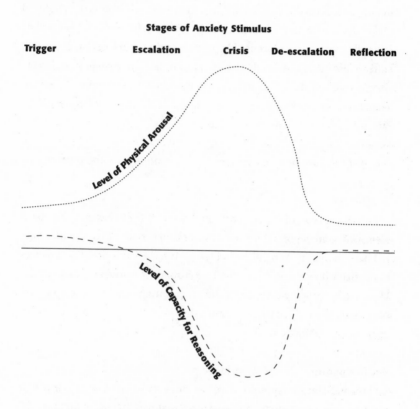

Stages of Anxiety Stimulus

Trigger   **Escalation**   **Crisis**   **De-escalation**   **Reflection**

Level of Physical Arousal

Level of Capacity for Reasoning

When emotions run high, reason runs low.

An exploration of the relationship between feeling, thinking, and doing yields insight into conflict. A growing body of evidence indicates that even relatively mild shifts in a person's current mood can exert strong influences on important aspects of thinking. One effect has been called the *mood-congruent judgement* effect. It suggests that people's current mood often tends to influence the way in which they think as well as their social judgement.[29] For example, when someone is in a positive mood he tends to think happy thoughts and to see his world in a more positive way. The glass is at least half full. In contrast, when someone is in a negative mood he is more receptive to negative interpretations of events and a cynical outlook on life. Strong emotional arousal creates what has been identified as a cognitive deficit, a reduced ability to formulate rational plans of action, or a reduced ability to evaluate the potential outcomes of various behaviours. Thus, people in conflict who become aroused by perceived threats to their interests will suffer a loss of capacity to think rationally. In fact, we have observed many people take self-defeating actions, such as cheating, sabotage, or acts of vengeance, because of a heightened emotional state that interferes with the rational pursuit of their actual interests.

Just because one has an emotion does not mean one must act on it.

The concept of "emotional intelligence" (EQ) has recently been identified as an important quality of successful people.[30] People with a high EQ have the ability to regulate and learn from their emotional experiences rather than allow affective impulses to control their behaviour and decisions. Similarly, we propose that people and organizations need to develop a form of conflict intelligence that integrates the profit track concepts of insight, inspiration, and investment.

Social Cognition and Motivation

The second area of psychology we can draw substantial knowledge from regarding the perceptions and behaviours that perpetuate conflict is social cognition and motivation. Several theories have emerged over the years that explain how we perceive events, how we form judgements, and what motivates us to think and act as we do. Each of the following theories provides insight into understanding factors that contribute to the experience of conflict.

CAUSAL ATTRIBUTION

Attributions are conclusions people form regarding *why* someone acts or thinks a certain way. Attributions are our conclusions or, more accurately, our assumptions about what motivates another person. When we are in conflict with someone—when they act in a manner that threatens us or they pursue objectives that threaten us—we instinctively try to assess their underlying motives. We become naïve scientists searching for cause and effect. Such information is perceived to be useful for understanding the current behaviour of another party and predicting their future behaviour. We think that if we know why they are doing what they are doing we will be in a better position to protect or pursue our own interests. Yet our experience demonstrates that these initial attributions are often wrong, and that the tendency to focus on the "why" is often counterproductive. Paradoxically, not only are these attributions often wrong, we actually believe the opposite—*we "know" we are right.* As a result of this illusion, we can embark on a course of action that is entirely different from that which we would have pursued had we come to the conclusion that we cannot really know what motivates another person.

> *We act as if we know when it would be more productive to act as if we do not know.*

To explain the attribution process, Kelley, a social psychologist, developed what is referred to as the co-variation model.[31] This model describes how individuals process information to make causal attributions about the behaviour of the self and others. More specifically, these attributions aim to assess whether a behaviour or decision stems from one of two sources:

- **INTERNAL CAUSES**, such as characteristics, motives, and the intentions of the person
- **EXTERNAL CAUSES**, such as aspects of the social or physical world

According to this model, attributions are derived as a result of three criteria:

CONSENSUS—the extent to which others react in the same manner to a stimulus or event, such as the person we are considering. Is the reaction unique to the person in question?

CONSISTENCY—the extent to which the person we are considering reacts to a specific stimulus or event in the same way on other occasions. Do they react in a different manner to similar events?

DISTINCTIVENESS—the extent to which the person reacts in the same manner to other, different stimuli or events. Do they react in a similar manner to different events?

The model suggests that we subconsciously use these sources of information to make judgements about why someone is acting as he is, and that we do so to protect ourselves and pursue our interests. More specifically, we use these observations to determine if the actions or thoughts of others with whom we are in conflict are prompted by external causes, such as being sick, or internal causes, such as prejudice. For example, consider an individual whom we believe has lied to us. According to attribution theory, we can reflect on the following questions:

- Did the person react differently than we would expect others to (e.g., others do not or would not lie)?
- Did the person react in a manner similar to reactions he or she has displayed in similar situations (e.g., lies whenever threatened)?
- Did the person react in a manner similar to reactions he or she has displayed in different situations (e.g., lies all the time, regardless of the situation)?

If our answers are yes to these questions, we will judge that the person's behaviour is driven by internal causes (e.g., the person is just a liar). If we already have biases about a group to which this person belongs, we may extend this judgement to the whole group. This process is central to the formation of group stereotypes and prejudices and their application to individuals. If we conclude that someone with whom we have a conflict is acting in a malicious manner, we tend to increase our protective mechanisms. In contrast, if we conclude the person is driven by valid external forces, or is acting in good faith, we are more likely to open up to that person and disregard the lie.

However, social science research, substantiated by our own case experience, reveals that people often make significant errors in attribution because they rely on assumptions or stereotypes and not on actual observation. For example, imagine someone cuts you off while driving. Are they a bad driver (internal) or did something happen to cause them to swerve into your lane (external)? You have never seen that person before. What information will you use to draw a conclusion? We know that people effectively rely on other, less direct information (such as racial or gender stereotypes), one's own past experiences associated with being cut off, one's own view of his or her own driving competence, and so forth. Similarly, we rarely have enough quality information in the context of workplace conflicts to make reliable attributions on a fair and individual basis, yet we proceed to do so anyway. We rely on our fears, stereotypes, past experiences, and recollections of similar experiences to judge whether the other party is flawed and we are justified.

One established attribution error particularly relevant in conflict situations has been identified as the *hostile attribution bias*. This bias refers to the tendency to perceive that hostile intentions or motives drive others' actions when their behaviours pose a threat. For example, people accused of harassment will perceive complainants to be malicious when they make a complaint and that they intend to harm the respondent; they do not assume the complainants are being self-protective and intend to improve their work situations. Managers who are told lies by their staff will perceive the motives of these staff members to be purposefully manipulative rather than responsive to a perceived threat, perhaps in response to the threatening behaviours of the managers themselves.

In a similar vein, a second well-known bias involves attributing internal causes of behaviour (e.g., he is a liar, she is selfish, he is lazy) to those who threaten your interests, rather than consider external or situational causes (e.g., he is under stress, she has different information than I do, he has taken ill).[32] In contrast, people are more likely to attribute external causes to their own behaviour when it causes offence or harm to others (e.g., I am stressed, he made me do it, I thought that was how I was supposed to act). Research has documented that pronounced attribution biases occur in corporate disputes, particularly when the behaviour of one party negatively affects the attributing party (i.e., when the two parties are interdependent).[33]

Together, these two biases lead people in conflict, particularly people in substantially heightened states of anxious arousal, to judge their antagonists to be wilfully attempting to hurt them and to be driven solely by internal factors. This dynamic is why we often hear people in conflict say that efforts to resolve a given conflict is "hopeless." They reflect this mindset of despair because they have attributed internal and hostile motives to the other party. In contrast, they have attributed well-meaning and external attributions to their own harmful behaviour.

If our initial attributions of others' intentions are consistent with these biases, our feelings of threat will increase. We are prone to view any new actions in which the other party engages in a manner that confirms these attributions, even if the actions are ambiguous or suggestive of a more neutral or positive motive. This dynamic is consistent with the notion of the "self-fulfilling prophecy." As suggested above, the phrase "seeing is believing" is perhaps not fully descriptive. Here we suggest a rephrasing of this common assertion:

Believing is seeing.

Therefore, countering biases at the beginning of any conflict, either by rejecting these attributions as likely flawed and unimportant, or by forming attributions based on transparent negotiation and an objective assessment of the three sources of information, will help support the move into convergence.

ROLE THEORY

In a study referred to as the "Stanford Prison Experiment," healthy male college students were randomly assigned either to be guards or prisoners in a mock prison setting on campus. Although the study had been planned to last two weeks, they had to stop it after six days because of the extreme conflicts that occurred. Prisoners first became rebellious and even attempted an uprising; after the uprising was crushed, they became passive and depressed. Guards became hostile and aggressive. In short, the students came to act more and more like actual prisoners and guards.[34]

This study demonstrated the power of one's *role* on the perceptions, interpretations, and actions of each individual. We have encountered managers who believe their role is to shape up incompetent staff, union leaders who believe their role is to defeat management by using whatever means are at hand, CEOs who believe their role is to "role model" the values of the organization, and CEOs who believe their role is to govern the organization with an iron hand. Role theory suggests it is the role that defines the person rather than the person who defines the role. More often than not, the role defines perspectives of what is right or wrong, acceptable or unacceptable, good or bad. Many times, over the years, we have heard clients say, "I'm just doing my job," and offer this rationalized defence of engaging in destructive behaviour. From a business standpoint, the CEO of Union Carbide, after the Bhopal tragedy in which thousands of people were killed or made ill by a deadly release of toxic gas, most likely believed he was doing what any CEO in his position would do when he denied the harm and distanced the company from responsibility. From a global perspective, dictators throughout history have justified their tragic and abominable actions as the means to achieve some larger, noble end.

As in the case of the prison experiment, individuals may reject reasonable alternatives to their behaviour because of their perceptions of the obligations of the role they fulfill. They will act in a manner that they think is congruent with the role, even if the action contradicts their personal values or evidence is presented indicating the damage they are causing.

We worked with one manager of a long-term care facility who clearly viewed her role as the "enforcer" of policies and regulations. Any employee who deviated from established policy, no matter how reasonable the deviation was in a particular context, became the target of her ire and disrespectful supervision. On one occasion, the staff at this long-term care home baked a cake and was preparing to present it to one of the residents, who was turning 90 years old that day. The manager walked into the employee lounge where the cake sat, topped with a few lit candles ready for presentation to the resident. The manager responded by berating the staff for violating fire regulations; she demonstrated no appreciation of the extra effort made by the employees to provide a positive experience for the resident. By "swinging the rod," the manager suppressed her staff's enthusiasm and innovative spirit and created an unnecessary conflict. When asked why she acted as she did, the manager responded by saying it was her job to ensure all policies were followed, despite the fact that the fire risk was negligible in this circumstance. She said, in effect, that the role made her do it. In contrast, the staff attributed her behaviour solely to "internal" factors. They said, in essence, that she was just a "bitch." Rather than create a huge divergence between herself and her staff, the manager could have achieved her goal of policy compliance and supported the enthusiasm of her staff simply by responding in a manner that respected both sets of interests. She did not do so, however, because she did not think she needed to—it was not her job.

The concept of *role* is one of the strong external factors that influences individual behaviour. The power of a *role* should not be underestimated. Managing role expectations is an important feature of conflict prevention and movement out of the Conflict Trap.

SOCIAL INFLUENCE

One powerful but often under-appreciated influence on behaviour is our desire to fit in with the group to which we belong or wish to belong. Although this influence does not affect some people, most of us feel pressure in group settings to act in a manner that is consistent with our perceptions of the expectations or general pattern of the group. Whether spurred by the need to manage the impressions of others, or by a lack of confidence in oneself, many people tend to adapt their thoughts and behaviour in response to group pressure.

A classic demonstration of this influence involved a study in which subjects were asked to respond to a series of visual perception problems, such as comparing the length of one line to three comparison lines.[35] A group of six to eight people were asked to respond. All participants but one, the last one to respond to the researcher, were accomplices of the researcher. Results showed that 76 percent of the subjects acquiesced to the group's selection of a given line even when the selection was clearly wrong.

Thus, people will deceive, hide their true feelings, and suppress socially unacceptable interests, ideas, and opinions to accommodate the social pressure that may exist in a situation. In addition, people may engage in harmful actions directed towards others in response to pressures experienced from a group. One type of this phenomenon has been referred to as *mobbing*. Mobbing is a form of social influence in which members of a group experience de-individuation, the loss of a sense of personal responsibility for the negative impacts of the group's behaviours.[36] People are particularly susceptible to the influence of others when they are in this state of de-individuation.

Often, a particularly charismatic supervisor or employee with whom other workers identify, at least initially, initiates mobbing in the workplace. Studies characterize people who are capable of gathering others into a state of de-individuation—such as leaders of extreme fringe groups and cults— as classic workplace bullies.[37] Bullies understand how to use social influence to build a following and exploit the vulnerability of co-workers they perceive to be "lesser" than themselves.

One would think that a person who is perceived to be a bully in the workplace would either be dealt with immediately or would develop some insight into the errors of their ways. However, having observed hundreds of bullies in many workplaces, we have noticed that bullies are, ironically, often rewarded for their "results-oriented" approach, even if it is detrimental to team functioning. Focusing on getting the task done, and knowing how to use power, regardless of how others feel about it, can get a lot of tasks completed in the short term.

On the other hand, focusing exclusively on getting tasks done, with no concern for relationships, ignores the connection between tasks and relationships. Popular reality television is rife with images of contestants "voted off the island" because they failed to pay attention to the importance of relationships and were, instead, over-focused on completing tasks. Like a country's foreign policy that focuses exclusively on its own needs, regardless of the needs of other countries, this short-sighted approach can win a few battles but ultimately loses the war as a result of intractable resistance. The resistance and rebellion of co-workers ultimately interferes with achieving goals over the long term.

With regard to people's insight into their own bullying behaviours, workplace bullies, contrary to popular belief, seldom see themselves as bullies. Instead, workplace bullies see themselves in three ways:

- The Champion: this bully is the self-appointed champion of professional standards who protects the "right" way to get things done amidst a sea of incompetent others.
- The Victim: often a bully will report how others are abusive to him. He will point out how others have not responded to his complaints about his lack of control and how he is under attack by "political correctness" or unreasonable expectations.
- The Warrior: a combination of both of the above, the warrior perceives that others seem to get all the breaks, and so the warrior will take on the job of being the great equalizer—to make sure that others do not get ahead and to set things straight.

In our work with over three thousand employees and leaders in hundreds of work environments, we have yet to sit down with someone who is reportedly engaging in harmful, bullying behaviour and have that individual say, "Roy, Larry—I'm so glad you're here. I'm a bully and I need help." It doesn't happen. It never will. Bullying is always something that someone else is doing. As with the defence mechanisms of projection and displacement, we have a tendency to distance ourselves from negative characteristics and to associate them with others; we do this so that we can simplify complex inter-actions by seeing ourselves as *good*, others as *bad*. While many people report being bullied, few acknowledge being a bully. So it is that a bully is able to enlist support from colleagues who wish to join the Champion, aide the Victim, or protect themselves from the Warrior. The pressure upon co-workers to participate in mobbing in the workplace is a powerful form of social influence that keeps organizations trapped in conflict.

Understanding the pressures some people feel when in groups offers some insight into how to help individuals involved in group conflict find ways to mitigate these pressures, overcome barriers, and pursue congruence.

IMPRESSION MANAGEMENT

Impression management can be understood as the positive, proactive side of the defence mechanism of rationalization. Impression management involves the process of modifying the presentation of oneself in order to increase one's influence in relationships and maximize profitable outcomes.[38] For example, people may express support for certain values or objectives— even if they do not actually embrace those values or objectives—if, by doing so, they are more likely to get their interests met. We all experience some level of narcissism, and most of us want others to see us as professional, competent, ethical, principled, and caring. In conflict situations, impression management can serve to build bridges by demonstrating characteristics that are valued by others.

Nevertheless, some of our most challenging cases have involved individuals who either engage in little, if any, impression management, or engage in far too much. In some situations, a lack of investment in what others think causes individuals to be overly aggressive, competitive, or rigid when responding to conflict. Such individuals do not care if they appear to be unfair, unethical, or abusive. To these people the ends justify the means and, if their ends are achieved, why should they care if people think poorly of them? They believe any reasonable person will ultimately support their efforts if the goal is achieved. However, in the end, the attainment of profit at any expense usually backfires, and the residue of conflict may last forever.

In other situations, some people become overly invested in the views of others and invest their self-worth in the control of others. In one case we encountered, a middle-level manager was having difficulty with her director. The director was highly esteemed in the organization and the manager located her value as an employee completely within his control. Over the time they worked together, she had done everything possible, from her perspective, to create a positive impression on the director.

During a stressful work period, he began to question certain decisions she had made and suggested she was falling behind in her work. She was devastated. To address her feelings of despair, her initial reaction was to perceive him as a harasser and thus insulate herself from her negative feelings. In this way she also sought to protect her sense of herself as a highly skilled and productive employee. Through our discussion, she realized she had given the director too much control over her self-worth and that she was over-reacting to his criticism of her work. Her conflict with him was resolved through her own self-discovery and she developed a healthier perspective of her view of their relationship. Through building her own insight, she was able to stay inspired on the job and use the feedback provided by the director to enhance her performance.

A healthy dose of impression management is valuable in conflict situations. Equally important is the recognition that most of us are motivated, to some extent, by the goal of impression management. It is challenging to not overreact to others' attempts to embellish their strengths or minimize their weaknesses, particularly when conflicts arise. However, not caring at all about what others think, or caring too much, will result in behaviour that exacerbates differences and perpetuates divergence and dysfunction. We have heard from many managers who become frustrated with employees who claim they understand something when in fact they do not. Teachers and trainers experience the same frustration. The force that is likely at work, here, is a need to engage in impression management on the part of the employee or trainee involved. Rather than see the other's response as a lie, they can choose to understand it as an attempt to manage impressions. Managers and trainers need to help such individuals learn—and believe— that, consistent with the old saying, "there are no stupid questions" and that they do not have to fear being honest.

GROUP SERVING BIAS AND STEREOTYPE-DRIVEN CONFLICT

One unfortunate but natural aspect of conflict is that conflict, by definition, divides people into opposing forces. These "opposing forces" then compete for resources based on their practical and psychological interests, particularly when the availability of these resources is limited. One powerful psychological process that influences our perceptions of others, particularly those with whom we clash or compete, has been called *the group serving bias.*[39] This bias involves seeing persons or groups with whom we compete as markedly different from and inferior to our own group or ourselves. This phenomenon is also referred to as the *in-group/out-group effect.* In other words, conflict can lead to prejudicial views of those with whom we have conflict, to stereotyping our adversaries. We also observe that the opposite is true: prejudicial views based on stereotypes can lead to conflict among people because of group serving biases that cause one to think, "I deserve more than you because I am better than you."

Psychologically, we organize our understanding of people at the most simple level—there are those who are like us and those who are not—in order to simplify our view of society and determine who is deserving of fear and loathing, and who can be trusted and valued. The resulting prejudice, as noted in chapter 1, is a crucial factor in the causation and perpetuation of conflict. Consider the following classic field study:

> In a classroom of grade three students, a teacher divided the class into two groups based on eye colour. On the first day, brown-eyed children were assigned an inferior status. They were ridiculed by the teacher and described as more dull, lazier, and sloppier than blue-eyed children. They were denied classroom privileges and, as a sign of their low status, were made to wear special collars. This treatment was continued for several days and then reversed. The students in both groups found the experience of being the target of discrimination quite upsetting, with the consequence that their school performance decreased and physical conflict erupted between students who were previously friendly.[40]

Our need to organize our perceptions of the world in absolute, or "black and white," terms is strong. Such groupings are typically based on observable characteristics such as gender, skin colour, ethnic background, behaviour, or expressed values or preferences. In workplaces, groupings tend to be rooted in differences such as levels of authority (e.g., management/staff), types of affiliation (e.g., management/union), and types of work (e.g., sales/production), in addition to personal characteristics, as noted above. Once the perceived difference creates an "out-group," people will interpret all new information associated with that group in a manner consistent with their predisposed negative view. This psychological practice is related to the desire to view oneself as "better than," rather than simply "different than." It also serves to rationalize actions undertaken to harm others (e.g., sabotage, deceit, even murder) when such actions serve as a means to affirm one's own superiority and self-esteem.

Consistent with this bias, we grow to judge members of "out-groups" based on stereotypes developed for the specific purpose of fostering negative views of that group. Thus, stereotyped views lead individuals to assess the actions and interests of out-group members with suspicion and disdain, and to subject them to *hostile attribution bias*. When actual or perceived conflict arises with members of an out-group, the typical response is to pursue one's own interests with even more vigour, competitiveness, and rigidity, even if to do so means turning to devious and malicious means. Studies have shown that individuals will choose less beneficial, even harmful options for themselves as long as the outcome they experience is better than that experienced by those in an "out-group."

Understanding the power of *group serving bias* and the tendency to (mis)apply stereotypes can help individuals and organizations develop more collaborative approaches to resolving differences. Strategies effective for developing awareness of this bias include working within ourselves and with others to revise our view of who constitutes the "out-group" and who the "in-group" comprises; strategies also include the debunking of stereotypes and promoting the evaluation of people and situations based on current and meaningful information. Retraining in these cognitive processes is particularly important for leaders who must recruit, hire, and appraise employees, and those who must find ways to manage conflict that support both employees' and organizational objectives.

COGNITIVE DISSONANCE

Most conflict gurus focus their efforts on defining and dealing with interpersonal conflict. However, conflict, as a clash of interests, can be both intra-personal and interpersonal. In fact, most workplace conflicts that we observe involve both intra-personal and interpersonal aspects.

More specifically, two types of intra-personal conflict can occur. The first entails a person who seeks to satisfy two needs that appear to be diametrically opposed (e.g., the desire for career advancement and the desire to spend more time with family; the desire to lose weight and the desire to eat fattening food). This type of conflict typically involves distinguishing a priority from among different needs and searching for ways to "have one's cake and eat it too."

The second type of intra-personal conflict involves a more powerful, but often underestimated, influence on a person: the psychological motivation to hold consistent views or to act in a manner consistent with ones own stated views. Leon Festinger, an early psychologist, first defined this form of intra-personal conflict as cognitive dissonance.[41] Simply put, he postulated that dissonance occurs when an individual has two or more cognitions, or thoughts, at the same time that have contradictory implications for his or her behaviour. Dissonance theory has been most relevant when accounting for the reactions of individuals who do something that may be viewed as unreasonable, improper, or harmful. The person needs to reconcile the clash between their beliefs (e.g., "I am a reasonable, good person") with the reality that she just did something unreasonable or unsupportable given an objective assessment of the situation (e.g., "I was mean to that person").

In a work context, this drive leads individuals to defend previously stated viewpoints, also referred to as *positions*, even in the face of contradictory evidence or information. For example, a marketing manager who expresses his opinion about the viability of a new product is prone to resist changing his opinion in subsequent discussions because of the discomfort he will experience if he acknowledges his initial misjudgement. Because of this drive, some people are extremely reticent to ever change their minds. Some might view changing their minds as a demonstration of weakness and poor judgement. In fact, experts on the practice of good leadership suggest the opposite is true—that good leaders are fully prepared to acknowledge their mistakes and change their minds if it is reasonable to do so, even without "new" information.[42]

Many experiments that examine the effects of cognitive dissonance demonstrate the capacity of people to re-organize their belief system, or their *perception* of what they have done or believed, in order to be more congruent with and to justify their actions or decisions. This may reflect an overt attempt to reorganize perceptions or a subconscious process to harmonize dissonance. The following studies demonstrate the power of cognitive dissonance on individual decision-making in business settings.

In one study, subjects were asked to divide $20 million in R and D funding between two company divisions. Subjects were told that, three years earlier, Division 1 received $10 million in funding but had experienced a drop in earnings since that time. Subjects were then divided into two groups: a "high responsibility" group, in which they were to imagine that they had made the previous funding decision, and a "low responsibility" group, in which they were to imagine that they had not made the previous decision. The results showed that subjects in the high responsibility group gave most of the current funds to the previously funded division; subjects in the other group did not demonstrate the need to be congruent with a previous decision, albeit a poor one.[43]

In another study, managers were asked to evaluate the performance of clerical staff in a large organization. Managers evaluated employees they had hired or recommended for hire more favourably than employees they had recommended not be hired or those in whose hiring they were not involved. Objective measures found no differences in the performance between the groups of clerical workers. The study's conclusion was that managers feel a drive to be congruent with previous decisions, even in the face of contrary evidence.[44]

We have observed many situations that initially involved differences of opinion escalate into full-fledged conflicts, simply because opinions were expressed before all the relevant interests and issues were discussed. Parties fell subject to the *hostile attribution bias* in their interpretation of the underlying motives driving the other party's opinions. These attributions resulted in escalating hostilities between the parties and, eventually, the expression of inflammatory comments, including accusations of incompetence, harassment, and misconduct. In one case, defamation lawsuits were filed in response to a conflict that originated over a relatively simple disagreement about the legitimacy of procedures that specialists should use in certain surgical situations.

The strong drive to maintain internal cognitive consistency is a key factor in assessing conflict situations and managing responses to conflict. The drive is so strong that people who unintentionally share wrong information, or make decisions based on evidence later proven to be false, may well feel compelled to use deception, obfuscation, or other means to justify their initial behaviour or decision.

Dissonance can also manifest subconsciously, as it does when people truly believe their rationalization of incongruent behaviour. In one case, we investigated an organnzational leader who had allegedly been hostile and threatening towards numerous colleagues and staff. His behaviour had caused lost productivity, ineffective decision-making, and widespread team dissension. He clearly saw himself as a noble and kind person, which he could well have been in other circumstances. He rationalized his abusive conduct as (a) necessary to support quality, and (b) a reasonable reaction to his own mistreatment by others. He reconciled the dissonance he felt between his self-image, as a good person, and others' view of him, as abusive, by denying some of his conduct and dissociating himself from any responsibility for the outcomes of his conduct. He also reported significant despair in terms of hurt feelings and loss of dignity. Even though this person was a leader in his field and by many accounts "brilliant," the organization removed him to restore efficiency, productivity, and a positive balance in the workplace. He was unable to distinguish between disagreement and being disagreeable, and he responded to perceived conflict with aggression—what we refer to as the *charging-into predisposition*.

An additional research illustration of the subconscious manifestation of dissonance occurred in an early experiment conducted by David Glass.[45] This research found that subjects who opposed the use of electric shock nevertheless proceeded to apply electric shock to a partner in an experiment; they altered their original view of their victim as someone who was a nice person to someone who was not very nice and therefore deserved, implicitly, the harsh treatment they imposed on him or her.

Dissonance, as a form of internal conflict, motivates the bully to blame the bullied, the abuser to blame the victim, and the abused to blame him- or herself (e.g., "I must have deserved it"). Blaming occurs in order to shift responsibility as well as to reconcile perceptions that an individual was justified in perpetrating or accommodating a given negative act, and that the individual was justified in his or her effort to satisfy a given need even at the expense of the needs, desires, and even the rights of others. Yet, as we will demonstrate in Part 3, the motivational power of dissonance can be used effectively to prevent and resolve many workplace conflicts.

Personality and Psychopathology

In attempts to aid people dealing with conflict, many books (e.g., *Please Understand Me*; *Toxic Coworkers*[46]) and speakers spend considerable effort organizing people into personality types to explain problematic behaviour and why it is that people end up misunderstood and in conflict. Others suggest that personality and psychopathology are the root causes of conflict.[47] However useful and comforting it is, from a cognitive perspective, to place people in these types of personality "boxes," we have observed that this practice can generate increased conflict and misperception amongst people. The reason is that an individual has little reason to expect another person's behaviour to change: "Now, not only do I dislike, distrust, and fear you, I've come to believe your behaviour is intractable because, after all, it's your personality to act this way." In fact, the labels associated with categorizing people can leave us with a false understanding of others and a misimpression of our own role in conflict.

From our view, the concept of the "personality conflict" is a misnomer. For the most part, all conflicts are "personality conflicts," but this does not help us resolve them. Personality has a strong influence on how one thinks and acts. Yet to effectively grapple with the reality of conflict, we need to focus on the issues and interests, on the thoughts and behaviours, on the processes and the outcomes, and not on each other's personalities. The notion of a "personality conflict" provides an easy and socially sanctioned excuse for parties to avoid dealing with the real contradiction of interests they have. Drawing on direct personal experience, we appreciate that behaviours associated with personality disorders can make people very hard to deal with. Anyone who has had conflict with a person diagnosed with a personality disorder will attest to the frustration that his or her symptoms, such as dependence and self-absorption, can cause. However, divergence is created by beliefs and behaviours, not personality. The desire to recognize personality as the source of conflict has been identified by psychologists as the Fundamental Attribution Error (FAE).[48] FAE, which is consistent with the previously mentioned *hostile attribution bias*, is the human tendency to overestimate the influence of basic character traits and underestimate the role of context that shapes behaviours in a given situation. We oversimplify in this way in a misguided attempt to explain undesirable behaviour. In one experiment, equally qualified basketball athletes were divided into two groups. One group played in a well-lit gym; the second group played in a poorly lit gym. As a result of poor lighting, the second group missed more shots. When the spectators were asked which athletes were more skilled, the players in the well-lit gym were judged to be superior.

We have had cases involving people diagnosed with schizophrenia, depression, adult attention deficit disorder, obsessive-compulsive disorder, and other psychiatric difficulties. In one case, the functioning of a team at a small consulting firm had completely deteriorated because most of the team sought to avoid one individual who had been diagnosed with depression. His behaviour was causing considerable stress and conflict within the team. However well meaning the team members were, their avoidance of the person and the behind-the-scenes gossip only served to exacerbate the conflict. Situations that involve mental health issues are delicate and warrant clear-minded and well-informed consideration. However, there is little value in labelling. With very few exceptions, people, if properly understood and motivated, can adapt their behaviour to pursue convergence and profitable outcomes from conflict regardless of "mental health."

Two case studies illustrate this point. In one case we were contracted to consult on a conflict occurring between the son of a long-term-care patient in a hospital and the nursing staff. We learned the staff members were petrified of him due to his erratic, weird, and threatening conduct. Management and nursing staff reported he was coming to see his mother on a daily basis and always did so at the same time. He would often ask questions about his mother's care using accusatory language and did so in a hostile manner. He would regularly complain to management about his mother's care. The nurses often heard him have loud arguments with his mother. They had observed him go into other patients' rooms and take their blankets to his mother's room. On one occasion, they reportedly observed him shaving his mother's face with a machete. He had resisted giving the hospital any information about himself; in fact, the hospital had no phone number or home address for him. Scared, and feeling helpless, the nursing and management staff went to the hospital administration to enlist its support to get a restraining order to prevent the son from coming on site and visiting his mother. They were convinced he was mentally unstable, unreasonable, and that removing him was the only way to protect their psychological and practical interests.

When we entered the picture the hospital was about to pursue the process of obtaining a restraining order, adopting a *charging into* strategy. We also learned the nurses had been using a *leaning away* strategy through their avoidance of him and by not responding to his questions or complaints. This strategy only exacerbated his frustration and prompted even more aggressive behaviour on his part. Yet several high-level nursing leaders did not want to deny the patient the opportunity to see her son, who was her only visitor and whose visits she appeared to enjoy.

To attempt to resolve this conflict, we teamed up with a nursing leader who first met with the nursing staff and local management to learn more about their experiences. We then invited the son to meet with us to learn about his experiences and determine if he would respond positively to a "leaning into" approach to resolve the conflict. During the meeting we were able to ascertain that the son had some very rigid, likely pathological, needs regarding hygiene, and that most of his complaints were related to substandard hygienic practices, in his view, involving his mother. We could also see how his other "odd" behaviour was consistent with characteristics of obsessive-compulsive tendencies. We also learned he had an apparently pathological mistrust of administration. Notwithstanding all these psychological challenges, when we presented the nursing staff's concerns about their interactions with him, the son was responsive and interested. He was surprised to hear how afraid of him the nursing staff members were and he was able to recognize how his conduct was part of the problem. He agreed to change his conduct. After the meeting, we informed the nurses of this outcome and provided some training to deal with similar difficult situations. As a result of the intervention, the son was able to continue to visit with his mother and the staff felt more confident and less fearful working with the son.

In a different case, we were asked to consult on a situation in which an employee was put off work pending a psychological assessment of his "emotional stability." We entered the picture after the employee's supervisor, the unit manager, and a human resource consultant had implemented this strategy to, in their words, "support" the employee. The supervisor had prior information that this employee had had past "mental health" problems and knew he had taken time off work previously due to stress. A recent incident had occurred in which the employee allegedly became agitated with another employee, to the degree that he exhibited threatening and erratic behaviour (e.g., he aggressively pointed his finger and raised his voice). This was the second complaint management had received in the past month about his behaviour. Rather than try to address this conflict situation through regular performance management processes, or even through alternative dispute resolution approaches, management decided to mandate that the employee submit to a psychological assessment and placed him off work until the completion of that process. Their stated practical interests were concern for the safety of others and the well being of the employee in question. In fact, the supervisor stated she thought this approach would be less damaging to and embarrassing for the employee.

Not surprisingly, the employee felt more damaged and humiliated by this strategy, and was highly motivated to protect his psychological interests, which he now perceived to be under threat. From our view, management used this tactic because of its misunderstanding and misattribution of possible psychological dimensions in this conflict. After being assessed as healthy by a physician hired by the organization, the employee made a human rights complaint against the organization for discrimination based on the protected ground of mental disability, a suit the organization settled at significant cost. If management had focused on the issues involved in the conflict, on the behaviour of concern, and on the interests important to the involved parties, management would have avoided incurring several damaging outcomes, including emotional damage to the employee, operational damage to his work team, and financial costs to the organization.

There are times when psychiatric or psychological factors are so central to a conflict that they must be considered and addressed. In one such case, an employee reported to us that his colleagues were harassing him. He described how they would move his things around on his desk and send subtle messages to him in their behaviour. He described how one of his female colleagues was making unwelcome sexual advances towards him simply by bobbing her foot up and down while she sat with her legs crossed in a neighbouring cubicle. Over a period of weeks he reported how his co-workers behaviour was escalating: they were now breaking into his home and moving his things around when he was at work. These co-workers were accomplishing this feat even though he had installed the latest in security locks in his home, which he could describe in minute detail. He also reported feeling physically threatened at work and was considering how he might defend himself. At this point, he agreed to let us meet with his managers; they informed us the man's co-workers had been reporting very strange behaviour on the part of our client for several months. With no evidence to support our client's reports, and in cooperation with his union, we all agreed this client was in need of help, and he was placed off work for assessment and treatment. This action also helped serve the interests of the department in which concerns were mounting and productivity was decreasing due to the individual's erratic and paranoid behaviour. All this was accomplished without grievances, lawsuits, or increased group conflict.

In summary, we have, in this chapter, covered a range of psychological and sociological factors that influence individuals' perceptions and shape their motivations when conflict is perceived. These intra-personal factors lock people in the Conflict Trap and impair their ability, and the ability of leaders, to engage with conflicted parties in attempts to discover mutually profitable solutions. In chapter 5 we turn our attention to the interpersonal aspects that contribute to the emergence, interpretation, and perpetuation of conflict.

Conflict Within at a Glance

- Conflict manifests within each of us psychologically as intra-personal perspectives and defences.
- The adoption of the principle that "all behaviour makes sense" is helpful for beginning to understand how we view conflict.
- There are Seven Deadly Defences:
  Denial
  Suppression
  Projection
  Displacement
  Reaction formation
  Identification
  Rationalization.

  Though we use them naturally and they provide effective means to protect our own egos, the Seven Deadly Defences ultimately function as barriers that keep us stuck in the Conflict Trap.
- Deception is a common defence we employ to hide reality from others and ourselves. While initially perceived as protective, like armour, this type of shielding also desensitizes and blinds us, keeping us trapped in conflict.
- When in conflict we tend to judge people and their motives rather than objectively assess the situation. We form attributions about ourselves and others to determine why we and others act in certain ways. These attributions are typically misguided.
- Believing is seeing. We remain stuck in the Conflict Trap because our perceptions are biased by our experiences, expectations, perspectives, and fears, and by our belief that our view of the conflict is the only true view.
- Role theory, social influence, impression management, stereotyping, and cognitive dissonance are all psycho-sociological factors that drive how we experience and respond to conflict.

- All conflicts are "personality conflicts," and yet personality and psychopathology are not usually helpful in understanding and resolving conflict. In fact, we are able to move out of the Conflict Trap with even the most difficult individuals when we employ optimal skills and strategies.

5

Conflict Among

THE INTERPERSONAL MANIFESTATION OF CONFLICT

Eugene hates staff meetings. He tried to function without them, noting they were not cost-efficient. But then his staff said they did not receive some information, and others complained that they did not have any "input." As the supervisor, Eugene implemented a compromise: he held some meetings, but he did so as infrequently as possible. During the next meeting, it seemed to him that Sally challenged everything he presented. When he informed the group of a new policy or directive, she would mutter or roll her eyes. When he asked her if she had something to contribute, she would say sullenly, "Nope. Nothing at all." At another point, she was more explicit and made a counter-argument: "That will never work—we simply don't have the resources." Even when Eugene asked the group for input, Sally muttered, "What's the point? You never use it anyway."

In performance management interviews with her, Eugene and Sally had discussed her attitude. She became defensive, and quoted her lawyer's advice on employment standards, threatening to go to the media with the company's abuses. Eugene felt paralyzed, and in meetings he now expected that any point he raised would meet with either her aggressive or passive-aggressive response. Some staff seemed to side with her, while others just looked at their feet, apparently embarrassed for him.

IN CHAPTER 4 WE EXAMINED PSYCHOLOGICAL FORCES and motivations that influence the conflict experience. In this chapter we turn our attention to the interpersonal dynamics that create, escalate, and perpetuate conflict. We observe that when interpersonal conflict is mishandled it can erode into something far more expansive and insidious—an infestation of negativity, hostility, and tension. Even getting staff together in meetings to discuss issues can become a mechanism that only creates more conflict. To understand these interpersonal dimensions of conflict we take the following steps:

- Examine models of communication and dispute resolution theories
- Explain how communication influences conflict
- Relate our model of conflict to an ecological model developed in the area of pest management
- Reveal insights into how conflict manifests interpersonally and how it can become a type of infestation that traps individuals and organizations in conflict

Senders and Receivers

> Three slightly deaf seniors went on a cruise together. As they were standing out on the deck one of the seniors said to the others, "My, it's windy, isn't it?" Her friend replied, "No, I think it's Thursday." The third senior responded with, "I'm thirsty too; let's get a drink." So, she headed indoors while the other two ran to a lifeboat, fearful that the ship was about to sink.

Often times, what we mean to convey is not what ends up being understood by the other person. To understand this dynamic process we refer to a model developed in the context of cross-cultural communication.[49] This model characterizes communication as a process that occurs between two parties: a Sender and a Receiver. In sending a message, a Sender must determine what to say and how to say it. More specifically, the Sender selects words from a range of vocabulary that will best articulate her thoughts and that do so in a manner that best matches the Receiver's ability to comprehend. The Sender then packages the message, usually subconsciously, using an appropriate tone and volume for the context in order to convey the words, and adds gestures and facial expression. This process has been referred to as "encoding" the message. Typically, this encoding process takes mere fractions of seconds and happens at a subconscious level. Once the thoughts are encoded into words, tone, and body language, the Sender then sends the message to the Receiver who, in turn, decodes the message. The decoding process involves interpreting the meaning of the communication. As dialogue continues, the Receiver becomes the Sender, and so goes the communication process.

The process sounds simple, but in reality it involves myriad complex factors that can interfere with the message's successful communication and its decoding in a manner congruent with its encoded form. Consider the scenario at the beginning of this chapter. Whether intentional or not, every decision and expression made by Eugene will be recognized as a message and will be interpreted by his staff. His body language and tone of voice may convey to some the message that he hates meetings. His reluctance to hold meetings may send a message that he does not want staff input into decisions. His recent decision to hold meetings again may be seen as a patronizing attempt to placate the staff. His manner of presenting issues and solutions may seem domineering and exclusionary and thus foster defensiveness and resistance. The same interpretative process will transpire for Eugene and others as they observe Sally's communication in the meetings. Even the absence of communication is often interpreted as sending a message. Think how powerful the "silent treatment" can be in workplaces and at home. The process of communication and interpretation, of encoding and decoding, is rife with possibilities for miscommunication, misinterpretation, and misunderstanding, depending on who you consider responsible for the gaps that arise from the communication.

Surprisingly, research has demonstrated that in some contexts body language and tone of voice can convey more than 90 percent of a message that is received.[50] This is surprising because we observe that a Sender typically thinks that most, if not all, of her message is encoded in her words. For example, a staff member who greets a colleague entering the work area fifteen minutes late and does so with a wave, a smile, and a cheerful,

"What happened, you're late?" conveys a very different message than the staff member who glares at their co-worker with arms crossed over their chest and coldly, through clenched teeth, asks, "What happened, you're late?" Same words, completely different message sent and received.

Pretty straightforward, right? Wrong.

If you and I have a good relationship—that is, you know me well and understand my values and attitudes—I am lucky if any more than 80 percent of the message I really intended to send to you is actually received as it was intended. If I am a stranger, or you cannot stand me because I am that guy who is never to be trusted, it is more likely that you will receive about 10 percent of what I intended to send. This is because of the role of *filters*. (See Figure 5.1 below.) Filters are personal and contextual factors that shape the message and our interpretation of it. Filters generally come in three types:

- Those that relate primarily to the Sender, such as previous experience and knowledge, current emotional state, language skills, values, self-awareness, self-esteem, gender, ethnicity, and communication or conflict style
- Those that relate primarily to the Receiver, which, in addition to the factors associated with the Sender, include factors such as attention, open-mindedness, and personal or professional biases
- Those filters that arise due to the context of the interaction, such as ambient noise level, the place of discussion, the comfort of the setting, and the time available for discussion, to name a few

FIGURE 5.1
Cross-cultural Communication Model

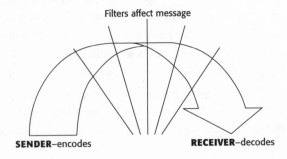

Filters affect message

SENDER–encodes   RECEIVER–decodes

The application of this model to workplace conflict is an important part of the conflict experience: when individuals or groups are in conflict, the growing number of filters that distort messages compromise the clarity of their communication. As a Sender, the more I deny, despair, or detach when in conflict, the less my messages are carefully and clearly encoded. As a Receiver, the more I deny, despair, or detach, the more messages are distorted as they arrive; I am likely to decode them as I assume the worst of intentions, and thus further distort what was meant to be sent. Even when a Sender carefully chooses words in order to be absolutely clear (e.g., express displeasure, disappointment, expectations), the emotion underlying the message will come through in tone of voice and body language in the encoding and decoding process. The trap becomes increasingly problematic when a Receiver responds to an already misunderstood communication with his own confusing message.

For example, consider driving a car as a metaphor for communicating. While you drive, your primary attention may be on what to prepare for dinner, an unresolved situation at work, problems with your children or family, how your make-up or hair looks, or any number of other thoughts, even as you focus your secondary attention on driving. You may be talking on your cell phone, eating, shouting at the kids, looking for a parking place, or engaging in other activities that divert your full attention from the act of driving. Blocks, or even miles, may pass before the act of driving becomes your primary focus once again. Usually, we multitask well and remain sufficiently attentive to react quickly enough to avoid accidents. However, accidents are clearly more likely to occur when the act of driving takes a back seat to the multitude of other issues on our minds.

The same dynamic is at work when communicating. We often encode our messages and decode the messages of others at subconscious levels. We simply engage in discussion without taking the time we need to thoughtfully encode our messages or thoughtfully decode the messages from others. Normally, this free-flowing pattern of communication works fine, particularly in social settings, and communicating goes well. On the whole it must go well, otherwise we would spend countless hours deconstructing our day-to-day communication, which, gratefully, we rarely have to do. However, we are prone to have communication accidents when we do not take time to consider our messages or to understand the messages of others. We can either cause the unnecessary perception of conflict or escalate a conflict because of a lack of control exercised during the communication process. Such was the case with Eugene and Sally.

Although the Sender–Receiver model was developed in cross-cultural settings, there is a good deal of evidence to support this notion:

Every communication is a cross-cultural communication.

When I am communicating with another party, my message will be filtered by that individual's family background, her values and goals, her previous experience with the subject, her current state of mind, and so forth, even if the two of us share the same cultural background. Gender filters are sufficiently significant to gainfully employ dozens of bestselling authors who go so far as to claim that gender differences in communication are so extreme that men and women appear to come from different planets.

In summary, this model underscores the importance of *how* we communicate and indicates that conflict surfaces because of how communication is sent and how it is received. Conflicts induced by this dynamic fall into the category of "process" conflicts, described in chapter 1. We next turn to an examination of the importance of what is communicated when in conflict.

Positions and Interests

Diane was steaming mad. After years of hard work and receipt of neutral to relatively positive feedback, her manager, Ahmed, gave her a scathing performance appraisal. The feedback ranged from general comments about her poor attitude to specific allegations of misconduct and poor practice standards. Diane claims she was never given the opportunity to respond. She now alleges that the performance appraisal is patently unfair and a failure of due diligence on behalf of management. Martin, the union representative, has told Diane her case is a "slam dunk" because the manager should have given her verbal feedback and allowed her opportunities to amend her behaviour. Martin said these cases are a union's dream, and that if the union is not able to put management in its place, an arbitrator will.

Ahmed has had it. After years of trying to support Diane to positively change her workplace conduct, he has resorted to describing his concerns in her performance appraisal. Despite her claims that he has not discussed the allegations with her, Ahmed maintains he has tried to do so in the past but that Diane becomes defensive, denies the allegations outright, and shuts the discussions down. Sherry, the Human Resources representative, has advised him to stay the course, as Diane's conduct is clearly inappropriate and needs to be addressed. Sherry is confident that the employee will back down and, if it goes to arbitration, the company would certainly win.

Positions

One of the ways that conflict manifests in workplaces is that parties take firm, unyielding positions on issues. The negotiation, or the exchange regarding each party's perspective, then becomes a spiralling argument during which each party escalates their rhetoric in order to defend and justify their positions. For example, in the unionized workplace mentioned above, management took the position that it had every right to give the employee a negative performance appraisal and spent considerable time and energy to document, investigate, and substantiate its argument. For every witness, document, or citing of rules that management presented, the employee had a couple of witnesses and documents, paired with her own interpretations of the rules, with which to argue back. As the parties became more entrenched in their positions, the case started to steamroll ahead on a seemingly inevitable course towards arbitration. In the meantime, both parties lost time, energy, and money in the process. Although an arbitrator eventually declared a victor, the victory was short-lived because the employee returned to the workplace with unresolved negative feelings. The loser had silently promised to make the other party miserable. And succeeded in doing so.

Alternatively, employees in many non-unionized workplaces do not have a support system that empowers them to respond to perceived unfairness, or they choose not to use support systems that may exist. They simply accept perceived unfairness and comply with directives, at least on a surface level. However, in such situations a type of passive conflict results that generates a costly legacy for employers in numerous other ways.

Much modern dispute resolution practice has its roots in the work of Fisher and Ury and the Harvard Project on Negotiation.[51] In their influential work, *Getting to Yes*, Fisher and Ury describe a distinction between two phenomena in communication that are typically lumped together in conflict: positions and interests. In basic terms, they define positions as what people "want." They define interests as the "needs, desires, concerns, and fears" related to a situation. Fisher and Ury go on to say, "Your position is what you have decided upon. Your interests are what caused you to so decide."

Positions and interests arise within the context of an *issue* that requires that some decision be made and where there is some opportunity for negotiation. An *issue* is the concern over which the parties are in conflict, and *positions* are the parties' stands on the issue. For example, the *issue* of the performance appraisal has each party taking opposing *positions*. Ahmed's *position* is that the performance appraisal was justified and will stand; Diane's *position* is that it was unjustified and should be retracted. Underlying these positions are numerous *interests* for both parties. For example, Ahmed needs to ensure quality service in his department and needs to feel respected as the manager; Diane needs to protect her job and to feel respected for the work she does.

In most western cultures, among others, society encourages us to take positions on issues. Positions often masquerade as opinions or solutions to problems. Having an opinion is a hallmark of thinking, and having an informed opinion is widely respected as a sign of intellectual and critical thinking. Critical thinking implies keen problem-solving skills. After all, what constitutes problem solving if not the ability to deconstruct key issues and form confident conclusions by means of research and drawing on informed opinion? Positions can be healthy responses to problems *when parties agree*.

However, positions, often expressed as opinions, become significant barriers to resolving problems when parties disagree. A position becomes a stand on an issue that gives the other party something to resist. As time passes and negotiations persist, that stand becomes linked with psychological interests, such as identity and self-worth; the position becomes more rigid and the person more close-minded. The resistance that each party experiences in response to the other solidifies and, like a newly poured cement wall, strengthens as time passes. Functioning under the hostile attribution bias, we come to see the other person's resistance as unreasonable and malicious. We misperceive their resistance as belligerence. However, our experience reveals this:

Resistance is really an unmet need.

For example, consider the case of an executive director of an environmental organization who works with her second-in-command, the chief managing administrator. Both of them agree the most significant issue that confronts the organization this fiscal year is the 30 percent drop in donor contributions and grant income. The executive director takes the position that all staff will have to "hunker down" and compromise to meet budget targets for next year. In consultation with staff, she has laid out a detailed action plan of shared salary cutbacks and program redesigns that will allow the organization to move forward and rebuild. The managing administrator, in consultation with her staff, believes that key staff members have been under-compensated for too long. Many important and high profile staff members have threatened to leave, and some already have—taking donor contribution money with them to other organizations. Her position is that the best course of action for meeting the compromised budget would be to complete a thorough review of the organization's goals and job descriptions in order to eliminate less important and costly jobs in the interest of building up priority roles. The issue is "meeting new budget goals with less resources." The executive director's position is for everyone to compromise together so that the program can be redesigned and move forward; the managing administrator's position is to downsize, restructure, and rebuild.

As each leader presents her ideas in her discussions, they each become more entrenched in the notion that her position and her way is the only way. They begin to see "just how wrong" the other person is and how risky it would be for the organization to follow the other party's plan. They each think to themselves, "No wonder things are so messed up, with this kind of misguided leadership in our organization!" It is not long before the two women seldom communicate directly and instead try to drum up support for their ideas from staff in their different offices. In turn, the staff members' take on the two positions and begin warring among themselves.

Ultimately, positions are lethal ways of encoding messages when in conflict.

Interests

In contrast, maintaining focus on interests provides a more effective means to communicate when parties disagree. Interests are not only the basic needs, desires, and goals associated with an issue, they also include the often less tangible hopes, expectations, emotions, priorities, beliefs, fears, and values that positions may represent. Interests are difficult to argue against because they represent what parties have *invested* in the disputed issue and do not represent an opinion or an interpretation of fact. For example, if I feel frustrated about what is going on and state that I want my sense of dignity to be respected, it is difficult for the other party to argue, "No you don't." They might be able to say, "Well, you shouldn't feel that way"; however, just as saying that we should all be millionaires does not suddenly mean that we are, saying someone should or should not feel something will not suddenly cause her to feel one way or another. A party has simply put forward another position in the guise of a solution that makes sense to them (i.e., "Just don't feel that way"). Feelings are more complicated than that. An individual's feelings about her situation is not likely to shift unless the triggers of those feelings, which can be understood from that person's interests, are at least acknowledged.

The most direct path to understanding interests is to start with any position and ask, "If that happened, what would it do for me? For you? For others?" Returning to our example above, the interests behind each position could be clarified by asking the executive director, "If all staff took salary cuts and the program redesigns went through, what would that do for you and the organization?" Responses might include a range of options: a sense of fairness, equality, hope, extra incentives to work to rebuild, shared pain rather than singling people out, empowerment of staff, fulfill-ment of the organization's community-based values, a demonstration of commitment to the donor community, and so on. All of these needs and objectives are interests. Interests drawn from the other perspective could be clarified by asking the managing administrator, "If the review occurred and jobs were scaled back to rebuild, what would that do for you and the organization?" The range of responses might include these elements: increased efficiency, cost-effectiveness, retention of star employees, fairness, hope, acknowledgement of staff value, a demonstration of commitment to the donor community to manage their donations well, and so forth.

In conscientious communication, dozens, even hundreds, of interests can be unearthed. The relationship between the positions on an issue and the interests that are important to the parties can be viewed in the diagram below:

FIGURE 5.2

Distinguishing between Positions and Interests

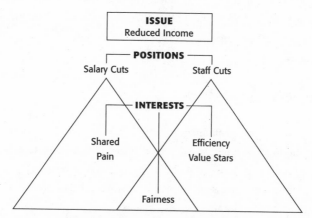

Fisher and Ury's Positions and Interests

So, conflict manifests interpersonally when communication is crudely encoded and/or erroneously decoded, and when parties argue about positions on an issue rather than focus on interests. By failing to carefully encode and accurately decode the true interests of parties in conflict, perceptions of events and people swiftly grow distorted and are misperceived. We can be wrong without having any idea of how wrong we are. To underscore the phrase presented earlier by a client of ours, we can be "so far behind we think we're first."

Even though many of our interests may be shared by others—a condition that offers compelling opportunities for convergence—in order to retain a sense of cognitive consonance we tend to focus on a destructive path that entails positions, argument, and divergence. Although this path seems reasonable at the time, it typically moves both parties farther from their true goals and interests. Even when we "win" or overpower the other party by sheer force, or through the "crap shoot" of arbitration or litigation, we only further entrench the opposing party's resolve. By winning in this way we have created losers. We have given the other side justification to resent us and resist us in the future. We have created a need in them to triumph over us next time.

Many of our clients often use the phrase, "two wrongs don't make a right." We propose that this assertion does not effectively address the real dynamic at work. In conflict virtually all parties believe they are right, that their position is just and fair, and that their "rightness" will prevail. Quite often the reality that both parties believe they are right results in a shared experience:

Two rights make a wrong.

We can see this phenomenon take place in international conflicts, as in the Middle East where parties to a conflict believe, in fact "know," they are right. The focus of most leaders has stayed on rights, with the disastrous outcome that many human beings are killed and global stability is threatened. More locally, we see organizations become stagnant, relationships become hostile, work teams become unproductive, individuals become ill, and workplaces even become unsafe as a result of conflict in which "everybody is right."

Manifestation and Infestation

The coddling moth is a pest that plagues apple orchards. It lays its larvae in the cores of healthy apples, which provide a sheltered environment in which its offspring develop while feasting on the moist sweetness of the apples' flesh. Lurking at the core of an apple, the farmer or consumer does not even know the moth is there until a bite reveals a blackened core squirming with worms. The moths can be so aggressive in their mating habits that entire orchards are wiped out and harvests cancelled; the scant number of apples at your grocer later that year cost as much as a steak.

In an attempt to combat the coddling moth, apple growers use a range of techniques. Historically, growers relied on toxic pesticides, sprayed heavily, to keep the little moths at bay. However, entomologists discovered that the insect pests eventually developed resistance to many pesticides. We also began to develop an awareness of how the toxicity of pesticides might be harming unintended targets. Other insects, such as bees, which are beneficial and critically important to the health of plants, were being killed along with the undesirable pests. In addition, the incidence of cancer and other baffling human diseases began to climb in proportion to our use of pesticides.

Biologists thus developed an approach to undesirable pests, such as the coddling moth, called Integrated Pest Management (IPM). IPM prevents pests from becoming resilient and reduces their impact. IPM also protects humans and beneficial insects. IPM first involves understanding what motivates and deters insect pests in nature, and then artificially duplicating certain conditions.

Now, as coddling moths arrive at an orchard pregnant with potential, many catch the scent of a pheromone trap and head off to one corner of the orchard, never to return. Others settle in lasciviously with a mate, but to no avail because most of the males have been sterilized in a lab and then released to compete with other males. Still others fulfil their destiny in a nearby field of apple trees established specifically for them as a distraction from the primary field of commercially produced apples. Ultimately, some coddling moths do leave their larvae behind in commercially produced apples, but very few. As a result of these methods, fewer toxins are required to address what is now a nuisance and not an infestation.

You may be wondering at this point what pest management has to do with conflict management. When conflict smoulders or erupts in the workplace, most leaders respond, as the farmers above might, with annoyance. The distraction from the many priorities competing for attention leaves management irritated and wishing that the pests who generate conflict would just get over it. As described earlier, the instinctual response for most leaders is to lean away from or charge into the conflict. Leaders lean away by denying that conflict exists or by detaching from conflict's negative impacts in hopes that the problem will just go away. Alternatively, leaders charge into the conflict by aggressively trying to eradicate negativity and legislate productivity.

So far, we have looked at conflict's psychological, sociological, and conceptual aspects in relation to this response pattern. We depart now, for a moment, to explore lessons that can be learned from an inter-disciplinary study of conflict. Current trends in research on biological systems can provide insights into how conflict manifests interpersonally in workplaces. Biology researchers and writers, like Sandra Steingraber and Mark Winston, advance arguments for the practice of Integrated Pest Management (IPM) to reduce undesirable outcomes—*resistance*, *fatigue*, and *dependency*—by addressing the threats created by insects and disease in plant crops. IPM is biology's strategy of "leaning into" pest control—and it has been proven to be a most effective strategy.[52]

Biologists and ecologists observe that humans typically respond to threats of pest infestation in three ways:

- By under-reacting, ignoring the problem until it is a crisis
- By over-reacting, using every chemical and defence they have
- By ignoring the problem until it is a crisis and then using every chemical and defence they have

These common responses to pest control essentially mirror people's responses to conflict: leaning away, charging into, or leaning away and then charging into a problem. Winston describes these responses as *infestation panic*. We under- or over-react to a perceived threat by greatly exaggerating the threat and thus our own fear. Public opinion surveys about attitudes towards insect pests reveal an interesting misperception. When people are asked if they would consider it an "infestation" if they noticed five cockroaches in their home, 97 percent of interviewees responded by saying, "yes." In fact, nearly seven out of ten of us consider the sight of one lonely cockroach to be symptomatic of an infestation.

It is this distorted perception that leads to infestation panic, according to Winston. We want to eradicate any possible threat. We call for zero-tolerance. We think, "These filthy, diseased cockroaches are just waiting to attack me tonight," as we spray toxins throughout our homes—in excess of four pounds every year for every person in North America. In reality, cockroaches only carry the bacteria that are already present in their immediate environment. So, take out the garbage! Cockroaches do not *attack*; they hide timidly from light. Like conflict, however, we develop assumptions about the risk and the intent of others to harm us, which leads us to respond to threats in these ways:

- Leaning away, by moving away from a home perceived to be infested
- Charging into, by blanketing our house in toxic pesticides
- Leaning away and then charging into, by ignoring the pests until they have proliferated to the point that one must use toxins

These three approaches to conflict, as with controlling insect pests, often lead to at least three key undesirable outcomes: resistance, fatigue, and dependency.

Resistance, Fatigue, and Dependency

Resistance

Both those who lean away from and those who charge into conflict encounter resistance. When others perceive you to be leaning away from their concerns, and disinterested in their interests, they develop the perception, rightly or wrongly, that you do not care about their needs. They, in turn, typically adopt the perspective that they will not care about your needs. It is not long before any request you make of them is challenged and resisted, sometimes simply because it is perceived to have come from you. As with Eugene, in the case study at the beginning of this chapter, it does not really matter what he says—as long as Sally has unresolved conflict with him she will perceive any communication from him to be focussed on his own interests, to the exclusion of hers. Similarly, when charging into conflict, others also tend to perceive that only the interests of the people leading the charge are being met, not the interests of those involved in the conflict. The others' unmet needs or interests become fuel for their resistance. This resistance then contributes to a growing sense of fatigue.

Fatigue

When leaning away from conflict, we become fatigued by our hopelessness and helplessness. Our perception that "nobody ever does anything to make it better" leaves us feeling despair characterized by a profound sense of being tired. In this state of fatigue we essentially give in and give up. At an emotional level, hopelessness and helplessness take over. At work, distraction, inefficiency, and absenteeism shoot up.

When charging into conflict, it is the person who is trying to respond, often aggressively, who gets tired of trying to improve the situation without success. They say, "I'm damned if I do and damned if I don't," and they give in and give up. Leaders who use competitive or aggressive responses to conflict report that managing staff becomes like trying to keep corks suppressed under water—"The minute I remove my thumb, they bounce away and are up to their old tricks again." Charging into conflict, whether a simple interpersonal dispute or a large, multifaceted conflict, can leave us drained and demoralized, even if we win the battle.

Dependency

In addition to resistance and fatigue, mishandled conflict can also create unwanted interpersonal dependency. Others in an organization often step in to address conflict when leaders are perceived to have abandoned the conflict by leaning away from it. A union representative or an outspoken co-worker starts to take on other people's battles for them. This can lead to a co-dependent working team wherein conflicts are not addressed directly and transparently. Conflicts spiral quickly into distortions because of a few self-appointed heroes or "leaders by default." These well-intentioned people typically form unhelpful communication triangles between themselves and the conflicted parties. Rather than functioning in a neutral and trained mediator role, these "toxic handlers," as they have been described, may help to reduce one party's discomfort, but they can enable harmful behaviour to continue.[53] In other words, unskilled but caring interveners in a conflict may help to prevent a crisis, but by preventing a crisis they can unintentionally prevent a lasting resolution. Others become dependent on these interveners in an unhealthy dynamic: interveners are needed and mistreated at the same time. Words to the wise toxic handlers:

No good deed goes unpunished.

Similarly, an unhealthy dependence can develop between staff members and leaders who charge into conflict. By rescuing their staff, well-intentioned leaders can disempower staff members and prevent them from developing the skills necessary to resolve conflicts successfully. Staff members develop a perspective that they are incapable of addressing issues and must involve management *every* time conflict occurs.

Leaning away or charging into conflict generates these unhealthy outcomes: resistance, fatigue, and dependency. We propose that, like the successful and counterintuitive strategies of Integrated Pest Management now employed by entomologists, successful conflict resolution relies upon leaning into conflict and an appreciation of the ecology of conflict.

An Ecological View of Conflict

If ecology is defined as the science of the relationships between organisms and their environments, the ecology of conflict addresses the relationships between conflicted parties and their environments. Similar to our strategy for handling conflict by resisting the urge to lean away or charge into it, and to *lean into it* instead, Integrated Pest Management (IPM) is an ecological approach for managing insect pests characterized by neither leaning away nor charging into the problem. IPM succeeds by leaning into the problem. IPM principles that can be applied to turn conflict into profit include these:

- Effectively manage a tolerable level of co-existence that may be inconvenient but is not a significant risk.
- Use the mildest means first and escalate measures progressively.
- Attempt to thoroughly understand behaviour and motivation.
- Adopt a range of creative, alternative, systemic, and contextually based methods that are the minimally invasive and have the least impact on other beneficial organisms and the environment.
- Utilize an ongoing and sustained approach.
- Follow-up with evaluations that inform the steps of the next intervention.

In contrast to traditional "lean away/charge into" pest control techniques, such as massive toxin spraying that harms beneficial insects, wildlife, and humans, examples of IPM strategies include interrupting the reproductive cycles of pests, baiting pests with their own naturally occurring pheromones and trapping them, and planting small bait crops near larger production crops wherein pests are allowed to live in order to inhibit their development of resistance to pest-control chemicals.

To illustrate the application of IPM strategies to workplace conflict, let us return to the example of the executive director and the managing administrator who were in conflict about how best to address their budget cut backs. In her frustration, the executive director could have enforced the authority inherent in her role to make the administrator comply with her direction. Indeed, the executive director attempted this, only to find it drove the conflict underground. The administrator began venting to her colleagues and threatened to leave the organization, taking a significant number of donors who were loyal to her along with her. If the executive director continued to charge into the conflict, she risked alienating key staff and crucial donors. If she leaned away, she risked losing the power struggle with the administrator. By leaning into the conflict, she first used IPM methods to clarify whether or not the organization's board supported her role so that she was prepared for any challenges to her authority. Once she was clear about the foundation of her power, she then started with the least confrontational approach and was prepared to become progressively competitive with the administrator if required. The executive director negotiated with the administrator to identify the key motivating interests beneath her positions. By managing her own "infestation panic" and anger, she was able to determine that the administrator's key interests were in retaining autonomy and receiving recognition of the fifteen years of service she had provided. The executive director then discussed how the administrator could have more autonomy and recognition by leading the movement to rebuild morale. Though the administrator resisted her at first, the executive director persistently linked her plan to the administrator's goals and modified the plan to ensure the administrator had an operational area that was autonomously her own; the administrator eventually accepted the executive director's modified plan. The two moved forward without damaging relationships within the organization and even ended up strengthening their donor base by presenting a consistent image to their donor community.

Essentially, IPM offers a metaphor for dealing with "pesky" behaviours that cause conflict in the workplace. The strategies involve an awareness of our psychological predisposition to perceive an infestation where there is none, as well as the impulse to eradicate the problems or simply deny the problems exist. The unrealistic goal to fully control our environment and others' behaviours only produces further resistance, fatigue, and an unproductive dependency. By better understanding the motivations and needs of insect or human "pests," we can employ strategies that reduce negative impacts and break the patterns that trap us in conflict. These biological metaphors serve to underscore the success to be gained from leaning into conflict rather than leaning away from or charging into it.

Spheres of Influence

These biological references also raise the importance of the element of *control* in understanding the means by which we can lean into conflict. According to Stephen Covey, there are aspects of our environment that we have direct control over and there are aspects that we have little or no control over. Somewhere in between lie those aspects that we cannot really control but can influence. These different levels of control can be conceptualized as spheres of influence (see Figure 5.3 below).[54]

For example, we live in the Canadian city of Vancouver. The region is a northern rainforest and is characterized by brilliantly sunny moments that break through torrential rains, and vice versa. We cannot control whether it will rain or shine tomorrow morning, or even by the time we step out for lunch. The weather lies in the "sphere of no control." Because we have learned, damply and annoyingly, that we cannot control or even accurately predict the weather here, we focus our attention on the aspects of the experience that we can control. In our briefcases we each carry a collapsible umbrella *and* a pair of sunglasses. Rather than lament getting caught in a downpour, or being blinded by sunshine, we plan for the fact that we cannot control the weather. Consequently, we do not have to suffer as a result. Making the simple choice to plan for and carry equipment to protect us from the weather lies in the "sphere of direct control." The issue of "the weather" could lead me to proclaim the position, "It better not rain tomorrow." But, if I focus on my interest of "keeping dry," I can come up with solutions that are under my control.

FIGURE 5.3

Spheres of Influence

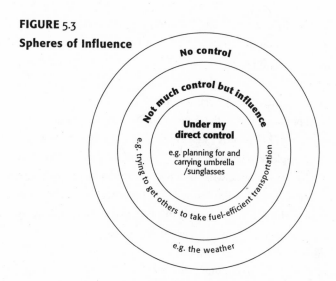

A more complex sphere, and the one most relevant to an understanding of the interpersonal manifestation of conflict, is *the sphere of influence* that lies between those aspects that we can control and those we cannot. There may be many things in life that lie outside our control, but there are at least as many elements that we can influence, even if we cannot control them directly. Other people's behaviour lies in this sphere. I may not be able to control the weather, and I may be able to protect myself from the weather by planning and carrying equipment, but there are still more things I can do. Most evening newscasts report stories of bizarre weather changes—raging fires of the sort never seen before, followed within days by freak snow storms, record-breaking flooding, new temperature highs and lows. I may not be able to control all the complex causes of climate change, but I can influence, even in a small way, how others around me either contribute to the causes of climate change or not.

One workshop we put on was for volunteers in various organizations who worked through a not-for-profit agency. Their goals were to encourage as many people as possible to use environmentally sensitive modes of transportation. These courageous volunteers risked being perceived by colleagues as "tree-hugging commies" because of their attempts to boost awareness of the value of sustainable transportation alternatives. Their success was predicated on the same principles of IPM—that is, they relied primarily on understanding and responding to others' motivations and behaviours.

The counterintuitive and "secret" insight that the Spheres of Influence model provides is this: those people whom we seek to influence the most, those whose behaviours cause conflict and negative impacts, are usually the same people who lie furthest away from our sphere of influence. It is likely far easier to get our closest friend to walk with us to work once a week, rather than drive his or her car, and thus influence their impacts on the environment in this way. It is far more difficult to get our worst enemy to even talk about environmentally sensitive transportation options. In fact, we assume that if they knew sustainability was important to us, they would go out of their way to pollute!

Those who are furthest away from our influence are precisely those people whom we must bring closer to our sphere of influence.

Leaning away from them, or charging into them, only serves to push them further away from our influence, and perpetuates our conflict with them. Ultimately, the only aspects of the environment we have complete control over are our own thoughts, emotions, actions, and decisions. Therefore, our best method of influencing others is through our own behaviour.

In summary, how we communicate and what we communicate when in conflict has a profound influence on how conflict manifests interpersonally and how it traps us in conflict. In response to the threat of perceived conflict, we either ignore the signs or perceive the signs as a potential infestation, which leads us to charge into or to lean away from conflict—to deny or detach—and to experience a sense of despair. Counter-intuitively, these responses tend only to promote resistance, fatigue, and dependency, which exacerbate unresolved and damaging conflict. However, borrowing from ecology research in general, and applying Integrated Pest Management ideas in particular, we can discover means to break through the trap of conflict. By letting go of the things we cannot control (and letting go of our complaining about them), and by focusing most of our energy on the things we can control or influence, options emerge for finding convergence and restoring productivity and profitability.

When conflict manifests interpersonally, it typically occurs on a continuum that ranges from low-risk erosion to higher-risk implosion, and on to high-risk explosion, as discussed in chapter 3. Conflict manifests as nasty gossip, chilliness between co-workers, union/management tensions, and low morale that erodes team functioning and efficiency. Mishandled, it typically degrades to higher absenteeism, negative reputations, retention and recruitment problems, income loss, and, ultimately, large deficits or insolvency for the organization. If the conflict continues to be ignored or fought, it further deteriorates into sabotage, theft, and violence.

Depending on our backgrounds, we all respond differently to these manifestations. You may perceive a conflict where I do not. I may have perceived something to happen that you saw completely differently. Taking positions on the issues, and encoding and decoding our communications in terms of who is right and who is wrong, typically serves only to trap us in conflict. One valuable lesson we can acknowledge about conflict is this:

There is seldom such a thing as a single truth.

What, you may ask? If we know someone is telling lies, am I supposed to just accept them as "different truths?" If so, then are we really saying that there are no standards? And, without standards, are we not all lost?

We are not suggesting that there are no useful standards, and no objective realities. We are suggesting that what we believe constitutes the truth, particularly in situations of conflict, is more belief than truth, and that a key barrier to overcome in efforts to find convergence is the knowledge that people in conflict focus on different truths. We learn more about this perplexing concept in the last chapter of Part 1, in which we examine cultural influences on the conflict experience.

Conflict Among at a Glance

- When we are stuck in the Conflict Trap, manifestations of conflict with others can look more like an infestation.

- Conflict is heavily predicated on communication. When we communicate we encode ideas, needs, and so on into words, tone, and body language, and then we send our message to another party. They then receive the message and decode the words, tone, and body language to interpret the meaning of our needs and ideas. Filters, such as context, gender, assumptions, biases, and culture, influence what is sent and what is received, particularly when conflict results in *communication mishaps* that perpetuate the Conflict Trap.

- The *interests* at stake in conflict are frequently expressed as *positions* that we take on *issues* that lead us to root our heels in and become further mired in the Conflict Trap. Moving others and ourselves from our positions and into a discussion of interests is crucial to breaking free of the Conflict Trap.

- Resistance is always an unmet need.

- The manifestation of conflict in organizations can be understood to be similar to the infestation of insect pests in agricultural settings. The most effective strategies for managing insect pests, referred to as Integrated Pest Management, provide a metaphor for the successful strategy of *leaning into* conflict, especially in contrast to the conflict-trapping approaches of *leaning away from* and *charging into*.

- In dealing with conflict, we need to appreciate what it is we have direct control over, what we can influence, and what we have no control over. Breaking free of the Conflict Trap involves focusing our energy on our *spheres of control and influence*, and letting go of the sphere of no control.

6

Conflict Across

THE CULTURAL ROOTS OF CONFLICT

When Adamah died and went on to the next life, she wanted to check out the possibilities and opted for a tour of hell first. The people there were gaunt and depressed, even though there were tables in front of them laden with food. The problem was that their eating utensils were longer than their arms so they could not get the food into their own mouths. In heaven, although the tables of food and the utensils were the same as in hell, the people were well fed and happy. The only difference was that the people in heaven were feeding each other.[55]

CONSIDER THE CULTURE IN HELL, where individualism and a lack of cooperation contributed to despair. In this culture, communication is suppressed and creative problem solving is compromised. In contrast, the culture in heaven fosters communication and collective problem solving, leading to health and happiness for all. This parable symbolizes the influence culture can have on individual and group behaviour in society and organizations. The parable suggests that two parallel organizations that have the same access to resources and opportunities can falter or flourish depending on the nature of the group culture.

In this chapter we consider a third level of influence on the generation of, and responses to, conflict. This level explores the emergence of conflicts that arise as a consequence of the growing diversity in our societies and workplaces. Cultural differences in beliefs and practices provide excellent examples of how people rely on assumptions and misperceptions as they either lean away from or charge into conflict. We review theory and research on the manifestation of cultural conflicts and foreshadow how leaning into conflict can create insight, inspiration, and investment.

Culture Defined

The concept of culture is used broadly to represent a number of concepts. Yet there is general consensus across disciplines that culture represents the acquired values and behaviours that are commonly shared within a group. In other words, culture represents the normative and expected "ways of thinking" and "ways of behaving" that are passed on from generation to generation within a given group. Those who exert the most control and influence over the group shape culture. As cultural researcher Trompenaars has stated, "social interaction, or meaningful communication, presupposes common ways of processing information among the people interacting. These have consequences for doing business as well as managing across cultural boundaries." He also points out, "what one culture may regard as essential, a certain level of material wealth for example, may not be so vital to other cultures."[56] Thus, all communication, all pursuits, and all conflict take place within a context of culture.

The study of culture also reveals that culture is not a stagnant concept: it evolves over time in response to changes in knowledge, abilities, and environments that influence individual thoughts and actions. This conceptualization of culture applies to society in general as well as to organizational or corporate cultures, both of which exert strong influences over the beliefs and behaviours of members of a given group. There is a reciprocal relationship between the culture of a social group and the membership of the group. Thus, people shape their culture and culture shapes people. Ultimately, culture helps individuals understand their place in their community and prescribes a range of behaviours considered acceptable by the group. In terms of the study of organizational behaviour, culture has been defined as "the way in which a group of people solves problems."[57] Similarly, we can extend the definition of culture as it relates to conflict :

Culture is the way in which a group of people perceives and responds to conflict.

We will explore the specific relationship of culture to conflict later in this chapter. We first explore, more deeply, some elements that define culture and how they influence individual thought and behaviour.

Values

Values, the key concepts underlying culture, are beliefs and ideas that determine what constitutes the proper ways to think and act in a group. They provide the social foundation upon which a group grounds and structures itself and also determines how the group pursues its goals and objectives. In other words, values are what individuals in a group learn to help them determine what is good or bad, right or wrong, fair or unfair, appropriate or inappropriate. Many researchers have recounted numerous descriptors of cultural values.[58] Drawing from their work, we highlight six cultural values that exert a strong influence on individual behaviour in organizations and, ultimately, determine how conflict is perceived and managed. To explore these continuums of cultural values, consider the six continuums in the following table and identify the number along the continuum that best describes your perspective.

FIGURE 6.1
Values Continuum Worksheet

Circle the number that best represents where you are on the continuum.

A. Whether I succeed or fail reflects on my work team.   1 2 3 4 5 6 7   Whether I succeed or fail reflects on me as an individual.

B. People should speak directly, no matter who they are talking to or what the situation is. Don't beat around the bush!!   1 2 3 4 5 6 7   People should be indirect with their feedback and use subtle words and references to convey their ideas without causing a loss of face.

C. What happens to me is my own doing.   1 2 3 4 5 6 7   Sometimes I feel that I do not have enough control over the directions my life is taking.

D. People should deal with   1 2 3 4 5 6 7   People should treat some
each other as equals, people with more respect
no matter what their age, because of their age, gender,
sex, wealth, or social class, or social status.
status.

E. Rules are more important   1 2 3 4 5 6 7   Relationships are more
than relationships and important than rules. Rules
should be applied evenly, should be adapted to fit the
regardless of who you are situation or relationship.
or what the situation is.

F. I respect people who   1 2 3 4 5 6 7   I respect people who
speak quietly, move express their feelings freely
calmly, and don't by letting me know they
embarrass me by are angry, upset, or excited
looking me in the eye. through their voices and
gestures.

Adapted from University of British Columbia Centre for Intercultural Communication

Each item in the table represents a values continuum. In most work groups we find substantial variability exists among group members on each of the continuums; we have also observed group cultures that reinforce certain values through the development of reward systems and policies.

Continuum A—Collectivist vs. Individualist

Cultures tend to reinforce one of two belief systems related to the identity of an individual within a group. In one view, the focus is on the achievement and functioning of the group as a whole, and the individual is important only as a component member of the group. This value has been identified as "collectivist." Cultures that function under collectivism reward achievement at the group level, require individual members to refer to the group for decisions, and structure themselves to reinforce the interdependent nature of the group.

In the contrasting "individualist" view, the focus is on the achievement and functioning of the individual and individual achievement supersedes group success. Cultures that adhere to an individualist belief system place value on individual achievement over group accomplishment, support individuals who make decisions on their own, and reinforce independent thinking and behaviour even where structural interdependence in relationships is necessary.

This value continuum influences many of the individuals and groups with which we have worked. For example, we have observed in academics how leaders appear to encourage collectivist collaboration among colleagues and interdisciplinary efforts. Yet the system rewards individual achievement over group success in terms of promotions and tenure (e.g., first authorship is far more valued than second authorship, Principal researcher status is far more valued than Collaborator); this creates a culture that breeds competition and conflict. We have observed individuals sabotage the outcomes of work teams when their own individual ability to be noticed, and thereby promote their own achievement, would be diminished in the context of team success.

In one case, we worked with a group that spoke the "language" of customer service and cooperation, but the members clearly acted on a personal interest basis. They took vacation, established hours of work, offered backup to each other, and made other such decisions solely based on their individual interests and not on the priorities of the group. They all said they supported the group goals of quality service, and yet when push came to shove many of them valued individual convenience over group success. They also worked in a system that fostered individualism because it set few, if any, group goals, and it tied rewards to individual markers. Conflicts arose between those members who were more "collectivist" in their worldview and those who were more "individualist," especially as the "collectivists" grew to resent others who were perceived to be selfish, uncooperative, and rigid. In this culture, divergence flourished in part due to these different value bases. We observe that conflict arises quite frequently between individuals who bring a strong individualistic mindset into their workplaces when their work involves some degree of interdependence with others.

Continuum B—Direct vs. Indirect Communication

This cultural continuum highlights the value placed on how people in a group communicate with each other. In some cultures, value is invested in people who use "direct" methods of communication, including the use of explicit language with parties directly involved. Many clients of ours who have been accused of being condescending, rude, sarcastic, and the like have defended themselves by expressing their compliance with the value of being "direct."

In contrast, some cultures value the use of more indirect forms of communication. In these cultures the meanings of messages are channelled through suggestion and non-verbal behaviour; communication through a third party is common. Other clients have told us of their frustration when their attempts to communicate with others fail to achieve their goals. When we explore the circumstances we typically find the person in question attempted to use indirect channels of communication and expected the other party to "get the message." Movies depict one character saying to another, "If you don't know why I'm angry then I'm certainly not going to tell you"—leaving both parties befuddled, frustrated, and, more importantly, trapped in conflict.

Although western culture tends to assert the value of direct communication, we observe that the culture of communication in western organizations remains indirect in many ways. For example, in many organizations employees are encouraged to go to their manager to complain about the behaviour of a co-worker rather than attempt to work it out directly with the co-worker. Many people use sarcasm as a means to communicate a negative message—an indirect method of relaying a loaded message. In still other organizations, communication travels indirectly—and often inaccurately—via gossip and rumours because the administrations are either too preoccupied to communicate clearly or they believe transparency is not required. As previously mentioned, many people, when involved in conflict that has arisen due to perceived mistreatment, avoid dealing with the conflict in the hope that their avoidance will be seen by the other person as tacit disapproval of the originating behaviour. Not surprisingly this approach rarely works, if ever. In fact, it frequently contributes to the escalation of conflict.

Yet, as noted previously, being very direct or disrespectfully honest can cause or reinforce conflict as well. Thus, abiding by and implementing either value orientation—direct or indirect—can be either helpful or problematic when it comes to addressing conflict, depending on the specific context and the orientations of the individuals involved. Specifically, many conflicts involve a clashing of these differing orientations and result in confusion, tension, and further divergence.

Continuum C—Internal vs. External Control

A third cultural orientation involves beliefs about the ability we have to control our own destiny and environment. On one hand, some cultures support the belief that you can control your own destiny and that natural systems and events are there to be conquered. In contrast, other cultures reinforce the belief that your destiny is predetermined and that you should focus on how you can live in harmony with nature and others. Statements such as "It was destiny" or "It is just fate," made in response to negative events or problems, reflect this orientation.

In western society we often hear messages that reinforce an internal belief system. These messages tell members of the society or organization that they can and should "control" their environments. Reward systems are created that value a "conquer" mentality rather than a convergence mindset. Conflict arises between individuals who hold these different values and beliefs about control. Whether or not one can or should "control" one's environment is not our concern here. We are simply pointing out how different views about control can produce differences in interests, perceptions, and behaviour that, in turn, result in perceived conflicts and missed opportunities.

Continuum D—Achieved vs. Ascribed Status

On one end of this value continuum status is attributed to achievement. Achievement means a person is judged by what they have recently accomplished—that is, by their deeds. In contrast, when status is attributed to ascription, people are judged by comparatively "stable" personal characteristics such as birth, bloodline, title, age, gender, education, and the like. In an achievement-oriented culture, the first question someone may ask is, "What do you do?" or "What have you done?" and thus emphasize accomplishments. In an ascription-based culture, the first question will more likely be, "Who is your family?" or "Where are you from?"— emphasizing inherent characteristics.

One way in which this dimension manifests itself in workplaces is related to communication and the use of job or professional titles. In health care, doctors usually refer to nurses, social workers, managers, and so on by their first names, while they are usually referred to by their title (e.g., Dr. Smith). Conflict can arise when people's interactions are based on different paradigms along this continuum. These differences can result in misunderstandings of expressions related to status. Most professionals who have worked with colleagues from countries that have established hierarchies or castes have likely observed how status tends to be more ascribed than achieved in such cultures.

In one case we are familiar with, a Hospital Director was in constant conflict with the Medical Manager of the program. They were considered to have equal authority and status within the organizational structure, yet the Director clearly entered negotiations with the Medical Manager, when discussing program issues, in a manner that ascribed more status to the Medical Manager than to herself. Even though the Medical Manager had no desire to be referred to by title, and was called by his first name by most of the unit staff, the Director continued to refer to him as "Dr. Smith." The Medical Manager subsequently used this apparent deference to his status to control the negotiation process: he often referred to his medical standing as a source of authority rather than emphasize his experience or knowledge. In other words, he argued that the hospital should do what he wanted because he was a doctor and the Hospital Director was not. The Director expressed frustration with and resentment toward the Medical Manager because of these dynamics, but she did not appreciate how she had contributed to their development by showing such high regard for the doctor's status. In this case, the dynamic changed for the better when the Director adopted a new approach with the doctor based on equality and respect, a move symbolized by calling him by his first name. In other situations, however, we have observed the opposite dynamic to be at work: there, maintenance of a more formal approach to recognizing status was important in attempts to communicate effectively and convey respect.

Once again, we are not suggesting that one value system or culture should be considered superior or that one is better aligned to achieve convergence than the contrasting value system. Simply put, people, organizations, and nations clash as a result of how they view, implement, and acknowledge status in their communities. Interests and approaches to negotiation differ. In fact, denigrating the status of the other, in mindset or practice, directly affects attempts to resolve conflicts.

Continuum E—Absolute Rules vs. Relative Relationships

To understand this dimension, consider again the manager who chastised her staff for lighting candles on a birthday cake in violation of fire safety rules. To this manager's understanding, rules and policies are established for sound reasons and must be rigidly enforced to maintain order and safety in the workplace. She sees rules as solid guideposts, and even minor deviations are unacceptable. On the other hand, the staff members who lit the candles knew about the fire safety policy. They also considered the importance of interpersonal relationships in their work and chose to reasonably break away from the policy in order to emphasize the importance of relationship building—with each other and with the client.

On a cultural level, some groups focus more on rules and policies than relationships. These groups will rely on formal contracts and other written mechanisms to govern conduct and decisions as a means of relationship building. The rules inform and dictate the nature of relationships. In contrast, cultures that focus on relationships spend time building associations rather than contracts, per se, to secure and inform future interactions and involvement.

We have observed substantial conflict arise between individuals who hold different values on this continuum. A "rules-oriented" person will often be heard to assert the need to comply with a policy or a directive simply because it is the policy or directive. Once established, rules should not be broken. For example, a policy that says fire is not allowed means that all fire has been determined to be unsafe. Therefore, employees who knowingly breach policy are considered reckless, unsafe, and insubordinate. In contrast, a "relationship-oriented" person will question rules and directives because of how they may affect relationship building, which can lead to a clash of interests. In a "rules-oriented" culture, meetings will typically follow a strict agenda (with timeliness as a key value), use an ordered approach to manage discussions (e.g., Robert's Rules of Order), and emphasize outcome-based discussion.

In a "relationship-oriented" culture, meetings will offer more opportunity for tangents and storytelling as components of relationship building, they will be more relaxed in their approach to managing discussions, and will emphasize the need to build relationships in order to reach quality outcomes. It is striking to observe a "rules-oriented" person involved in a "relationship-oriented" business meeting—their confusion and frustration with what they perceive as a lack of direction and inefficient style becomes evident quickly. The opposite is also evident when a "relationship-oriented" person becomes disenchanted with meetings that impose rigid boundaries around discussion and prevent tangential interactions that some believe are so important in building connections with other group members.

In a progressive attempt to integrate the value of rules and relationships into a culture, we have observed a movement towards a "standards-based" approach to decision-making and behaviour. This movement in some areas of society is a response to dissatisfaction with "rules-based" control over people and practices. Health care, and its evolution of medical ethics, provides a good illustration of this movement.

For years, four ethics have served as pillars of ethical medical practice. These elements include:

- Autonomy of and respect for the preferences of individuals
- Beneficence, or doing good
- Nonmaleficence, or doing no harm
- Justice, or fair treatment of like cases

These ethics are considered standards rather than rules because they do not prescribe a specific course of action.

Standards are interest-based, while rules are position-based.

Standards offer guideposts for decision-making that leave room for the development of specific practices; they also recognize the importance of relationships in the sense that they respect people's preferences. Historically, "do no harm" was considered the paramount virtue of medicine. Of late, autonomy has emerged as the paramount ethic in western medical care.

The shift towards standards offers insight into changes in many industries. The change moves away from the use of rules to control the choices and actions of people. Many hospitals, for example, instituted rules regarding visiting hours for patients. Some still have them. These rules were established to control the care environment and access to patients in a manner that served the interests of the nursing and medical staff. These rules had little to do with patient preferences or the interests of patients. While some conflicts were suppressed through the application of these rules, many more conflicts were created for patients who preferred to have family and friends visit on a more regular basis. The original rules also failed to accommodate people from more relationship-based cultures who found it difficult to recover from illness or injury without the presence and support of their family and friends.

Consistent with the emergence of autonomy as a standard, most hospitals have replaced rule-based visiting hours with a standard that allows hospital staff to restrict visiting hours on an as-needed basis, as promoted by the four ethical standards. The general rule is that visitors can be with the patient as long as they do not interfere with the effective care of the patient. This new approach is consistent with the pursuit of congruence when in conflict rather than reliance on unilateral rules imposed by those in authority. However, the new approach also challenges the communication skills and attitudes of care providers. No longer can they use the rule that designates specific visiting hours as a tool for control (a "charge into" approach to conflict). Instead, they now need to address the potential conflict between themselves, patients, and visitors by means of explanation and respectful negotiation. This approach can take more time and requires more skill. However, it ultimately saves time and allows for opportunities to develop more adaptive solutions that effectively meet the needs of all parties.

Continuum F—Neutral vs. Affective Interaction

A sixth continuum of culture involves the acceptability of emotional expression in communication. In some cultures, the suppression of emotional expression is expected. Physical contact, gesturing, or strong facial expressions may also be considered taboo. Many professions, such as ambulance paramedics and army personnel, encourage the suppression of emotion because of its capacity to interrupt the duties of the job. The expression of emotions is frowned upon and considered trite. In other cultures, the expression of thoughts and feelings are encouraged in both verbal and non-verbal modes. Touching, gesturing, and strong facial expressions are common. Among people who share and value this practice—"Oprah Moments," as people who do not share this value might described them—are welcome. Think about your own family environment in which you grew up. Did it allow for you to express yourself and participate? Did your parents fight in visibly emotional ways or did they suppress their emotions in order to maintain an illusion of decorum and dignity? Who was allowed to have feelings in your family? A person's cultural upbringing affects their approach to dealing with issues involving emotional content. Considering the close relationship between emotion and conflict, our place on this continuum will influence our method of dealing with conflict. Clashes between emotional people may seem loud and unacceptable, yet this may be their way of discussing important issues and finding resolution. We have heard many clients tell us that they fight it out and then its over, solutions are eventually found. In contrast, conflict between an emotionally expressive person and an emotionally restrained person can be extremely difficult to manage—they just cannot connect with one who perceives the other as repressed while the other sees the first as uncontrolled and a bully.

In business settings, this values continuum can have a strong influence on organizational culture. Trompenaars has made this observation:

In North America and Northwest Europe, business relationships are typically instrumental and all about achieving objectives. The brain checks emotions because these are believed to confuse the issues. The assumption is that we should resemble our machines in order to operate more efficiently. But further south and in many other cultures, business is a human affair and the whole gamut of emotions is deemed appropriate. Loud laughter, banging your fist

on the table, or leaving a conference room in anger during a negotiation is "all part of business."[59]

This value continuum, and the others, lead people to view diverse
behaviours and responses to conflict as acceptable or unacceptable, reasonable or unreasonable, abusive or normal, good or bad. In the end, these
orientations are neither good nor bad in and of themselves. However,
behaviour arising from one's cultural value base may be more or less
effective when dealing with others depending on the culture of the other
individuals in a group, or the culture the group has fostered as encouraged
by the organization. Seeking to understand core value differences between
conflicted parties can offer parties insight into identifying approaches to
transition out of conflict and toward convergence.

FIGURE 6.2

Values Orientations Described

Collectivist
- Focus is on the group
- People refer to the group for decisions
- People ideally achieve in groups, which assume joint responsibility

Individualist
- Focus is on the individual
- People make decisions on the spot
- People usually achieve alone and assume personal responsibility

Direct communication
- People communicate using explicit statements made directly to people involved
- Focus is on words, not context

Indirect communication
- Meaning is made indirectly through suggestion and non-verbal behaviour
- Communication through a third party is common

Internal Control
- A belief that you can control your own destiny
- A sense of conquering nature
- A focus on the self (i.e., one's own group, organization)

External Control
- A belief that your destiny is somewhat predetermined
- A sense of living in harmony with nature
- A focus on the "other" (e.g., a client, colleague)

Status achieved
- Status is earned through accomplishments
- Titles are used only when relevant to the situation or task

Status ascribed
- People have status because of age, gender, position, etc.
- Extensive use is made of titles, especially to clarify one's status in an organization or interaction

Rules
- Focus is more on rules than relationships
- Frequent use of formal contracts before a relationship is built
- There is only one truth: that which has been agreed upon

Relationships
- Focus is more on relationships than rules
- Time is spent building relationships in order to secure future interactions and involvement
- There are different perspectives on reality, depending on the people involved

Neutral
- Thoughts or feelings are not revealed
- Emotions that are often dammed up will occasionally explode
- Physical contact, gesturing, and strong facial expressions are often taboo

Affective
- Thoughts and feelings are openly revealed (verbally and non-verbally)
- Emotions flow easily without inhibition
- Touching, gesturing, and strong facial expressions are common

Culture's Influence on Perception and Interests

As noted in chapters 4 and 5, self-perception and other perceptions are products of individual psychology and interpersonal dynamics. Perceptions are also a product of cultural beliefs and identity. If you learn from your culture that individualism is good and collectivism is bad, that directness is good and indirectness is bad, or that rules rule and relationship building is time destroying, you will perceive people and events through those lenses. In conflict, you will have more difficulty with others who value communal responsibility, third party communication, and spending time to get to know each other. If you learn that aggressiveness is strong and passiveness is weak, your primary interest in strength will likely manifest as aggressiveness.

Consider the following questions used by psychologists specializing in anger management.[60] What colour is a lemon? Now, if you put on blue-tinted sunglasses and look at the lemon, what colour is the lemon? If you are like most people, you will say *green*, knowing that yellow and blue combine to make green. However, the lemon is still yellow: you only see it as green. Furthermore, you see it as green because you are the one wearing the blue glasses, not others. Such is the power of the cultural filters that we all wear. These filters, informed by our values, directly influence the way we assess our own interests and the interests of others in conflict situations.

For example, people who value rules in their workplaces tend to value the completion of tasks, even if completing a task involves the loss of relationships. People with this value orientation see a relationship as a means to an end, rather than as an end in itself. In contrast, people who primarily value relationships will pursue relational outcomes even if this compromises tangible task outcomes. People with different value orientations who have interdependent tasks, interdependent relationships, and disparate interests in both are far more likely to become trapped in conflict.

Cultural values are the source of individual and group judgements about the correct nature and appropriateness of one's own and others' behaviour and interests. Thus, people will likely view all conflicts through their own cultural lenses.

To illustrate, there is a concept in communication referred to as *pause time*. Pause time is the period of time between when one party in a conversation stops talking and the other party begins talking. Research about pause time has revealed that significant cultural variability exists. Some cultures have very short pause times (i.e., a fraction of a second) while other cultures have more extended pause times (3-4 seconds). We have heard numerous stories about communication that has failed due to differences in pause time. In one situation, a therapist in a medical clinic was interviewing a client from a different cultural background. The therapist would ask a question, wait a second for a response, and, when no response came, would go on to the next question. After several questions the therapist gave up, left the room, and wrote "non-compliant" on the client's chart. This interview had been video taped, and when a clinician with cultural knowledge reviewed the tape he saw the possibility that the issue was not one of non-compliance but might simply be one of differences in conversation patterns. A second attempt to interview the client met with success when the therapist allowed the client more time to respond to the questions.

This scenario demonstrates how differences in cultural practice can lead to misunderstanding and conflict; however, judgements of the communication gap are equally, or more, important than miscommunication when it comes to contributing to conflict. For example, some cultures use what can be descriptively referred to as negative or overlapping pause time, which involves a second party starting to respond in a conversation before the first party finishes his thought. Another description of this dynamic is "interrupting." Cultures in which this practice is common will view interrupting as a normal pattern of communication. In some families, if you did not interrupt you would never get to talk. By contrast, cultures that practice longer pause times may consider interrupting to be rude or disrespectful. In such a case, the real experience of being interrupted is replaced by the judgement of the other party as rude. The key interest of the first party is to be allowed to finish her thought. Yet, rather than approach this conflict with consideration of the interests at stake, we observe that people focus on and communicate their judgement, either directly to the other party (e.g., "stop being so rude!") or to others behind the other party's back. The cultural lens that determines what is considered appropriate replaces a more objective understanding of the situation, and the expression of judgement only exacerbates the conflict.

An important focus of moving from conflict to profit involves replacing judgement (e.g., assessment of what is rude) with curiosity (e.g., "I wonder why he keeps interrupting") and assumptions (e.g., "He is a rude person") with openness (e.g., "Maybe he's just over-excited about this topic"). In fact, many behaviours have vastly different meanings for different cultures, groups, and individuals.

Behavioural Interpretations and Misinterpretations

The cultures in which we grow up not only infuse us with certain value preferences, they also instruct us on the meaning of different behaviours. For example, what does direct eye contact mean to you? Does it convey a sense of respect and deference or does it mean the individual is challenging you? How about people who stand very close to you when you are talking with them? Does it mean that they like you or that they are attempting to intimidate you? How about someone who is always quiet in business meetings? Is he disinterested, attentive, shy, stupid, or simply unable to find an entry point into the discussion? Our interpretations of these behaviours add to the complexity of conflict situations and contribute to the emergence and perpetuation of many conflicts.

A doctoral student at a Canadian university was researching eye contact. In her phenomenological methods she asked subjects to carry notepads with them to keep a journal of what they observed about eye contact. One subject, a heterosexual man, described standing alone at a bus stop one evening except for another man. He reported in his journal a "game" wherein he noticed the other man would hold eye contact until the subject looked away. Then the other man would scan up and down the subject's body before holding eye contact again. The heterosexual man expressed amusement that he had never noticed this kind of "eye game" before. He expressed surprise when the other man, now revealed to be gay, approached him and asked him for a date. The subject interpreted his eye contact as a non-verbal game, whereas the other man clearly interpreted it as an expression of romantic interest. The intended message, encoded and sent from one party to the other, was clearly different from the message received and decoded on the other end, and these were based on the different (mis)interpretations of the behaviours the two men perceived.[61]

In one case, a leader in a small firm was having difficulty with one particular direct report, as well as with several other staff members. The female direct report described being intimidated by the male leader's aggressive nature and bullying tactics. He seemed to value directness (to the point of abuse), individualism, control of people and environments, status ascribed by position (his, that is), and the expression of thoughts and feelings. In contrast, she valued collective approaches, was more comfortable with indirect communication, believed status is achieved, and was more neutral in her expression. On one occasion the leader entered her office to discuss "what her problem was." She was sitting in her chair with her arms crossed—a typical position for her. He perceived her arms being crossed as a sign of rejection of and disrespect for him and told her, in no uncertain terms, that she was never to cross her arms while in discussion with him. Not surprisingly, his interpretation of her posture and his authoritarian response only exacerbated the conflict that already existed. This leader's belief in his absolute authority and his rightness on all issues contributed to ongoing conflicts with numerous staff members and resulted in the deterioration of the work environment, the suppression of productivity and creativity, and, in this case, the erosion of the group was too deep to repair.

When tensions arise, the potential for the misinterpretation of confusing behaviours increases and the application of the hostile attribution bias is more prone to surface. Rejecting initial interpretations and replacing them with curiosity about the behaviour or about the interests in dispute can prevent conflicts and divergence.

Culture and the Interest of Saving Face

A rumour was spread during Richard Nixon's presidency that while he was visiting China he tried to steal a priceless Chinese teacup by slipping it into his briefcase. A Chinese official supposedly spotted him. But instead of confronting Nixon directly, the dignitaries entertained him with a magician who, while performing, retrieved the cup and substituted a worthless replica. Nixon did not realize it until he got back to the U.S. Allegedly, this rumour was started by a Chinese news agency to reinforce a Chinese self-image. It symbolized the victory of the resourceful Chinese over the crafty foreigner in a manner that avoided anyone having to lose face.

The concept of "face" has been studied and applied to cultures across the world.[62] A loss of face involves the condemnation of the society as well as the person. In Chinese culture, the individual ego is often shared with group ego and thus interdependence is created between person and group. Damage to individual face is equivalent to damage to the group face. In the U.S., face is often more individualistic and is used to account for conflict, shame, embarrassment, compliance-gaining tactics, social status, and politeness strategies. In Japan, face is often considered an important concept, particularly in reference to politeness strategies.

In our experience, the desire to save face is an important aspect of most conflict situations. Saving face is related to the use of psychological defence mechanisms, the pursuit of cognitive consistency, the development of reputation, as well as numerous other aspects of social interaction and interpersonal conflict. Whether deeply ingrained in a cultural landscape like China, or merely a need to maintain one's individual dignity or reputation, protecting face is a drive that seems virtually universal. However, in contrast to the rumour involving President Nixon, where saving face for one's adversary was as important as protecting one's own face, many individuals in western society see face as one-dimensional, particularly when in conflict. Not only do many people appear to prefer strategies that may damage the face of whoever is threatening their interests, they seem to relish the opportunity to do such damage. In fact, rather than try to "save the face" of our adversaries, we tend, instead, to want to "rub their faces in it." We observe in western culture that teachers still use tactics to embarrass students, managers to embarrass employees, competitors to embarrass rivals, and so forth, with little, if any, regard for the concept of saving face. These strategies, when used in interdependent conflict situations, can only lead to further the conflict by creating needless despair in the other person.

Dominant Features of Western Organizational Culture

From our work and study of organizational culture in Canada and the U.S., we have observed several features of our value system that warrant specific consideration as influences on the experience of conflict.

A Culture of Individualism: The Golden Rule

A fundamental principle emphasized in most households, schools, and workplaces in North America has been called "The Golden Rule." This rule, referred to as the ethic of reciprocity, is endorsed by most of the large world religions and key historic religious leaders. Jesus, Hillel, and Confucius have used the rule in their ethical teachings.[63] In its simplest form, The Golden Rule states that people should "treat others as they themselves would wish to be treated." The Golden Rule is held up as the highest standard of moral principle. It is reinforced in our society by parents, teachers, managers, and others who ask, in response to bad behaviour, "How would you like it if someone did that to you?"

Yet for all of The Golden Rule's positive contributions, it conveys a counterintuitive message that fosters egoism and individualism. It does this by suggesting that we should judge behaviour through our own lens rather than through the lens of another. It assumes that what I desire, appreciate, and value should be what another desires, appreciates, and values. It proclaims that if I do not feel offended, violated, or threatened by a behaviour then the behaviour should be judged moral and acceptable, even if another person was offended, violated, or threatened. It teaches that my way of viewing the world is the standard by which to judge everyone else.

This rule forms the philosophic basis of a common form of rationalization. We have heard many clients comment, in response to a complaint, that "If they did it to me I wouldn't care," or, "I wouldn't be offended," or, "They're just too sensitive." These statements imply that the individual would not have taken the comment or conduct as sensitively. The Golden Rule can be a means of absolving oneself of responsibility for harm because one views the behaviour and the outcome as acceptable based on the individual's own standard. Thus, a strict interpretation of this rule leads people to view the morality of their conduct through their own lenses and not the lenses of those affected. It also teaches that we have little reason to listen to others' experiences in conflict situations because we can simply rely on how we would have perceived a given situation to "know" how it should have been perceived. Thus, rather than foster understanding and connection between people in conflict, it breeds the opposite effect—it impedes the development of the mindset that is necessary to learn, to appreciate difference, and build convergence. You can see yourself as ethically intact even while great damage is being inflicted on others. You can be so far behind you think you are first.

In response to the counterproductive message of The Golden Rule, an alternative ethical principle has been developed and coined "The Platinum Rule":

Treat others as they wish to be treated.

The Platinum Rule allows for there to be differences in beliefs, desires, interests, and needs, and it emphasizes that understanding these differences is vital to fostering ethical treatment and establishing functional and fair relationships. For example, The Platinum Rule is consistent with the modern priority given to the medical ethic of autonomy. No longer is it acceptable or ethical for physicians to force people to undergo medical procedures to which they object. The new ethic is based on informed consent as determined by the patient—not the doctor.

The Platinum Rule is not without its limitations. There are situations, such as violent or abusive situations, that call upon each of us to consider our own moral or professional obligations and to not "treat others as they wish to be treated." However, The Platinum Rule, as a guiding principle, prevents more conflict than does The Golden Rule. As previously noted, resolving conflict in a manner that seeks convergence and profitable outcomes requires one to understand all the interests involved, including those of other parties. Simply rejecting the interests of others as either improper or unreasonable, as they may be perceived through our own cultural lenses, places us at a disadvantage when we seek to find solutions that meet our needs and the needs of the individuals and groups with which we work.

A Culture of Adversarialism

Another common feature of western society and business is a strong tendency to see conflict in terms of protagonists and antagonists, in terms of enmity, and in terms of supporters and adversaries. In turn, this belief system fosters communication patterns consistent with this value system. The Socratic method is held in high esteem as a means of teaching and debating. Posing a thesis and debating it—often arguing for it aggressively—is the central process of government and organizational decision-making, as anyone can tell you who has witnessed the exchange of viewpoints and insults that occurs in the U.S. Congress or the Canadian Parliament. The legal system is premised on the belief that justice is best secured through adversarialism. Adversarialism is a key strategy in the training of many professionals, such as doctors, lawyers, and academics.

Linguist and author Debra Tannen described western culture as The Argument Culture. She posits that a pervasive, warlike atmosphere makes us approach public dialogue, and just about anything we need to accomplish, as if it were a fight. She states that argument has served society well, to some degree, but the culture of argument has become so exaggerated that it is getting in the way of solving our problems. Tannen concludes that people's spirits are being corroded by living in an atmosphere of unrelenting contention.[64] We would add that while spirits are being corroded by argument, relationships, organizations, and profits are also being eroded.

We observe that some people thrive in a culture of argument and adversarialism, and that some systems benefit from their ability to detect weaknesses in arguments. An example is how the justice system works to challenge testimony in order to discover truth. We also accept that there are times when this approach to public and organizational discourse is productive. The approach can challenge the logic of one's position and motivate further reflection when arguments fail to meet the test of logic. It can also spur a form of healthy competition to develop the most cogent evidence-based ideas. However, like Tannen and countless organizational researchers, we also observe the substantial damage this approach causes to individuals and organizations. While many people respond well to debate-style decision-making, many others prefer less vitriolic means of communication and decision-making. Every issue and every difference does not have to be a "fight." The obsession with being right can interfere with the achievement of being happy.

Do you want to be right or do you want to be happy?
In conflict, there are times when you do not get to be both.

How many people have you known who got to be right, won an argument with his spouse, but spent the night sleeping on the couch? Our case experience supports the clear conclusion that when people are in argument mode, they are less able to listen, learn, or problem solve—in other words, they are less able to be creative or innovative with their efforts to find solutions to difficult conflicts.

Interestingly, the current thinking in management and leadership emphasizes the need for openness, listening, and relationship-building. Current management research supports approaches like brainstorming, 360-degree feedback programs, shared governance, and similar strategies. However, the success of each of these innovative management strategies is dependent on the ability of the parties to express themselves and listen in a manner that is accepting, not rejecting. In our experience, many minor conflicts escalate because of the tendency to contest rather than contemplate, to debate rather than discuss, to fight rather than facilitate. When we express different views as adversaries—even when we are on the same team—and approach every issue as a debate, we create such tension that we often lose sight of the real issues and concerns in an adversarial atmosphere.

A Culture of Intimidation

Growing up in a culture of individualism and adversarialism leads individuals to learn and adopt an ethic summed up by this familiar saying "the ends justify the means." Consider that the dominant ethic in business is "caveat emptor": let the buyer beware. Within this ethic, sellers have minimal responsibility for potential errors in judgement made by buyers, even if those errors are strongly influenced or created by sellers. Also consider that the dominant structure of institutional governance is hierarchy, wherein those in power have the right to control the actions of those under their authority. Combine these concepts and we observe that those in power learn that they are culturally sanctioned to absolve themselves of any harm done by their reports because the operative philosophy is, "let the employee, student, client, etc., beware."

In various ways, western culture teaches us that others are out to get what they want, with little regard for us—so we better learn how to use our power to get what we want. We are taught that this ideology of "to each their own" results in the best and most just outcomes. Thus, a dominant practice in western culture when conflict occurs, or is even remotely possible, is for one side to use its power to intimidate its adversaries as a means to pursue its own interests. The problem with this culturally endorsed win–lose dynamic is that it fails to seek opportunities for win–win outcomes. Instead, win–lose scenarios often lead, ultimately, to lose–lose outcomes, as we observed in chapter 2. For example, an arbitrator may decide in favour of one party and against another, but if the parties need to continue to work together the legacy of the adversarial process will damage both of them well into the future. Under the free use of power, and an "ends justify the means" ethic, people and organizations erode, implode, or explode far more often than is natural or necessary. The "winners" can distance themselves from the devastating consequences they cause because they can claim they were just doing what they have been taught to do: pursue your own interests as effectively as you can, using whatever means are available. They say, "You have to compete, and I was just competing."

In this culture, arguably, the dominant paradigm is to view the "other" as the "adversary." Even individuals who are your colleagues, employees, trainees, and clients can be viewed as adversaries because they can block your achievement. We assume, when in conflict, that they will in fact do so if given the chance. The image of the military drill sergeant comes to mind as the quintessential authority figure. The use of intimidation tactics has been shown as effective, if not virtuous, in western media and entertainment through the years. Thus, in this culture you are free to exert your power in whatever ways are available; as long as your "adversary" (e.g., your employee, student, client, colleague, team mate) buckles under the pressure, it is the other's inherent weakness that caused the implosion—not you.

Power is very much perception-based. We tend to think about all of the people and circumstances that have more power and control than we do. We do not tend to think about all the ways in which others might perceive us as powerful. We do not tend to think of all the conflicts that can arise because others perceive us as powerful and as a threat, even when we do not see ourselves in this way. We come home from a difficult day at work, where our skills, knowledge, and expertise were challenged by others. Our bills for the telephone, heat, and cable television have all arrived on the same day and are waiting for us. We go to the fridge to discover how empty it is. We rush to the store to hunt and gather canned food for dinner. Walking into the store, we do not feel powerful, and yet others in the store—those who came home from crummier days, with bigger bills to pay, and with less in their fridges—may perceive us as very powerful. Potential for conflict arises, even in the grocery store.

We all tend to compare up with power.

Power comes in various forms.[65] Consider these:

- Reward power—the ability to use or provide reinforcement
- Coercive power—the ability to threaten or punish
- Legitimate power—the sanctioned right to require or demand
- Referent Power—influence derived from respect for the power holder
- Expert power—influence derived from the perception of superior skills and abilities

These forms of power are exploited in two ways: positional or personal. Power is granted to an individual through the assignment of a position of authority in an organization. The higher one's position in the hierarchy of an organization, the more power one can usually exert. Stakeholder groups in organizations, such as unions, boards, lobby groups, customers, and the like, can also exercise power. In addition, power can be exploited through personal attributes such as physical size, one's level of experience, confidence, personality, passion, communication skills, and culturally defined elements, such as gender, race, education level, attractiveness, and so on. Any of these bases or sources of power can be used as means to intimidate others in order to achieve one's goals.

Intimidation

Intimidation is defined in this way: "to frighten or overawe, especially to subdue or influence."[66] In its attempt to halt the common use of intimidation in postgraduate medical education, the College of Physicians and Surgeons of Canada has defined *intimidation* as "any behaviour, process, or tradition that is likely, on reasonable grounds, to induce an unwarranted fear or have a detrimental effect on the learning environment."[67] Thus, intimidation involves using power to threaten other parties in a manner that exceeds natural feelings of "awe" or "fear" with the loss of some valued practical or psychological interest (e.g., denial of opportunity, a poor evaluation or grade, damage to reputation, financial loss, embarrassment, loss of self-esteem). All business, professional, academic, and personal activities that challenge us also create some level of anxiety or intimidation. This naturally occurring sensation of anxiety can be difficult to cope with.

When this sensation is exacerbated by a "behaviour, process, or tradition that is likely, on reasonable grounds, to induce unwarranted fear," the level of intimidation becomes unnecessarily high and can result in potentially dysfunctional responses that undermine the goals of all parties. A number of dysfunctional behaviours occur within intimidating organizational cultures:

- Withholding opinions
- Working in an overly cautious manner, or not taking reasonable risks

- Withholding new ideas
- Hiding (e.g., not participating in events)
- Avoiding others, particularly individuals with whom you have conflict
- Accepting the status quo
- Self-blaming for outcomes that one is not actually responsible for
- Venting and gossiping
- Protecting oneself by lying, cheating, and sabotaging others

Although these behaviours may also be rooted in other causes, such as personality or cultural differences, they are noticeably more evident as responses to intimidation.

We know some people will not share this view of intimidation. During a presentation on this topic, an organizational leader suggested that the dysfunctional behaviours listed above are more a product of personality than of a culture of intimidation, and that she simply does not hire individuals who display these characteristics. This viewpoint runs counter to our experience—and a great deal of study done on organizational behaviour—that supports the key role that organizational culture plays in either exacerbating or mitigating feelings of intimidation. We have observed even the strongest individuals become repressed and dysfunctional in response to acts of intimidation and a group culture that condones such practices.

We have encountered many rationalizations for acting in an intimidating manner. We have summarized these justifications as goals and representative statements in the following table. Yet, while these goals are reasonable, the approaches identified in the representative statements reflect a "charging into" approach to conflict that has the effect of creating undue intimidation and unproductive resistance, and undermining the actual goal.

FIGURE 6.3

Goals Associated with Intimidating Behaviour and Culture

Goal	Representative Statement
To Motivate	"Get off your butt and get to work."
To Advise	"You don't have time for other things—don't be selfish."
To Protect	"Do it the way I showed you, or I'll have to do something we will both regret. You have to trust me."
To Support	"Watch your back—others are out to get you."
To Test	"Let's see if you can cut it."

We had a case in which a surgeon was having conflict with the nursing staff in the area. When things ran smoothly the surgeon was fun, respectful, and a joy to work with. However, when things were a bit chaotic the surgeon was prone to vitriolic outbursts directed at the nursing staff, regardless of whether or not they had control over the situation. At these times, the surgeon used both professional stature and personal power to intimidate others into serving his needs. This approach created a legacy of fear among the nursing staff, rather than respect. The conflict shifted from a slow erosion to an implosion on the day that staff decided it would no longer accommodate one of the surgeon's personal practices. He liked to stand on a towel while performing surgery. Through the years, the nursing staff put down the towel for him as they prepared the operating room for surgery. In light of the surgeon's aggressive and disrespectful behaviour toward them the nurses decided they would no longer put his towel at his feet for him—the practice of bowing at his feet became too denigrating to their self-esteem as professionals to continue. Their resistance initially led to increased tension, and some power plays, but conveyed a valuable message to the surgeon who, with assistance, learned how to deal with his work frustration in a manner that did not lead to unhealthy conflict with the nursing staff.

Control of Information

A Government Minister in a Canadian province gave a press conference about a new plan for liquor sales in the province. During his presentation he did not mention any policy position regarding the obvious exclusion of corner stores in the plan. When asked about this omission he responded by saying simply that corner stores were not included in the plan. When asked why, he again responded by saying they were not included—end of story. The problem with his response was what was not being said, and what would likely be inferred by the omission. It was hard to believe the Minister did not know why corner stores were not included in the current plan. More likely, he simply did not wish to discuss the reasons for this exclusion at a press conference. He probably thought the real reasons would cause more conflict than his attempt at obfuscation. Yet, in the absence of authentic information, as we explored in chapters 4 and 5, people fill in the blanks. They will also conclude that the reasons for exclusion are likely unfair, at best, or malevolent, at worst. Otherwise, why would the Minister not present them?

Another way in which power is used to control is through the release of information. After all, information is power. The above situation represents a common experience in many workplaces. Information is often withheld for the purpose of controlling dissatisfaction and preventing overt conflict. If intimidation is equivalent to charging into conflict, then the common practice of withholding information is an attempt to lean away from conflict. Yet the uncertainty, assumptions, and misperceptions that emerge from an absence of information only lead to increased despair, which, in turn, leads to heightened tension and conflict and more rigidity in attempts made to resolve disputes.

A Final Thought on Culture

Anthropologist Ruth Benedict explained her perspective on why it is that some cultures are fundamentally peaceful, cooperative, and respectful while others are not. She posited that the difference is related to one primary concept: our need as social beings for self-esteem. In what she called "good or synergistic cultures," she posited that "selfishness and altruism are merged by granting esteem to those who are generous." She added, "Cultures that reward behaviour benefiting the group as a whole...while not allowing behavior (sic) that harms the group as a whole are peaceful, respectful of women and children, and cooperative."[68] In such a culture, individual members are found to be secure. On the other hand, cultures that grant esteem to those who acquire and hold onto wealth, and that reward behaviour that benefits the individual at the expense of the whole, will be "warlike, abusive toward women and children, and competitive." In this culture, individuals will constantly feel insecure. Benedict also reported finding that members of the former culture were happy for the most part. In contrast, she found that members of the latter culture were not.

When one applies Benedict's observations to organizations, they suggest that cultures that primarily value individual achievement and reward behaviour that benefits individuals at the expense of others will cultivate work environments that are rife with hostility, abuse, competitiveness, and suspicion. When conflict arises in these organizations, its people will respond with denial, despair, and detachment; the effects are compromised achievement, growth, and profitability.

In contrast, organizations with cultures that reward the pursuit of communal goals over individual interests, and that prohibit behaviours that harm the organization and its people, will have work environments characterized by peace, respect, and collaboration. When conflict arises in these organizations, its people will pursue insight, will be inspired to find meaningful and productive solutions, and will remain invested.

Conflict Across at a Glance

- All communication is cross-cultural communication.
- Culture is the way in which a group of people perceives and responds to conflict.
- Cultures share similar values, although there will always be members of a culture who adopt different sets of values.
- These values can be arranged along several continuums:
  Collectivist vs. Individualist
  Direct vs. Indirect Communication
  Internal vs. External Control
  Achieved vs. Ascribed Status
  Absolute Rules vs. Relative Relationships
  Neutral vs. Affective Interaction
- Culture significantly influences perception and interests.
- Frequently in conflict, we must make a choice: "Do I want to be right, or do I want to be happy?" We will not be able to be both.
- The more the other party represents *otherness*, the more different they are from us, the more likely we are to misinterpret what they encode in conflict. Yet we typically see our own misinterpretations as accurate.
- Often, we become stuck in the Conflict Trap because we ignore the need many of us have to "save face." Rather than "saving the other's face," we tend to want to "rub their nose in it."
- Western organizational culture tends to be individualistic, adversarial, and intimidating. These traits contribute to the denial, despair, and detachment that keeps us stuck in the Conflict Trap. Turning conflict into profit requires that we adopt new approaches to deal with each other and with the conflicts that are bound to arise in our working lives.

PART
2

MOVING THROUGH THE NARROW PLACE

7

Moving Through the Narrow Place

FIGURE 7.1

The Narrow Place

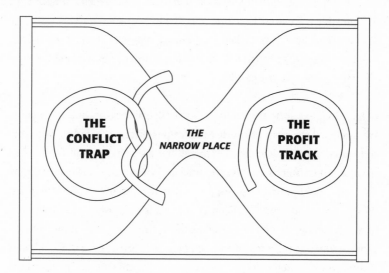

A man was walking along a beach at midday. The ocean's tide had retreated far out into the bay and the midday sun was blazing down. He could see thousands of sea stars lying on the sand and rocks. Fingers of deep purple and bright orange coated the crescent of the bay. Though some, closer to the water's edge, seemed content to sun bathe, hundreds of others further up the beach had died and countless others were clearly perishing in the baking sun. As the man walked along he came across a nine-year-old girl. She was skipping among the sea stars and bending over to examine them before selecting one or two. She then carried those to the water's edge and threw them into the water. He watched her playing in this way for a few minutes before he approached her, asking, "What are you doing?"

"Oh, I'm throwing these sea stars into the water. Some of them are drying out and will die if they don't get wet again," she replied without pausing in her work.

The man watched for a few more minutes before he said, laughing, "But little girl, there are thousands of sea stars drying out on this beach. Hundreds of them have already died. You can't possibly hope to make a difference!"

The little girl picked up another sea star, skipped to the water's edge, and tossed it in. "Made a difference to *that* one," she said, as she skipped past him.

IN PART 1 WE EXAMINED THE CONFLICT TRAP of denial, despair, and detachment. We discussed the crisis of conflict that causes divergence within, between, and among us. Conflict involves threat and risk, anxiety and fear, defensiveness and resistance, and the potential for loss. Yet each and every conflict also presents opportunity—opportunity for discovery, development, achievement, and profit. In Chinese, the translation of the English word *crisis* is a pictogram of two different ideas: "danger" and "opportunity." When trapped in the crisis of conflict, most of us experience the dangerous aspects most acutely; denial, despair, and detachment bring unwanted negative consequences to us and those around us. However, when conflict is handled well, it also presents opportunities that would not have existed had there been no conflict in the first place. When we lean into conflict and resolve it, people report experiencing a deeper understanding of their own and others' needs. They report more authentic and deeper relationships, improved communication, and greater efficiencies. They report synergy and convergence.

We can be so overwhelmed by negativity and crises that we deny there are problems or detach ourselves from them. As with the man in the story above, we walk along seeing problems but we are conditioned to not think of them as "our problems." But unlike the man in the story above, the problems we encounter in conflict are not as easy to dismiss as sea stars drying out on the beach. Perhaps he did not care or have to care about their suffering; however, if his family members, friends, co-workers, clients, or even his enemies are suffering, he will most likely suffer too. As in the story above, we may not be able to address all the suffering we encounter; if that is our goal, we will be disappointed. Nevertheless, like the girl in the story, we can choose the standards by which we measure our success. We may not be able to make a difference to everyone, but we can make a difference for others and ourselves. To do so requires us to break free of the Conflict Trap and to lean into conflict as a bridge to profit.

We characterize the bridge from the destructive Conflict Trap to the opportunity of the Profit Track as the "Narrow Place." This bridge, to return to our metaphor of the Conflict Hourglass, is an "aperture." It is an opening that leads from the denial, despair, and detachment of the Conflict Trap to the insight, inspiration, and investment of the Profit Track. Like the aperture of an hourglass, it is a passage that is narrow. *Narrow* means thin, or of small width. Other meanings of *narrow* include fine, precise, exact, tight, and focused. Definitions of *place* include these: a portion of space occupied by people, a natural position, a residence or home, space for a person, an area for a specific purpose, and a position as a member of a team.[69] When we put the two together we get this:

The Narrow Place is a naturally occurring, thin opening that creates a precise opportunity for people to accomplish a specific purpose, individually or as a team.

The image and concept of a Narrow Place arises cross-culturally in most major religions, philosophical works, arts, and politics:

- William Bridges describes the "neutral zone" as the confusing and tense space between endings and beginnings.[70]

- Scott Peck's best selling book, *The Road Less Travelled*, discusses how human potential and growth are achieved by taking an approach that is uncommon, narrow, and requires attention and persistence in order to follow it.[71]
- "Enter by the narrow gate; for the gate is wide, and the way is broad that leads to destruction, and many are those who enter by it. For the gate is small, and the way is narrow that leads to life, and few are those who find it."[72]
- "Two roads diverged in a woods, and I—I took the one less traveled by. And that has made all the difference." Robert Frost.
- "Do not go where the path may lead, go instead where there is no path and leave a trail." Ralph Waldo Emerson.
- In Greek, *narrow* means "pressure, suffering, and tribulation."
- In Hebrew, one of the meanings of *mitzriyim* is "finding redemption by going through a narrow place."
- Leaders sometimes refer to taking a narrow path from deficit to profit, implying the need for difficult decisions and short-term discomfort in order to achieve long-term goals.
- Books, television and movies are rife with suspenseful images of heroes and antagonists doing battle on narrow mountain ridges or deteriorating, thin bridges.

Finding the Narrow Place

Curiosity

Perhaps you have been locked in a Conflict Trap. You have noticed how you and others alternately deny there are problems, despair that things will ever improve, and detach from the situation, and thus contribute to divergence among teams and compromised growth. How do you move from this negative cycle towards resolution and profit?

The transition from threat to opportunity means moving from assumptions to inquiry, and from judgement to curiosity. Adopting a spirit of inquiry is the first of two approaches that take us from the negativity of the Conflict Trap into the Narrow Place of opportunity that leads us, ultimately, to the Profit Track. Curiosity involves de-personalizing the negativity of the Conflict Trap by taking the approach of the naïve scientist. Rather than react to conflict with thoughts such as, "I can't believe they said that!" or "Those jerks! Now I'm going to make their lives miserable," a spirit of inquiry involves thinking along different lines: "I wonder why they said that?" or, "Those jerks! I need to find a way to change this situation." It can seem a little canned at first, but there is a reason why the Vulcan race in the popular "Star Trek" television programs are depicted as peaceful, prosperous, and evolved beyond most cultures: they are dispassionate about conflict and thus avoid getting trapped in it.

Certainly, one does not have to become an unemotional Vulcan to successfully move from conflict to profit. Emotions play a key role in transforming conflict's negativity into positive outcomes. However, it is the *role* of emotions that must change. Though we want to move emotions out of the driver seat, we do not want to kick them out of the car. Conflict is most successfully addressed when emotions are in the passenger seat, offering information and navigating us through the conflict. Reason, however, should be firmly planted in the driver's seat, reminding us what our true goal is. For example, when I feel frustration, the emotion carries important information. However, the emotion alone often seeks a goal different from that which I might ultimately be seeking. I might want the person who frustrated me to change their behaviour so they no longer cause me frustration. The feeling of frustration alone may simply want to protest, or to punish that individual. One of the most significant transitions we must consider and integrate when we move from conflict to profit is that we can learn from our own emotional responses how to better achieve our true, overarching goals. Otherwise, we get trapped in conflict when we indulge our emotional responses individually, when we treat them like drivers rather than messengers.

Emotions are messengers.

Negative emotions carry important information that there is a problem, that there are costs to others and ourselves, and about what needs to happen for all to profit from the situation. Transitioning from negative reactivity to the "proactivity" of curiosity involves three related elements: awareness, attention, and acknowledgement.

Awareness

In the story at the beginning of this chapter, the first thing the girl had to do in order to problem-solve was notice that there was a problem. This seemingly obvious observation is completely lost on us when we are stuck in the Conflict Trap. Unlike the man who saw the problem but did not notice it was a problem for him, the girl would have come to the bay and *witnessed* a problem for others. Like the man, she could easily have chosen to deny the problem and look past the dying sea stars to the inviting ocean, then skipped between their carcases to go splash in the sea. She could just as easily have despaired, noticing only the cruelty of nature and viewing the sea stars' deaths as a metaphor for the futility of all life. Indeed, she could have detached by saying to herself that dying sea stars are just a part of nature, and skipped on.

Alternatively, she could have thrown herself into the task of rescuing all the sea stars, frantically racing against time in a marathon she could never win. We have discussed anger and its attendant anxiety as attempts to *rush towards* the Profit Track from the Conflict Trap. Often, when people are immersed in despair, or immersed in defending against despair by denying or detaching, anger and anxiety build. We then make attempts to break through the Conflict Trap, typically in one of two ways. We give-up, or we lean away—sometimes by quitting our jobs. Sometimes, in desperation, we rush towards the aperture of the Narrow Place, or attempt to charge into the situation and try to force others, or the situation, to change. This rushing towards the Profit Track can be visualized as grains of sand in one side of an hourglass being forced through the aperture to the other side. Rather than allow the sand to pass through grain by grain, pulled through naturally by gravity, we cause the grains to become jammed when we force them. The attempt to force the sand through the aperture only contributes to sealing off the trap.

Developing an awareness that we are in the Conflict Trap moves us towards the aperture of the Narrow Place.

Attention

Most of us, when confronted with a challenge, automatically respond with a combination of denial, despair, or detachment. After all, this Conflict Trap resembles the grief cycle and thus prompts a normal response to loss or the threat of loss. It is normal and, though it may not feel like it, it is also healthy to despair in the face of threat or loss. It is normal and healthy to deny and to detach as defences against the despair triggered by a threat or loss. The normal and healthy grief cycle becomes an abnormal and unhealthy Conflict Trap over time, particularly when we remain stuck in these responses. In other words, the Conflict Trap describes the symptoms of problems, not their causes or their cures. If everyone denied, despaired, and detached when they saw creatures like sea stars suffering and dying, if we did not have groups who work to protect endangered species, we would have far fewer species by now. This ordinary response to negativity does not, on its own, resolve any problems.

So what is the point of this normal grief reaction if it only traps us and prevents us from solving the problem? The negativity of the Conflict Trap makes us aware that there is a problem. When we stop fighting the conflict by leaning away or charging into the problems and, instead, simply "sit in the problems" for a while, we take our first steps towards entering the Narrow Place. By sitting in the problems, we allow ourselves to be pulled towards the aperture without trying to force our way through, which inevitably creates an impasse.

All jobs essentially comprise people who are hired to pay attention to a particular role or function. The CFO is paid to pay attention to the financial health of an organization. The custodian is paid to pay attention to the cleanliness of the work environment. Questions that professionals ask themselves in the successful execution of their roles include these: "What is in the best interest of preserving the organization's financial health?" "What will keep the environment most clean with minimal effort and cost?" Questions that people who wish to move from conflict to profit can ask include these: "What is going on?" "What might be the possible interpretations of the behaviours of others?" "What do I want and, given what I know about other people, how can I get what I want from them?" "What else do I need to learn about this situation?" Paying attention moves us further along towards the Narrow Place.

Acknowledgement

In nearly every one of the thousands of conflicts we have worked with, the issue of fairness arises. Typically, fairness surfaces in the form of someone's objection: "Why me? Why do I have to make the first move? They're the ones that started it and they're the ones who continue it! It isn't fair that I should be the one to do this!" In response to this, we have one observation: You may be completely correct. It may be completely unfair. However, these facts do absolutely nothing to resolve the conflict, to end the negative consequences you suffer from, nor do they move you towards growth and profit.

It is not fair that we live for only about eighty years when trees live for hundreds. It is not fair that I have to rely on breathing air in order to survive when it would be so much easier to not require oxygen. Many things are unfair but continue to happen. Rather than be consumed by the issue of fairness, studies indicate that when we focus on our needs and employ a range of strategies to get our needs met we experience much less conflict than people who continue to try to fashion the world into their own image. Typically, it is unfair that you should be the person to make the first move to resolve conflict. Typically, though, if you do not, you will continue to stay locked in the Conflict Trap. The acknowledgement of this fact moves you towards the aperture and opportunities for achievement.

Acknowledging that there not only *might* be problems or that there *are* problems, but that problems left unaddressed or mishandled will continue or worsen—this is the last aspect of curiosity that moves us towards the aperture of the Narrow Place. Acknowledge that this is not fair and that you do not like it. Acknowledge that it does not have to be fair and you do not have to like it. This acknowledgement frees up your capacity to generate ideas about what to do about what confronts you.

Into the Aperture

Courage

A hero is no braver than an ordinary man, but he is braver five minutes longer.

—*Ralph Waldo Emerson*

Becoming aware of potential sources of conflict, paying attention to the signs and symptoms that problems exist, and acknowledging there are steps we can and should take to move out of the Conflict Trap, even if those steps may not seem fair to us, are the three steps of curiosity that leave us with an overarching question: "Now what should I do?" In part, you are already doing it. We cannot overstate the importance of curiosity in the profitable resolution of conflict. Thus, one key strategy to take away from this book is this:

Be curious at all costs.

Curiosity has costs. It takes courage to take risks and incur those costs. When I am curious it might cost me an opportunity to "tell it like it is." It might cost me some time to spend an extra four minutes trying to figure out where someone else is coming from. It might cost me some pride and cognitive dissonance to imagine that the "jerk" I am confronting might actually have legitimate dreams, hopes, and wishes, even if the way that person is trying to achieve them is so upsetting.

Yet "leaning into" strategies, founded on curiosity and courage, are your best means to draw profit out of conflict. In karate lessons, self-defence workshops, and in training to manage aggressive behaviours, all successful responses to violence involve a form of leaning into. Consider these examples:

- Resist the urge to look away from or to challenge a potential attacker; instead, look them in the eyes.
- Walk tall and purposefully, and neither wander aimlessly nor run desperately.

- If an attacker grabs your arm, the best strategy to break the person's unwelcome grip is not to try to forcefully pull your arm away, nor is it to passively let the individual hold your arm. It is to use all your weight to lean towards them, shift their balance, and then firmly draw your arm away.

All of these strategies involve courage. All of these strategies work. You have choices before you. You can choose to lament how cruel some people are, and how unfair life is. You can choose to be temporarily comforted by others who share your frustration but who do not help resolve it. Indeed, you can choose to remain stuck in the Conflict Trap. Alternatively, you can start to ask questions to increase your awareness about what is going on. You can choose to pay attention and learn from what you observe rather than just react to it. Even though a given problem is either "not your problem," or "should not be your problem," you can, if there is some cost to you or others, choose to acknowledge a role for yourself in addressing the concern. Sometimes your role in resolving conflict may not generate a direct benefit for you; you may, however, simply be in a position to help others. You can feel anxious, even fearful, and still choose to take some calculated risks, which we describe in the next section, to move onto the Profit Track. Building insight, feeling inspired, and becoming more invested enables you to reap more profit from your investment. It may be a tight fit. It may feel as though you cannot get through. It may feel like living in denial, despair, and detachment is preferable to expending the energy required to manage your emotions, release your judgements, and try new ways. While the risks involved in engaging conflict may appear insurmountable, the risks are more perceived than real, and are controllable when you implement the steps and practices we outline in Part 3.

The Narrow Place at a Glance

- The conflict cycle is a trap for individuals and organizations because denial ultimately leads to despair, which ultimately leads to detachment, which, in turn, brings more denial, and so on.
- There is a path out of the Conflict Trap and into profit, but it is a path less travelled through—a metaphorical Narrow Place.
- Moving away from the Conflict Trap and towards the aperture of the Narrow Place requires curiosity and making conscious choices to employ a spirit of inquiry.
- Curiosity involves three key aspects: developing *awareness* that there is a problem, paying *attention* to what the problem is, and, if it is a problem for people who are in any way associated with your own profiting, *acknowledging* that it is a problem worth addressing.
- Pulling ourselves through the Narrow Place and onto the Profit Track also involves courage. It means refusing to deny issues, refusing to collude with others' despair and hopelessness, and it means resisting the urge to detach, avoid, and lean away from problems.
- To convert conflict into profit requires us to use curiosity and courage to lean into that conflict.

PART
3

TURNING CONFLICT INTO PROFIT

8

The Profit Track

INSIGHT, INSPIRATION, AND INVESTMENT

FIGURE 8.1
The Profit Track

THE
PROFIT
TRACK

Every path to a new understanding begins in confusion.

—*Mason Cooley*

AS WE DISCUSSED in Part 1, the Conflict Trap is a negative cycle of denial, despair, and detachment similar to the grieving process. However, as individuals and organizations, even those of us most mired in conflict can move out of "grieving" and onto the positive growth cycle of what we call the Profit Track. By implementing the skills and strategies discussed in the following chapters, individuals and organizations can move through the aperture of the Narrow Place from conflict to profit.

In this chapter we outline the stages that are critical to handling conflict in a manner that keeps us on the Profit Track. We refer to these stages as Insight, Inspiration, and Investment. It is important to remember that, like the stages of the Conflict Trap, the stages of the Profit Track are not necessarily linear or sequential. Though most individuals and groups generally move, over time, from a Narrow Place that requires curiosity and courage to develop insight, experience inspiration, and become invested along the way, many will not move in this order. Some may immediately begin by investing, and others may feel inspired by some external stimulus and enter the Profit Track at that point. We present the Profit Track in overlapping and non-linear stages because we observe that often the curiosity and courage people employ build insight as they pull themselves through the aperture of the Narrow Place. As their insight builds, we observe that most people begin to experience some measure of hope and a sense of efficacy that we characterize as feeling inspired. As inspiration grows, most people develop the interest, time, and resources to invest in further growth, which in turn assists in building more insight and further inspiration. With perseverance, the Profit Track becomes a self-reinforcing cycle of growth and profit, where future conflicts serve to build further insight, create deeper inspiration, and leave previously conflicted parties more invested. Consequently, the organization as a whole is more profitable.

FIGURE 8.2
Insight on the Profit Track

Insight

One day a mother asked her young son to run to the store to pick up a few groceries for dinner. The errand should have taken about 30 minutes, and when the boy wasn't back after an hour the mother was angry. Anger turned to worry when he didn't return by suppertime. When he finally arrived home with the groceries, two hours after being sent, she demanded, "Where were you? I've been worried sick and now supper will be late."

He responded, "On the way to the store, I saw Cindy crying on the street. She had broken her favourite toy."

"Well, I don't see how it could take so long to help her fix it!" the mother said.

"I didn't help her fix it—I just helped her cry," was his reply.

The first stage we enter as we emerge from the Narrow Place is into insight. The spirit of inquiry that we used to find the Narrow Place, and the courage we used to do something different than what we usually do, always leads to new and creative ideas. Creativity and innovation do not always happen in a blinding flash of brilliance when you need them most. Often, when confronted with conflict, we feel pressure to do something, to resolve the issue or at least make it better. However, we may not have any ideas about what to do. The temptation to lean away from conflict is powerful when we do not know what to do. So our modus operandi is to stick to the status quo in the hope that at least we will not make anything worse. However, leaning away from conflict will likely make it worse. One powerful insight that occurs for most of us as we emerge from the Narrow Place is that leaning into conflict does not necessarily mean "doing" something right away to fix it. As a colleague of ours has said, "Don't just do something, sit there!"

This insight is a basic formula for growth, profit, and the successful resolution of conflicts. Keep doing whatever it is you are doing that is working, and stop doing whatever it is that is not working. If what you are doing is minimizing the number of unhealthy conflicts and maximizing the creative energy drawn from conflicts to move you forward, keep doing it!

If what you are doing in response to conflict is not moving you and others forward, it is time to build insight and generate new strategies.

Another key insight that arises as we emerge from the Narrow Place is that shifting our mindset can amount to 90 percent of the necessary work. First, simply being curious—and acting on this curiosity by staying aware, attentive, and being ready to acknowledge—and having the courage to lean into problems moves us closer to understanding the nature of the conflict. Then we can begin to explore resolution options. Leaders with whom we have worked commonly request a quick solution to their conflict problems. "Just tell me what to do and I'll do it," they say in their frustration and exasperation. Typically, we suggest resisting the urge to lean away or to charge into conflict.

There is a lot to be said for just showing up.

"Showing up" involves being visible and listening. Listening involves a range of skills:

- Paraphrasing aloud what others have said
- Reflecting what you have understood to be the impacts on them
- Asking for more information
- Summarizing their perspectives and interests
- Acknowledging what is important to them
- Framing carefully, clearly, and tactfully what you want them to understand
- Reframing positions into interests
- Making conscious choices about what is conveyed by body language

Insights flow from building on a spirit of inquiry. Like the boy in the story above, insights come from having the curiosity and courage to sit in the problems for a moment without stampeding to fix them. This does not mean that busy professionals must find hours in a day to "help someone cry." Sitting in the problem does not take long. Becoming more aware, paying attention, and building your insight by acknowledging what you know and notice can take just one minute.

The One-Minute Money-Maker

As an experiment, try this exercise. Promise yourself that for a week, each day you are in your work environment, you will take one manageable step towards moving onto the Profit Track by spending 60 seconds with people you ordinarily either ignore or walk by with only a brief "Hello." Be strategic. Have a 60-second conversation with as many people with different roles in your organization as you can reasonably have. For example, when you walk by a senior VP with whom you typically do not speak, dump your assumptions that she is too busy to talk to you and make a One-Minute effort. Next, when you are in line behind the union representative (who may have been making your life a living hell), dump your assumptions about how they might interpret your intentions and make a One-Minute effort. As you show up for an appointment with a colleague, dump your assumptions about what you think you are expected to do (like sit in the waiting area quietly) and make a One-Minute effort with the administrative assistant.

In a Randstad North America survey of nearly 1,500 workers, 83 percent of employees who characterize their bosses as excellent communicators said morale was high where they worked. Additionally, almost four out of five participants said morale was high in companies that acted on employee comments.[73] Just showing up and listening boosts morale and profits.

These "One-Minute Money-Makers" produce insights in spades. It is not as though each conversation reveals shattering new information. The way this works is that, over time, the information you collect from various perspectives gives you access to your organization's brain trust—for just minutes a day. Moreover, the few extra minutes you invest in a given week create mini Narrow Place apertures throughout your organization. It does not matter if you are the CEO, a frontline worker, the human resources professional, or the information systems consultant—your One-Minute efforts to plant seeds move you, others, and your organization out of the Conflict Trap and onto the Profit Track.

Insight Brings Profit in Sight

As we will explore later when we look at cultivating innovation, insights and new ideas can spring from unlikely places. Insight begins with having the humility to recognize that our knowledge is incomplete. Insights flow from the awareness, attention, and acknowledgement that we employed to move through Narrow Place. When we are "so far behind we think we're first," insight is compromised—we cannot grow when we assume we know. We grow when we have the insight to know how much we do not know. Insight grows with listening. The more we listen, the more insight we develop; the more insight we develop, the better we can find resolutions to our conflicts and the more growth and profit we can achieve.

FIGURE 8.3
Inspiration on the Profit Track

Inspiration

A union representative at a large organization had a reputation for her unreasonable demands, aggressive style, and "management-busting" bullying tactics. Most managers, and all human resources professionals, had heard about her and dreaded having her show up to support a staff member. For years she fought angrily for her union colleagues' best interests, but she often encountered tremendous resistance from management. The more resistance she encountered, the more she developed the perception that management representatives were stupid, evil, or both. The more she came to believe this, the more unforgiving and unreasonable she became. Though she still won the odd case, many of her union members' situations became grievances and were bogged down in drawn-out arbitrations. Members lost confidence in her. In her frustration and rage she lost sleep, gained weight, and became depressed.

One day she stumbled across a brochure on workplace conflict. Somewhere inside was some rather cliché advice: "You will always get much further with honey than vinegar." For some reason this notion struck her at a profound level. She thought about it for days. It had simply never occurred to her to try to overcome resistance by leaning into conflicts rather than charging into them. She had grown up in a poor family with eight siblings and had only learned how to fight—not how to negotiate. Even with her first attempts with "using honey" she began to see some shifts. Excited, she was motivated to learn more. She signed up for training on conflict resolution and negotiation. Today, both staff and management respect her as one of the most successful union representatives in her organization.

In 1990 Mihalyi Csikszentmihalyi, who had been studying the achievement of happiness and working cross-culturally for decades, published his findings in a book that became a national bestseller. Years and years of researching thousands of people's experiences with how they achieved, or were prevented from achieving happiness are summed up in his book, *Flow*.[74] The secret formula for happiness was remarkably simple: Skills = Challenges, where skills are developed to better handle increasing challenges. If the challenges became overwhelming and moved beyond one's skill set, the task created anxiety and frustration. If the challenges were too far below one's skill set, the task became boring and mundane. When we are challenged by situations that push the limits of our skill set and require further development, whether it is with mountain climbing, taking on a new job, getting married, or just reading a book, we become inspired and achieve happiness.

On the heels of the first stage of the Profit Track, Insight, comes the stage of Inspiration. From the moment we glimpse that there might actually be another, better way, to approach conflict, we begin to feel inspired. One of the most rewarding aspects of conflict resolution work is encountered when we are training in workshops. Most conflict resolution practitioners can describe the excitement they feel when they see insights creep into the minds of workshop participants. Bright, professional, and highly-skilled people see, for the first time, how some very practical strategies and their strategic use of skills can break up conflicts that they had lost hope over. Many participants have heard of the skills, and some are even aware of the strategies, but as they come to understand how to use them in a new way that might actually just work, their inspiration becomes infectious.

Csikszentmihalyi established that inspiration comes from being confronted with challenges that are exciting enough to be interesting but are not overwhelming. Thus, we are stimulated to build our skills to match the challenges. In terms of the Profit Track, inspiration flows from being confronted with challenges that are stimulating enough to generate insight but are not so overwhelming that we lack the resources, time, energy, money, or skills to invest in tackling the challenge. If the challenge is not interesting enough, or if it is overwhelming, we all have a natural impulse to lean away or to charge into. That natural, unconscious response keeps us stuck in the Conflict Trap. The Conflict Trap arises when we say, "It's hopeless, I give up, it's not my problem, I can't do anything about it anyway, and it will never work." The Profit Track requires us to say to ourselves, "I wonder what it would take to make the challenge more manageable? What would it take to get over the barriers?" Or, to even ask ourselves, "What needs to happen to make the challenge more exciting?"

A leading research university conducted a study of the performance of new teachers. The study looked at two groups of students who were training to become schoolteachers at the time they were completing their final-year practicum. The first group was given extra attention from their mentors; the other group was not. The researchers hypothesized that by providing more critical feedback to young teachers in training their performance would be better than that of other teacher-trainees who did not get as much feedback. In the first group, mentors reviewed with each trainee everything the individual did that needed improvement. Trainees in the second group received little feedback about their performance. The researchers then followed the teacher-trainees into their first year of professional teaching. They extensively surveyed the new teachers' students about their teachers' performance. They extensively surveyed the teachers' self-ratings of how they felt they were doing, how confident they were, and how inspired they were. As the data came streaming in, the researchers were shocked. The group that received the most mentor feedback rated themselves with the *lowest* sense of self-efficacy. In other words, they rated their confidence in their abilities to be good teachers significantly lower than did those in the group of teachers who received less feedback. The second group saw themselves as much more skilled, and they rated themselves as confident and inspired. The most dramatic finding was that students rated the teachers from the second group, those who had received less critical feedback, as more interesting, more knowledgeable, and as better teachers than those from the first group who had received more feedback.

So, just as for the union representative described above, the building of insight builds inspiration. Building inspiration in turn boosts performance. The more inspired we are, the more inspired will be our performance. Obviously, boosting performance generates better outcomes like achievement, growth, and profit. As we build momentum along the Profit Track, the insight and the inspiration that flows from it lead us to investment—that is, making investments and being invested.

FIGURE 8.4
Investment on the Profit Track

Investment

There is, of course, a significant difference between being interested in something, or even being involved in something, and being *invested* in it. Investment implies commitment. When we invest in something we commit to putting something that is important to us into a project or objective. To quote a popular truism about this distinction, we use the metaphor of a ham omelette: "The chicken was involved; the pig was committed." Fortunately, our investment in the Profit Track does not require the same level of commitment that the pig made.

Investment is obviously not simply financial. Investments of money are symbolic of how important we consider an investment to be. If I spend very little money on vacations and a lot of money on clothes, I likely value my public image and my sense of self-expression more than I value sightseeing, relaxation, or travelling. *Investment* is the commitment of resources that are important to you. While this can be money, it can also be your time, energy, attention, ego, or other "valuables." We can, and many of us do, invest significant amounts of our time in volunteer roles and in projects that are important to us, without money ever changing hands. We can invest precious energy—sometimes stealing from energy already mortgaged on too many projects—in a particular concern at work that we decide is a priority. We can decline a promotion in order to invest our attention in a new family member who is a higher priority for us than our work.

Investment is both a means and an end. We *make investments* and we *become invested*. We invest our savings into retirement funds, making careful choices about which options will take us most effectively into a comfortable retirement. Making investment choices is a means to an end. By investing a portion of our income every year, we move closer to a desired outcome. If we choose not to invest, or if we make poor choices, the profitability of the outcome will be compromised. Investing is an action that involves choices that affect outcomes.

At the same time, diverting some of our savings into mutual funds or other holdings means that we *are invested*. What happens to our investments is important to us because what affects them affects us. If they appreciate better than other investments, we have profited; if they depreciate, or they are not as profitable as others, we have either lost or have not maximized our return on our investment. When we make investments, we become invested. Investing is an action or choice that leads to a state of being invested.

Investment is the opposite of detachment. We are not apathetic about things we are invested in. We are not detached from something to which we are committed. This is why, arguably, detachment is the most dangerous and profit-threatening nadir of the Conflict Trap. When we, or others, are detached, we are at the point furthest from making investments and being invested. We make investments and become invested when we develop insight and become inspired.

The Myth of Return on Investment

At the end of the day, all profitability rests upon the return we reap on the investments we make (R.O.I.). This well-accepted business maxim is the fundamental standard upon which all strategic decisions are made. Yet, as we focus on our R.O.I., we lose perspective about what creates the I in the first place. Before we can analyse and anticipate a return on our investment, we must first consider where the capital comes from. What leads us to make an investment? What leads us to commit to this investment over others? What makes us want to invest in some situations and not in others?

Too many individuals and organizations with whom we have worked have approached R.O.I. decisions related to conflict with a blind spot about these questions. They seek a return on an investment that we do not understand. They just assume that the investment they are waiting for a return on—the number on that line of the budget spreadsheet—will either grow or diminish, depending on how strategic they were in analysing the opportunity, how sound the opportunity was, and whether or not they are lucky. They lose sight of the fact that the Profit Track defines Investment as the result of Inspiration and Insight. While they await a return on investment, what kind of return can they expect if their organization's insight is compromised? How big will that return be if our people are denying, despairing and detaching instead of being inspired? Just because they have placed dollars here or removed them from there, does this mean they have truly "invested," or have they just "tucked" some money somewhere else? We suggest that leaders in organizations who await returns on their investments but do not address where their investments come from (i.e., insight and inspiration) are really only *tucking* resources into different places. R.O.I. is often only a "return on tucking," or R.O.T. The following are some examples of R.O.T.:

- Training programs that do not build the insight and inspiration needed to deal with the real stimulants of conflict
- Developing policies on conduct and conflict that are expected to implement themselves
- Relying on managers and human resource staff to "discipline" their way to better productivity and performance

When in conflict, our decisions are often "penny-wise and pound-foolish": we choose not to invest the necessary resources (e.g., time, energy, consideration, optimism, or money) to successfully address the real interests at stake. Waiting for this return is a symptom of the Conflict Trap. With R.O.T., one awaits a return that will not come. Sure, some conflicts might appear to be prevented or resolved in the short term, but in the long run no meaningful or effective investment can be made without first developing insight and inspiration. Without investing yourself in the conflict you cannot achieve any positive return. A lack of investment, or investing without insight, will create conditions in which conflict will grow, fester, and eventually erupt. High returns, in terms of turning conflict into profit, come from decisions that reflect that R.O.I. is as much a return on Insight and Inspiration as it is on Investment.

The Profit Track at a Glance

- Emerging from the Narrow Place and breaking free from the Conflict Trap places us on the Profit Track. This process involves three stages: Insight, Inspiration, and Investment.

- Insight is characterized by and arises from leaning into conflict with curiosity. Just showing up and listening, even if only for a minute, yields insights.

- Insight defeats denial.

- As insight builds, we begin to feel inspired, which brings creativity, innovation, improved morale, and higher performance. Inspiration = skills + challenges, where our skills are adequate to handle challenges that are stimulating.

- Inspiration defeats despair.

- As we become more inspired we invest resources. We make decisions to commit to what has become important to us, and by doing so we lose our detachment. We are invested.

- Investment defeats detachment.

- If we do not consider Insight and Inspiration in our decision-making, we do not make a meaningful Investment. We are only tucking money away in one area or another. In order to achieve a high return on investment we must also develop our insight and inspiration, because true investment can only flow from these conditions.

- Achieving high returns on our investments (R.O.I.) requires investing in building insight and inspiration. When we respond to conflict by spending money on projects that do not build insight or inspiration, we can only expect a return on tucking (R.O.T.), which typically produces little.

- The Profit Track becomes a cycle of enduring learning, achievement, and growth—of personal and organizational profit. The more insight we develop, the more inspired we become. The more inspired we become, the more we invest and are invested. The more we invest and are invested, the more insight we develop.

9

Step 1
TAP THE ENERGY

Jane, a nurse at a major city hospital, was struggling with a patient. The patient needed hospital care but had decided to leave the hospital anyway. Upon seeing the patient preparing to leave, Jane immediately paged the physician and began to discuss with the patient his decision to leave. She spent over an hour trying to convince the patient to stay, but was unsuccessful. As chance would have it, the physician, Dr. Smith, arrived a few minutes after the patient had left. Hearing at the front desk that the patient had just left, the physician approached Jane and in an aggressive, loud voice asked her, "Why did you let the patient leave?" Paralyzed by Dr. Smith's intense and hostile approach, Jane did not respond. Dr. Smith waited for what seemed to him like an eternity, and when Jane did not respond he said to her, "You might as well go home, since you can't seem to keep my patients in the hospital. I'll make sure you never take care of any of my patients again."

Conflict and Energy Generation

Threat creates fear. Fear is energy.

Unfairness creates anger. Anger is energy.

Dissatisfaction creates frustration. Frustration is energy.

Criticism creates defensiveness. Defensiveness is energy.

Conflict creates anxiety. Anxiety is energy.

THE NATURALLY OCCURRING ENERGY that emanates from conflict will either lead you into the dysfunctional Conflict Trap or it will inspire you to seek new levels of insight and allow you to invest in achieving profitable outcomes. The *choice* is yours. And it *is* a choice.

Yet when we are in conflict, many of us do not recognize that we have a choice. People react out of instinct and either lean away from or charge into conflict in order to satisfy their needs without understanding or considering the downside of such automatic responses. As discussed in Part 1, in many ways our socio-cognitive constitution has not prepared us well to make this choice. Whether it is our innate defence mechanisms, our proneness to attribution biases, our prejudices, our adoption of culturally prescribed values, or other forces that affect our thinking and perceiving, we seem unprepared and untrained to effectively channel the energy generated by conflict into thoughtful and productive responses. We respond to conflict in ways that undermine our own interests and then continue the dysfunction by denying to ourselves and to others that we had any choice. Thus a core challenge at the heart of turning conflict into profit is harnessing the energy created by conflict and channelling it into productive and positive attempts to find convergence and growth.

Consider the above scenario. If you were Dr. Smith, how would you react? What would you think about? How would you have approached Jane? If you were Jane, how would you react? What would you think about? How would you respond to Dr. Smith? This type of scenario happens every day. It could be a sales manager threatening a sales rep, a foreman threatening an assembly line worker, a CEO threatening a marketing manager, a client threatening a sales representative, or any number of workplace conflicts that occur all the time. Many people, particularly those in supervisory roles, become frustrated when they perceive something is not done to their satisfaction or expectation and they respond with accusations, anger, and threats—they charge in. They instinctively feel their interests are at risk (e.g., job security, reputation, feeling respected, and so on); they respond without due consideration of all the interests at stake—without thinking. Many others become the targets of anger and unfairness because they do not meet expectations and they respond with avoidance or accommodation, with defensiveness or placation—they lean away. They also instinctually feel their interests are at risk and can respond without due consideration of all the interests at stake—without thinking. Do you want to be right or do you want to be happy? And what if being right means you will not be happy?

The energy generated by such an experience is felt internally, but quite commonly it is not well understood. The manifestation of the energy, in the form of anxiety, fear, or anger, is communicated to others even before we have decoded it for ourselves. We tend to act first and ask questions later. If we are lucky, an insightful receiver will respond to our emotional expression without judgement and in a way that helps the energy transfer be positive and helpful. However, in most situations our energy acts as an accelerant and causes the conflict to escalate. Even after we get a handle on our emotions, often the blaze has already become a wildfire that causes the Conflict Trap to tighten and fuels even more negative emotion.

To explore the issue of energy and the ability to seize opportunity out of despair, we will refer to the case example with Jane and Dr. Smith. As we develop this scenario further, we encourage you to consider this discussion in the context of a situation in which you have found yourself. Think about who you identify with, Dr. Smith or Jane, and what type of energy arises in you when you are confronted with unmet expectations, with threat, with disregard for your interests, with conflict. Do you typically walk away from conflict regretting what you did not say or regretting what you did say? After a confrontation, those of us who later think of all the things we wish we *had* said tend to be people who generally lean away from conflict. Those of us who later think of all the things we wish we had *not* said tend to be those who generally charge into conflict. Either way, confronting conflict by *leaning into* it offers a far more productive and satisfying experience.

Leaning Into Conflict

In the above case, Jane felt unfairly criticized, attacked, and threatened. Jane became anxious in the face of a perceived attack and was too paralyzed to respond. Her lack of response only served to frustrate and infuriate the physician even further and led to his threatening remark. Dr. Smith arrived as soon as he could after just dealing with another difficult situation. He was emotionally unprepared to arrive to find his patient gone. With frustration running high, he reacted to Jane out of emotion. Jane was equally unprepared for such an attack. She, too, was already frustrated and fatigued due to her unsuccessful attempt to convince the patient to stay. She was fully prepared to tell the physician what happened but was shocked by his condemning body language, tone, and words.

The typical outcome of an incident like this is that both parties walk away feeling more threatened or more frustrated, more fatigued, and more conflicted. Jane believes her job is at risk. Her self-esteem is damaged due to her failure to keep the patient on the ward and her inability to respond to Dr. Smith in the moment of crisis. She may decide to internalize her feelings and thus erode her confidence and emotional well-being. She may decide to attack in return, lodging a complaint against Dr. Smith, calling her union, and filing a grievance for harassment. Dr. Smith may be worried that his patient will become sicker or die, and that he, as the doctor, might be sued or blamed by the hospital. He may see the situation as a validation of his previous lack of confidence in Jane's competence as a nurse. On the other hand, he may feel somewhat badly about how he yelled at Jane without fully appreciating the intensity of his response or the impact it had on Jane and on their professional relationship. They both will believe that they did nothing wrong.

Each of them begins the spiral into the Conflict Trap of denial, despair, and detachment. If they do not stop the spiral, the conflict will continue and further damage will arise. Jane will avoid Dr. Smith. She may request that she not be assigned to his patients and thereby cause scheduling problems on the ward. She may complain about him to the other nurses and doctors, spreading her discomfort and expanding the sphere of the conflict. Dr. Smith may also avoid Jane, talk badly about her to his colleagues, and pre-emptively complain about her behaviour to hospital management. Each may get trapped in their positions, which assert that the other party was wrong, and exaggerate what happened in order to add strength to their arguments. Both may carry grudges against the other well into the future.

Alternatively, on his way home Dr. Smith may think about how he might have overreacted. He might realize that he could have asked about what had happened without accusing Jane. Jane, on her way home, might think of other ways she could have responded. She could have defended herself by saying how she tried for over an hour to get the patient to stay. On the other hand, she could have responded by yelling back, "The patient would not have left if you had got here on time." She may sense that the former approach would have likely ended the conflict in the moment but would have left her feeling like a doormat. The latter response, a "charging into" approach, would have likely escalated the conflict, but at least she might have felt better about standing up for herself.

The real concerns for Dr. Smith are for the patient and ensuring good care when in the hospital. His approach did nothing to address his real concerns. In the face of Dr. Smith's perceived attack, Jane's real concern is that she is being accused of not doing her job properly. Dr. Smith's language conveyed the message that she was responsible for the patient leaving; Jane does not like being *blamed* for a choice made by the patient that she tried very hard to change.

Both parties to this, and most, conflicts can approach the situation differently. They could choose to "lean into" the conflict rather than "charge into" or "lean away from" it. Dr. Smith could have managed his frustration and anger. He could have taken a fraction of a moment to breathe and think in order to encode a clearer message to convey his true interests. After all, he really only wanted to know what happened and what could be done to remedy the situation. He had the choice. Jane could have managed her anxiety. She could have taken a fraction of a moment to breathe and think in order to encode a response that would have put some balance into the dialogue. She also had a choice.

You may identify with Jane and believe that Dr. Smith is the one responsible for the conflict, and that people just should not act that way. And, to a great extent, you are right. On the other hand, you may identify with Dr. Smith and believe that expecting people to always be in such control over their emotions is unreasonable and unhealthy, and that Jane should have just responded to Dr. Smith's question—even though it was blaming. After all, he has a need and a right to know what happened. And to some extent you are right. The problem with these attitudes, however rightful they are, is that, as previously mentioned, two rights end up creating and maintaining a damaging wrong—a wrong of distraction, inefficiency, and divergence. Notice that the focus is not on the real issue—the patient and the need for effective communication. The focus is now on the problem the two colleagues have with each other.

Each party has the opportunity to change the conflict dynamic. Each party has the choice to stay focused on the important interests at stake. Each party has the capacity to tap the energy from the conflict and turn it into approaches that seek positive and profitable outcomes. As discussed in relation to the concept of "Spheres of Influence," both parties have control over their own behaviour and both can influence the other party's perceptions and behaviour through their own behaviour. Rather than making thoughtful, conscious choices, they collided in a significant communication accident, falling subject to many of the intra-personal affective and cognitive tendencies outlined in chapter 4.

So, you may be asking, what does the "lean into" approach look like? For Dr. Smith, it would involve understanding his level of frustration, consideration of his and their mutual overarching interests (such as care for the patient and the maintenance of an effective working relationship), and turning his emotion into a thoughtful and productive communication to promote these interests. For example, he could have said to Jane, "What happened with the patient, I got here as fast as I could?" Not feeling attacked, Jane would have responded by describing what happened and they both could have problem solved what to do next. If Dr. Smith's concern remained about Jane's performance, he could have expressed his frustration with her inability to manage the patient effectively and offered to give her some assistance with how to be more effective in the future—leaving her the option to accept his offer or not.

For Jane, she could have realized that her immediate concern with respect to Dr. Smith's message was her perception of being blamed, and with the unfairness of the accusation. Rather than getting defensive or becoming offensive, she could have attempted to respond to the actual issue of concern by leaning into the conflict with curiosity and courage. For example, she could have responded to Dr. Smith's initial question by asking him in response, "Just to be clear, are you saying you think I'm responsible for the patient choosing to leave?" Or she could have been more direct by saying, "It sounds like you are blaming me for the patient leaving even though you weren't here to see what happened. I'd like to describe what happened if you are willing to hear me out." These leaning into approaches should send a message back to Dr. Smith that Jane hears his message as an accusation, that she does not appreciate it, and that she feels the accusation is unfair. These are the messages that Jane actually wants to send—the ones running through her mind even while she says nothing. These messages can turn the conflict into an opportunity for reasonable dialogue, understanding, and problem solving.

Such an approach also allows Dr. Smith an opportunity to reframe his message in a more thoughtful manner. In our experience, most people who express negative and threatening messages typically have neutral or even positive intentions. Yet most targets of this type of attack will perceive or misperceive the situation and the perpetrator in terms of the attribution bias. Responding with curiosity enables other parties to clarify their message and their intentions before a conflict escalates. In response to Jane's "leaning into" responses, Dr. Smith might respond with a comment such as, "No, I'm not *blaming* you; I just want to know what happened." Then Jane could accept his reframed message and explain to Dr. Smith what had happened. The Conflict Trap is avoided with no loss of face for anyone.

In a more unusual situation, where Dr. Smith responds by confirming the accusation by saying something like, "Yes, you *are* to blame. You're the one who let him go," Jane still benefits from inducing Dr. Smith to clarify his message and intentions. She now does not have to act on assumptions and can respond to the criticism based on a more complete understanding of his perception. She has also given herself more time to get control over her thoughts and emotions and prepare herself to develop and implement a more effective response, one that attends to all her interests and keeps focused on the real issues. She might respond by saying, "So, you saw me as having more control over the patient than I did. Allow me to clarify my perspective...."

Managing Anxiety

The key step in this communication process is being able to interpret and manage your emotional response to a conflict, *and making the decision to do so*. Whether it is in the form of anxiety, anger, or some other affective response, the emotion is the energizing force. Unchecked, it tends to make you resort to ill-considered responses of fight or flight. Alternatively, the emotion of the conflict can prompt you to a heightened level of self-awareness, which can stimulate thoughtful and productive responses.

Research on anxiety has found that people tend to go through five stages in response to anxiety, referred to as an anxiety curve. The anxiety curve begins with a trigger. An event occurs that suggests to you that your interests are threatened in some manner: that you are in a state of conflict. Remember that the conflict can be with others as well as within you. The trigger for Dr. Smith was the patient not being on the ward when he showed up. The trigger for Jane was Dr. Smith's accusatory communication. Jane's anxiety may also have been triggered by her own feelings of despair or inadequacy because she was not able to convince the patient to stay. Anxiety, rather than anger, tends to prompt those of us who experience it to internalize a conflict and related concerns. Worry, despair, and self-blame are central features of internalized anxiety.

Triggers cause the stimulation of an emotional response in order to alert us that some interest of ours is at stake. Anxiety is part of all human endeavours and achievements. For example, in school the prospect of exams and reports can trigger anxiety, as well as the receipt of grades that we find unsatisfactory or unfair. At work, new tasks, performance appraisals, deadlines, and so forth are triggers that create anxiety. In life, speaking in front of groups, engaging in competitive sports, dating, and many other activities are all triggers that create anxiety. Anxiety tells us that some form of tension or conflict is at work and manifests itself in many forms such as fear, anger, excitement, and trepidation.

Despite how anxiety is discussed in common language, it is *not* an emotion. We say, "I feel anxious," but we are not describing an emotional state. Anxiety is a physiological state of arousal experienced in the body. You become anxious because of complicated emotions like anger, fear, sadness, elation, and so on, and your body goes into a physical state of arousal. How do you know when you are anxious? You feel tension in our shoulders, neck, and other muscles; you get "butterflies" or a sense of nausea; breathing becomes shallow; heart rate quickens; your face flushes; sweat appears; and sometimes dizziness or even fainting occurs from the sudden change in blood pressure.

Anxiety in its most productive form can be viewed as an energizing force that motivates us to properly prepare for, or respond to, a triggering event. However, anxiety that is misinterpreted or goes unmanaged can greatly interfere with thought processes and decision-making. As shown earlier in Figure 4.1, a little bit of anxiety has an insignificant effect on reasoning. However, as anxiety increases our capacity to reason decreases. Information processing physically shifts within the brain. For example, instead of processing information such as the sounds we hear with primarily one area of the brain, or thinking about what to say using another area of the brain primarily, information processing physically shifts in our brains to the Hind Brain, or the Old Brain. This is an evolutionary artefact of ours that responds to anxiety-provoking stimuli by distilling a highly complex conflict into two options: flight or fight. Leaning away from or charging into. Essentially, when you find yourself in a highly stressful situation with complex interpersonal dynamics and your own interests appear threatened, your brain, when you need it most, has silently departed on you. It has left the building.

When anxiety rises to a certain level we can end up in personal crisis, unable to think through what is really happening to us and unable to make good decisions that will reduce the anxiety. At some point after crisis, which can last a few moments or several days, the anxiety de-escalates and our ability to reason is restored. Finally, we are able to reflect on our experience and, hopefully, learn from it.

Unfortunately, the decisions made during the phases of escalation and crisis can leave a legacy of damage that may be irreparable. In Jane's state of escalating anxiety, she was unable to respond to Dr. Smith's perceived attack. Her lack of response resulted in Dr. Smith escalating his, causing even more anxiety to occur. Heightened states of anxiety lead people to engage in self-damaging behaviour ranging from avoidance to cheating, lying, or violence in order to self-protect. During escalation and crisis, our baser instincts, such as psychological defence mechanisms, attribution biases, and personality pre-dispositions, overwhelm our capacity for reason and we can make unfocused choices and engage in destructive behaviour. Normally these flawed decisions can be rectified through more reasoned action later on. Unfortunately, many conflicts do not end so well. The escalating anxiety that leads to escalating conflict can undermine even the most well-reasoned attempts to find resolution and understanding in future. You may get to the stage with an employer, co-worker, or client where the goal of resolution is replaced by the goal of justice and retribution—a highly contentious and adversarial form of detachment. For some people, whether the cause is embedded in their value systems or is learned from socialization, they move to this stage from the onset of a conflict. For others, it may be years of frustration and resentment that finally put their anxiety into crisis. Thus, a key to successful conflict management, for many of us, is effective management of the anxiety that is brought on by the expectation or the experience of conflict.

Managing Anger

In the tall grass and bushes surrounding an ancient Indian temple there lived a king cobra with a terrible and explosive temper. Many pilgrims who passed and innocently ventured too close to his den were fatally struck.

One day, the priest of that temple, learning of still another tragic snakebite, sought out the great snake. The priest asked, "Have you been striking my people as they come to the temple to do puja?"

The snake closed his proud hood, bowed his head in shame, and shook it in the sideways nod that means yes in the Indian subcontinent.

"You shall never strike another human being as long as you live. You shall not act in rash anger no matter what the provocation may be," the priest commanded. The snake's head moved sideways again in assent.

A year later, the priest happened on the cobra once more. The great king was now beaten and scarred. His once proud hood was stripped of scales; a fang was missing.

"What has happened to you, my friend?" asked the priest.

"Oh, it iss a ssorry life ssince I can no longer sstrike. Everyone ssteps on me. Children sswing me by my tail. I am sslapped, sstomped, ssmitten until I am ssore and sscarred. It iss a ssorry life ssince I have given up all anger," hissed the snake.

"But you must not give up anger," said the priest. "I told you that you dare not strike, but I did not say that you cannot hiss."

Folktale—Origin from India[75]

Anger, like anxiety, proceeds through a set of stages. Unlike anxiety, though, anger involves an aspect of antagonism in response to a conflict. Anger stimulates us to externalize a conflict and see others as the cause of our feeling dissatisfied, blocked, frustrated, abused, or neglected. Psychologist Joseph Shannon points out, "recognizing, labelling, and expressing anger in a healthy way is vital to our mental health."[76] As the above folktale suggests, it can also be vital to our physical health. Anger can give us energy in the form of strength and determination in response to threats and conflict. Anger tells us something is wrong that needs to be resolved.

However, anger does not tell us what is wrong and what will best set it right. As with anxiety, anger escalates when our capacity to reason and strategize diminishes. When anger overwhelms reason we make foolish decisions and engage in behaviour that harms others and directly undermines the interests we are trying to protect. The key is to understand the root of the anger and to choose effective and constructive ways to express anger to those with whom we become angry. To return to our earlier driving metaphor, the anger should neither be in the driver's seat nor be kicked out of the car. The best strategy is to have anger in the passenger seat, giving information while reason remains squarely in the driver's seat.

For example, Dr. Smith's frustration with the patient's leaving manifested as anger toward Jane and led him to approach her with little control over his communication. His immediate goal was to understand what had happened and try to redress the problem. His expression of anger blocked the achievement of his immediate goal, and this poor communication could have a lasting impact on Jane in the future. However, in the situation with Jane and Dr. Smith, they met a few days later and resolved their differences over the incident with the help of the unit manager. Dr. Smith apologized for his threatening approach and clarified his intention to simply understand what had happened. In addition, he committed to managing his frustration and anger more effectively in the future. Jane accepted his apology and acknowledged that she could have been less defensive at the start. This conflict ended well, and both parties recognized the interdependence of their working relationship and learned something about themselves, each other, and how to respond when in conflict.

Techniques for Managing Anxiety and Anger

There are some effective techniques for managing both your own anxiety and the anxiety of others. They are simple but they are not easy. With respect to your own anxiety, because it is a physiological response, you must take a physiological action to address it. Take a deep breath. Of course, this sounds trite: deep breathing will not make you suddenly feel calm and relaxed. However, it will prevent your anxiety from cresting to a level where your brain shuts down on you, overwhelmed by the hormones and chemicals that surge when the body is physiologically aroused in anxiety. Oxygenating, when the body wants to breathe shallowly and prepare to run or fight, short-circuits some of your physiological response. The second technique to use to manage your anxiety is to exercise some type of reality-testing cognitive intervention. Again, this can become trite when someone tells you what works for them and it does not work for you. Only you can choose, in advance, what strategy challenges your own natural desire to make attributions and assumptions. Here are few examples of things you can say in your head that work for some, but not all:

- "This is not dangerous."—It can feel dangerous, even though it is not life-threatening.
- "Neither I nor they will be thinking about this on our death beds."—This reminds you that although this is a stressful exchange or event, in

the context of your life it may not be the most critical thing that will ever happen to you.

- Count to 10—For some, the logical progression of numbers buys them a few seconds to slow their reaction.
- If you have a religious tradition, say a prayer or mantra—For some, tapping into a larger spiritual well for strength is helpful.
- "What's the worst thing that could happen?"—Sometimes the worst thing is pretty bad, so it can help to follow this thought up with a question like, "And how will I handle that?"
- "I'm not *The One*; I don't have to save the world."—It is a lot of pressure off your shoulders to remind yourself that though you are important, the planet will likely keep rotating on its axis even if you cannot resolve this conflict.

With practice, these strategies can be effective means to bring anxiety or anger under control. However, there is still the other party's anxiety and anger to deal with! There is one technique that can be very effective for addressing the anxieties and anger in others, but, again, it is not simple. If it is used with the wrong tone or volume, it can easily be perceived as condescending. When used appropriately, however, it brings anxiety and anger down very effectively. When confronted by an anxious or angry person, many of us, with the best of intentions, can manage our own responses well enough to not respond similarly. Often we respond by calmly trying to explain to the other person why things are happening the way they are.

People find information that they disagree with easier to accept if they understand its rationales.

However, why are you explaining something to someone when his or her brain has departed? Why are you appealing to logic when the other person's brain has left the building? Explaining rationales is very important once anxiety and anger have come down to a manageable level. The single most effective technique to bring the anxiety and anger down is to acknowledge it. *Acknowledgement* is when you say what you have understood the other person's perspective to be and what that person's interests are.

Acknowledging is not agreeing.

Many of us are so worried about being perceived to be in agreement with the other person that we do not acknowledge their perspective. This contributes to anxiety and anger and keeps us locked in the Conflict Trap. To break free, try acknowledging without agreeing. Acknowledgement is best executed in a tone similar to (not louder than) the tone of the person who is anxious or angry and is stated in as few words as possible. Remembering the importance of not sounding patronizing, these are some examples of expressing acknowledgement:

- "Clearly, this is frustrating—we need to work this out."
- "So, you believe that I had control over the patient."
- "So, obviously this is upsetting. What do you think we should do?"
- "I can see how annoying this is from your perspective. Let's talk about what happened and what we can do to resolve it."

Tapping Energy in Groups

Tapping energy involves leaning into conflict by showing up, asking questions, and listening. This technique is effective with individuals and with groups. However, where we see leaders get into trouble is when they mix individual issues and group issues.

Generally speaking, you want to address individual issues in individual processes and group issues in group processes.

For example, if either Jane or Dr. Smith decided to raise the issue of how they had communicated that day in a staff meeting the next day, they would have remained locked in the Conflict Trap. To raise an issue that occurred between the two of them in front of a group would contribute to negative impacts like embarrassment, miscommunication, and further defensiveness. We frequently see this happen, however, when unresolved conflict surfaces at staff meetings, in the form of under-the-breath negative comments or eye rolling, because an individual issue has not been addressed.

If, however, Jane's lack of communication and Dr. Smith's threatening communication were common styles of communication between nurses and doctors on the unit, there would be an opportunity to address this as a group. If the group is experiencing negative impacts it is a group issue; if only a few individuals are experiencing negative impacts, it is an individual issue.

These represent some effective strategies for tapping energy in groups:

- Clarify what the group issues and interests are.
- Build an agenda for discussion by seeking all group members' input.
- Generate guidelines for the group to promote respectful discussion.
- Keep discussion interest-based while reviewing the different perspectives on the issues.
- Resist the urge to rush to a resolution, which is a common dynamic in groups.
- Only after perspectives have been discussed, brainstorm options for resolution.
- Clarify, often in writing, a plan constructed from the options generated.

Tapping Energy at a Glance

- Negative impacts like anger, frustration, and anxiety create energy that can be harnessed and utilized to generate resolution and profit.
- The more we allow ourselves to be anxious and reactive, the further away we move from our real goals.
- Anxiety is a physiological response in the body to complex situations that create complicated emotions in us.
- Techniques to reduce anxiety include physically taking deep breaths, which short-circuits the physiological response, and keeping the conflict in perspective by using some type of cognitive intervention (e.g., reality testing).
- Techniques to reduce others' anxiety involve doing nothing but acknowledging what they are saying is important to them.
- Acknowledging is not agreeing.
- Tapping the energy generated by conflict involves leaning into conflict by resisting the urge to avoid. Show up, ask questions, and listen.

10

Step 2
FIND THE LEARNING

A large service organization had just finished recruiting a new Director for one of its high profile divisions. The division, already highly esteemed, was ready to grow to new heights and required strong and experienced leadership. Knowledgeable, experienced, and skilled professionals from a variety of complementary disciplines staffed the division. The group functioned as a consensus-driven, interdependent work team in which each member assumed responsibility for divisional goals as well as individual contributions. During the recruitment process, the new Director expressed support for the concepts of facilitative leadership and the team's approach, as well as respect for the various disciplines that were involved in the division.

Soon after his arrival, conflict began to arise. The staff in the division actually found his leadership to be autocratic and non-collaborative. He refused to hold regular staff meetings and, when he did, he would limit open discussion, particularly on issues he had no interest in discussing. At one point he stated, "I have a vision for the division and I will do whatever it takes to achieve it—no matter how many people I have to piss off." He made numerous inflammatory comments during individual interactions with staff and customers and was perceived to demonstrate disregard for the staff's knowledge and expertise.

The staff in the division went to upper management to get help. They asked the Vice President to intervene and reinforce the democratic and collaborative values of the organization and the division with the new Director. They also asked for support in implementing a team development process. The VP met with the Director, who responded with defensiveness and blamed the staff for not communicating with him. He refused to support a team development meeting, saying it was not worth his time. He did say he would attempt to respond to the staff's concerns. Over the next few weeks the staff observed no change in the Director's behaviour, even after several direct confrontations with senior staff members, and they wrote a letter to the VP requesting that the Director be fired.

In response, the VP arranged for the team and the Director to participate in a facilitation process. The staff gave the Director one more opportunity to express alignment with the values of the team. Even after hearing what the staff expected from him, the Director responded by indicating that he felt entitled, by the mandate of his role, to direct the division as he saw fit and to consult with the team only when he deemed necessary. The Team felt demeaned and disrespected by the Director and saw no hope in resolving their differences. Unable to convince the Director to adapt to the team structure or learn new methods of leadership, the organization felt they had no other choice but to fire the Director and incur the substantial financial and reputation costs generated by the termination process.

Learning: The Root of Resolving Conflict

CONFLICT IS ROOTED IN DIFFERENCE: different interests, goals, beliefs, values, work styles, expectations, and so forth. Responding to conflict when bolstered with a mindset that you are right and others are wrong impairs your ability to learn and discover the options to productively resolve conflict. This is particularly true before any meaningful exchange has transpired regarding beliefs, values, and interests relevant to the situation. Albert Einstein once said, "Problems seldom exist at the level at which they're expressed." To find answers, we need to look beneath the level at which the problem is expressed and find the real needs and goals at stake. The path to profit lies *inside* the conflict, not beyond it.

According to learning researcher Cameron Fincher, learning is defined as "a process of progressive change from ignorance to knowledge, from inability to competence, and from indifference to understanding."[77] Fincher adds, "In much the same manner, instruction—or education—can be defined as the means by which we systematize the situations, conditions, tasks, materials, and opportunities by which learners acquire new or different ways of thinking, feeling, and doing."

Accordingly, learning begins with the insight that you have something to learn. Without that recognition, learning is blocked and defensiveness is the norm. It follows that the insight that you have something to learn requires acceptance of the fact that your current state of knowledge, competence, and understanding is limited. Insight necessitates the recognition that what you want or believe may be shortsighted, unrealistic, or unfair. Psychiatrist Thomas Szasz writes about this recognition this way:

> Every act of conscious learning requires the willingness to suffer an injury to one's self-esteem. That is why young children, before they are aware of their own self-importance learn, so easily; and why older persons, especially if vain or important, cannot learn at all.[78]

So, learning necessitates an acceptance of our own limitations, our own biases, our own filters, and our own ignorance. It also necessitates listening and reasoning. That is why managing emotion, as reviewed in Tap the Energy, is the essential first step on the Profit Track. Only then can learning begin.

Learning in conflict involves the implementation of several cognitive practices that run counter to the normative processes and reactions we detailed in Part 1. For example, in the above scenario the new Director demonstrated resistance to learning despite the influence of several socio-cognitive and cultural factors. He entered the new position believing he was the voice of authority for the division. As role theory predicts, he engaged the role according to the template he had been taught about how a Director should lead. He made numerous attribution errors in appraising the conduct of the division's staff. The staff and he suffered from differences in value orientations as they applied to the culture of the division and the organization.

Finally, when he was confronted with these differences and concerns, he felt threatened and vulnerable. In this state of threat his inner defence system was activated in a misguided attempt to safeguard his interests and protect his self-esteem. He became stuck in the Conflict Trap. By becoming defensive, he blocked his ability to listen to the concerns and observations of his staff or consider their feedback in terms of what he might be able to learn. He chose not to pursue true insight into the nature of the conflict and the interests perceived to be at stake; he thus denied himself the tools he needed to effectively pursue his own interests by attending to the interests of his staff. He was unable to overcome their resistance by charging into the conflict. He expected that his expertise and formal contract with the organization would ultimately protect him. He was wrong. Even though he did receive compensation in the end, a promising career was significantly damaged and the efficiency and profitability of an important division was considerably compromised. These consequences would have been completely avoidable had the Director opened himself to the value of learning—the means by which he could rationally decide in what ways he should adapt and in what ways he should remain true to his current ways of thinking and acting.

This case, and thousands more like it, offer insights into the key practices we can use to exploit conflict as a vehicle for learning. The first set of practices involves learning about your own habits, patterns, and tendencies. The second set focuses the learning on the conflict situation in which you find yourself.

Learning about Yourself

MONITORING AND MANAGING DEFENSIVENESS
An initial, critical prerequisite for both preventing conflict and managing it well when it occurs is to reject our initial instinct to defend. As previously described, your subconscious habit may be to deny, to suppress, to displace, to rationalize, or to fall subject to one of the other self-protecting defence

mechanisms. Yet these mechanisms actually lead to counterproductive outcomes. In the short term, they may protect your ego; however, defensiveness rarely results in meaningful self-protection, at least when it comes to the workplace or personal conflict.

Learning involves understanding both our natural and nurtured approaches to perceived threats. Think about how you tend to respond to the possibility of loss or criticism or threat. Be honest with yourself. Then consider how you would prefer to respond. Keep in mind that the emotions triggering your defence system are important messengers and should not be ignored. Nevertheless, neither should they prompt an initial communication or action, such as retaliation or sabotage, that only serves to set the Conflict Trap.

When in doubt, when anxiety or anger is escalating, when feelings of frustration or vulnerability mount, refocus on the objective of learning. The more you understand about the perceptions, concerns, interests, and issues at stake—yours and others'—the better prepared you will be to make informed and constructive choices. You may still decide to defend yourself when you respond, but your decision about how best to respond will be made based on a more informed appraisal of your situation and goals.

One way to think about this approach is to turn conflict into curiosity, and defensiveness into inquiry. For example, rather than deny, rationalize, or blame, ask open-ended questions of yourself and the others involved. Open-ended questions, beginning with words like *what*, *where*, and *how* tend to gather more information than closed-ended questions that begin with words like *did*, and *were*, which lead to "Yes" or "No" responses. Consider the following examples:

- Closed-ended: "Did she talk to you?" This generates little information, such as "Yes."
- Open-ended: "What did she say?" This generates more information.

Ask about the other person's perception, her thinking, or her plans. Take the time you need, either in the moment or over time, to clarify the issues at stake and the interests involved. Then form a response based on your needs and interests, and manage your encoding process to ensure your message is decoded as intended.

In the situation with the Director, he never chose to inquire why the staff members felt the way they did. He dismissed their concerns from the onset and immediately fell subject to the hostile attribution bias. He did not learn. Because he was not open to learning and asking questions, he continued to be confronted with resistance. At some level, he probably thought he could change their minds about him by confronting them with their misinterpretations and "poor judgement." He thought he could convince them, or at least convince the administration, that he was right and they were wrong, and all would be fine if they followed his direction. In fact, many of us fall subject to the same type of misguided defensive process. Rather than change their minds, as the Director ultimately discovered, his defensiveness and rationalization in response to their concerns actually reinforced their concerns and led them to become bound more by their position and more adversarial. His use of denial to lean away from the conflict, and then charging into the conflict by blaming everyone but himself, led to his demise in the organization.

Thus, to resolve conflicts effectively, and even prevent conflicts from arising, a crucial strategy is to develop insight into your own defensive patterns, and to understand that others whom you perceive to be lying or manipulating may be responding to a need to self-protect. Then consider how you can use the situation to learn new "leaning into" strategies. Practice asking open-ended questions: this effort will also help you learn how to work through the resistance and defensiveness manifested by others.

Assumptions, Conclusions and Analytic Bias

As you lean into conflict and pursue learning, it is crucial to be able to understand the differences between assumptions, conclusions, and truth. Working with physicians and academics over the years we have observed how they approach scientific assessment. They use a standard approach referred to as "hypothesis testing." This approach involves thinking about an issue or problem, reading what others have thought and researched, and developing their own theory about why something happens. Then they develop tests to assess the validity of their hypothesis.

In Part 1 we reviewed how we all act as amateur scientists insofar as we form attributions regarding the causes of behaviour in others and ourselves. We examined how we rely on personal observation and the observation of trusted colleagues and friends to form conclusions about the causes of other people's behaviour and our own. We also discussed how these conclusions are typically formed based on incomplete information, flawed logic, and self-fulfilling prophecy.

The problems with these methods when we try to understand and manage conflict are three-fold. First, unlike scientific endeavours, real life does not offer a controlled setting within which we can effectively test hypotheses by eliminating other influences. Therefore, we are always engaging with others with some level of uncertainty. We cannot know for a fact the intentions of others—only they can know. We can only infer their intent, and sometimes our inferences might be logical inferences based on what others have said and done, but they are still inferences and not fact. In fact, we might not even be aware of our own true intentions due to our desire to see ourselves as good and honourable. For example, our own "little lies" are not intended to harm. Our own aggression is only intended as self-defence—not to harm. Therefore, what we believe about the intentions of others is only an assumption. Conclusions we draw are not facts. If our goal is to uncover facts, as scientists do, we should remain open to new information and to the possibility that our previous conclusions are not accurate or the truth.

Second, whether we are directly involved in a conflict or simply bystanders, our observations will be based on our own subjective viewpoint, our own beliefs in right and wrong, and our own values. Our perspective is also shaped by the angle from which we see the conflict. A popular TV advertisement a few years ago depicted a leather-clad punk rocker running into a businessman on the sidewalk, grabbing him, and knocking him to the ground. The camera angle then shifted to an aerial view of the same situation: the punk rocker, looking skyward, saw a piano breaking free of its support straps from a crane and hurtling toward the businessman, and the punk rocker ran and knocked him out of the way. One perspective led to one set of conclusions; the other led to a more complete set of conclusions. To manage conflict effectively, pay attention to your filters and biases in order to remember that your perception of reality may be different from the perceptions of others. The way something *should* have happened or *likely* happened, from your view or experience, is not necessarily the way it *did* happen. Therefore, it is important to replace assumption with learning and, when the necessary information is not available to achieve certainty, to allow for multiple interpretations rather than accept any one as "truth."

Third, in real-life situations the very act of forming and testing hypotheses will have its own impact on the conflict. For example, if you believe your boss has lied to you, how would you go about testing this assumption? If you share your assumption with others to seek confirmation and validation, you may be viewed as spreading rumours about your boss, which may escalate the conflict. If you confront your boss directly by asking her if she lied to you, you may trigger a defensive response that increases tension and exacerbates the conflict, perhaps by prompting her to lie to you now. If you attempt to stage a situation in an attempt to catch your boss in the lie, it may backfire and you will escalate the emotion and impede resolution.

On the other hand, if you reject the assumption right from the start, and consider alternative possibilities about what happened and why it happened, you set yourself up to learn as you prevent possible misinterpretations of your behaviour and intentions.

> *Unless you're the crown prosecutor of a murder case, typically the best response to lying is to work with the lie.*

For example, if the VP had confronted the Director with the information that staff members perceived him to be closed to their perspectives, the Director may have lied and described his many attempts to listen to and understand the staff. In response, the VP could have thought, "He's lying," and then set about attempting to reveal the truth. Alternatively, the VP could have responded with, "That's interesting—from your perspective, you say you've tried to listen and respond to the staffs' concerns. Yet they don't seem to perceive that you care about their concerns. What should we do about that?"

You can examine the circumstances surrounding the "lie" with an open mind and with the goal of resolution in mind. You can consider how the perceived lie is affecting you and maintain a balance between your emotional response to being lied to and your cognitive response, that of trying to stay rational and constructive. Thus moving from the Conflict Trap onto the Profit Track involves an understanding that assumption is not truth, and the avoidance of attribution biases that may result in critical misinterpretations and harmful communication.

Adopt The Platinum Rule

Learning necessitates accepting the nature of difference and seeking to expand intellectual horizons. If we have concluded that our way is the "right" way and that those who believe and act differently are "wrong," we block our capacity to learn. Ronald Heifetz, a leadership authority, makes this observation:

> *People don't learn by staring into a mirror; people learn by encountering difference.*[79]

Adopting The Platinum Rule—treating others as we have learned they like to be treated—enables us to enter into conflict without preconceived notions. The only effective way to understand the perceptions of others is to listen and accept what they have to say, even if it violates our basic understanding of people and how things work, and even if we suspect they are lying. "Treating others as they wish to be treated" necessitates learning how they wish to be treated. We may decide we should not or cannot treat them that way for a variety of reasons. We may find their needs require us to act in ways we would not normally act. That is fine. At least we are able to make choices based on learning rather than assumption, on personal values rather than imposed values.

Sexual and racial harassment are types of conflict that reflect the importance of this concept. For example, in response to complaints that men have harassed female colleagues and subordinates, many have responded, "What's the problem? She should be flattered!" In response to complaints that someone's attempt at humour was offensive, many people say, "I wouldn't have been offended if they said that about me." These Golden Rule reactions, of "treating the other as I like to be treated," only serve to escalate a conflict. These responses blame the other party for being too sensitive, or of misinterpreting the comments, or having the wrong values. It fuels the other party's sense of outrage or despair.

Acknowledging someone else's sensibilities, preferences, or values does not show weakness and does not mean we agree with them. It only means that we accept their rights to their own values and beliefs and that we will demonstrate that respect by treating them as they wish to be treated without compromising our own values and beliefs.

Learning about the Conflict Situation

TRACE CONFLICT TO THE SOURCE: PROCESS AND OUTCOME

As we described in chapter 1, conflicts come in two types: process and outcome. Either or both may be the source of your being in conflict. You may feel internally conflicted about the outcomes that you want or with respect to what you think you need to do to get those outcomes. For example, you can ask yourself, would you bend your ethical principles to improve your chances of getting a promotion that you know you deserve? You may be in conflict with others over the attainment of outcomes or over the process being used to achieve those outcomes. For example, ask yourself, "Am I upset about the possibility of losing an opportunity or am I upset about not being included in the decision process?" You may be in conflict with others because of things that were said or done or because of how things were said or done. For example, ask yourself, "Am I upset about the feedback my co-worker gave me, or the way in which he gave it to me because it sounded patronizing and critical?" Tracing the conflict to its source is a crucial element of your ability to focus your response where it is most needed and to remain stable on the Profit Track.

"Process" is not "content."

Often when we approach someone to address a conflict, the issue we wish to resolve may be one about process—that is, *how* that person talked to us. The minute we raise that with them, they will often want to bring it back to content—that is, *what* they were talking to us about. For example, I may approach a co-worker by saying, "I'd like to talk a bit about how we communicate generally, and specifically how we talked last Friday." He will likely respond with, "Yeah, I'm glad you brought that up because I still don't think you get how tough the workload is on me." How we communicated is a process issue and the workload is a content issue. The best strategy is often to acknowledge the content issue and bring it back to the process issue. For example, I might say, "Clearly we need to talk about the workload more and how it affects you and me. I'd like to focus first on how we can communicate more effectively."

At times it is important to distinguish between a trigger and a source. Triggers are more immediate and observable events that stimulate the feelings associated with conflict. Sources are the deeper concerns that often lie beneath the surface. Triggers may be the actual source, or they may only represent a manifestation of the real issues in dispute. Consider this illustration: in one case a male nurse reported serious concerns about a female colleague. The two had worked together for years on the night shift at a major hospital. He reported being harassed by her, to the point that he could not go to work. He wanted her fired, or at least transferred off the unit. He was very anxious and in despair. When asked what she was doing, he described three main events. First, she had recently opened a window on the ward, making a loud noise in the process in order to startle him. Second, she had referred to him as a "meathead" to another nurse on the unit. Third, she did not try to wake him up at the end of their shift so he could go home, and she left him sleeping in the lounge when the next shift arrived. Yes, you read that correctly. He was so distraught and so angry with her that he did not realize he was effectively reporting how he had violated hospital policy by sleeping on the job.

The level of his angst was disproportionate to the nature of the incidents that he described. While considering his complaint, we reserved judgement and set out to learn more about the whole story. He wanted a formal investigation. The events that he described would likely not have constituted a breach of the organization's policies or the law, so a formal investigation was not required. We agreed to try mediation. When we met with the other staff member, she acknowledged each of the incidents. She had opened a window loudly because it was stuck and she had to push harder to get it open. She had called him a "meathead" because she said he was acting like one. She had tried to wake him up by knocking on the door, but he had locked the door and, when her knocking failed to wake him, she decided to go home. These events were triggers rather than the deep sources of conflict. As we explored the conflict with them over a few weeks, we discovered that they had been friends outside of work and that they had had a personal dispute arise. With his consent, she had stored furniture in his garage for several months prior to a move she was making. When she went to retrieve her furniture, she discovered that his sister had mistakenly sold it at a garage sale. This incident occurred only weeks before he reported her harassment.

The above case represents an unusually large separation between triggers and sources, but is a useful reminder for us to seek to understand the authentic basis that causes us to feel in conflict.

Finally, an old proverb says this when it comes to learning:

Tell me and I forget.
Show me and I remember.
Involve me and I understand.

From our view, leaning into conflict is the best way to become involved and to develop understanding, for you and for others. Without the desire or will to learn, little can be accomplished to construct meaningful and profitable resolutions to conflict.

Finding the Learning at a Glance

- Assumptions and defensiveness, natural and controllable responses to threats, inhibit learning.

- In order to learn and grow, it takes humility and insight to recognize that what we know is likely incomplete—that there is always more information to gather.

- What we generally find ourselves in conflict about are outcome issues; the reasons outcomes get addressed (or not) are generally process issues. Separate the outcome issues from the process issues in discussions and seek what can be learned about both.

- The Platinum Rule of treating others as they wish to be treated trumps The Golden Rule of treating others as you like to be treated. The Platinum Rule encourages learning and growth along the Profit Track, while The Golden Rule encourages assumptions and misconceptions that get you stuck in the Conflict Trap.

- Finding the learning involves asking open-ended questions to identify interests and goals and acknowledging perspectives, even those—and perhaps especially those—that conflict with ours.

11

Step 3
BUILD RELATIONSHIPS

Julia, a regional manager with a high technology manufacturer, was confused. She valued good relationships with her staff and attempted to create a positive working culture and open communication. She offered advice to her staff about how to improve their productivity and professionalism whenever the opportunity arose. She found that a few of her staff seemed grateful and used her suggestions. However, she also observed a number of her staff exhibited resistance to her help. She made an effort to be available to her staff and told them that her door was always open. She couldn't understand what their problem was and why they were becoming more hostile towards her as time went on. She tried talking to each of them, but they just said that everything was "fine." Yet their tone and body language told her it wasn't. She learned from one of the staff members close to her that this group had initiated a petition asking upper management to fire her. She felt betrayed and fatigued and considered resigning, but she didn't want to give those staff members the satisfaction of winning. She didn't know what to do or why these valued relationships had deteriorated so much.

DAMAGE TO RELATIONSHIPS is one of the most significant costs of and contributors to conflict, and it is the most avoidable. As learning creates insight, and insight begins to counter denial, we need to allow for the possibility of agreement, change, and growth. We can then emerge from despair and become inspired to lean into the conflict in order to effectively protect and pursue our interests. As hope for improvement builds, conflict moves from blame to a desire to have some control and share responsibility for outcomes. When we blame others, we also give them control. The more we blame, the more control we give them. By seeing others as inflexible and unable to change, or as evil or insane, we are giving them power over us and we will remain trapped in conflict. At some point, it is productive to share control rather than take or give away too much. As trust develops, sharing control with others becomes a means to mitigate risk and maximize outcomes. In this step we review the attitudes and actions required to maintain productive and professional relationships, even with people who stretch the patience and good will of others, and especially with those people whom you do not trust.

In the above scenario, several key factors were at work that interfered with the development of productive relationships. Julia was very sincere in her efforts to be a supportive and accommodating manager. She gave freely of her time and shared her enthusiasm for the job. She genuinely wanted all of her staff to succeed and develop. However, what she did not realize was that her approach, while helpful to some, was seen as condescending and patronizing by others. For these long-time staff, the advice she gave was heard as criticism. When she offered to help, it was heard as condescension. When she asked what was wrong, staff members heard, "What is wrong with you?" And the more these staff members resisted her efforts, the more Julia's negative view of them was reinforced. Julia did not take the time to learn about the different needs of her various staff or develop relationships based on individual expectations, needs, and desires. She adopted a "one size fits all" approach and duplicated what worked with several to use with all. The case reveals how even the most generous and supportive leaders can run into relationship conflict that, in turn, can cause the decay of individual and group morale, and of overall productivity. Thus, we will take a closer look at practices that support the development and maintenance of positive and productive professional relationships.

Development and Maintenance of Productive Relationships

Counter Attribution Biases

We have reviewed the strong effect that attribution bias has on the formation of opinions regarding others. In an earlier case we described how a manager, in collaboration with human resources, placed an employee off work for a mental health assessment. This flawed decision was in part based on a flawed assessment of the foundational conflicts. The manager and human resources consultant attributed the conflicts that were occurring in the workplace to characteristics of the employee, even after receiving evidence to the contrary from the employees' peers and from direct reports. They concluded that because the employee was involved in recent conflicts and with several others during the years of her employment, and that she had taken "stress" leave on a previous occasion, that something must be wrong with her. They failed to recognize that the working environment and their own favouritism toward other staff had directly contributed to the ongoing conflicts. They chose the easy path of assigning blame for the conflicts completely to the employee instead of pursuing a strategy of learning. With the best of intentions, they chose a path they thought would be less humiliating for the employee, based on their own narrow view and biases and without understanding the needs and concerns of the employee. They did not build the relationship with this employee to find solutions to the ongoing challenges that would work for all of them.

When we encounter "troublesome people," as predicted by attribution research, we immediately conclude that something must be wrong with them. We also form the corollary conclusion that nothing is wrong with us. Yet this way of thinking is counterproductive, and it impedes a more comprehensive and dynamic assessment of conflict situations. It divests us from engaging in the relationship and limits our ability to think rationally and develop productive solutions. A key concept used in mediation applies here:

The "person is not the problem"—the "problem is the problem."

This concept aims to guide you to examine both personal and contextual features of a conflict and delay making judgements about people that can derail you from the Profit Track.

Reject Stereotyped Thinking

Stereotypes are a form of mental laziness. They provide mechanisms for us to quickly assess and categorize others by endowing them with characteristics that we believe are common among people like them. If they are like us, we are immediately more comfortable with them and more ready to develop a trusting relationship. If they are different from us, and perceived to be less worthy, capable, or safe, we withhold our efforts to form trusting relationships. We do all this without learning anything meaningful about particular individuals. Thinking in stereotypes neglects the reality that each person is unique. Even if patterns can be seen generally among some groups, there will always be individuals who do not conform to these patterns. We may share common ways of thinking and acting with individuals from a shared culture or ancestry, but these common traits are not reliable predictors of professionalism, skill, or performance. Relying on stereotypes blocks the development of productive and respectful relationships.

For example, a senior executive we worked with was hiring a new financial director. The executive was known as a respectful and open-minded person, yet he had formed a narrow vision of the type of person he wanted for the job. There was one qualified internal candidate who also happened to be from a different culture and had a different skin colour. This candidate had a gentle, relaxed, and kindly manner consistent with people of his culture. He also had been an effective manager and had acquired an advanced degree and several professional certificates during his tenure with the organization. The executive did not even consider him for the promotion. When asked why not, he said that the manager did not have the right "style" for the job. What the executive actually believed was that "gentle and kindly" equated with "weak," and that people of the manager's culture are not executive leadership material. The executive hired someone external for the job that he perceived to be more dynamic and, therefore, more fitting for the job. The external candidate cost the organization significantly more money because of the need to cover relocation costs. Six months later the new director was fired for causing too much disruption in the department, due to her "dynamic" personal style.

In addition, the executive damaged the company's relationship with the valued manager, who left the organization for greener pastures within a year. Rather than encountering difference with openness and curiosity, and building on established relationships, the VP relied on stereotypes and personal bias to the detriment of his division and the organization. Stereotyped thinking is a strong impediment to learning, as well as to developing effective and profitable work relationships.

Develop Trust through Honesty

Without some level of trust there can be no meaningful exchange of ideas, no meaningful collaboration, and no development of interdependent relationships. And without honesty there cannot be trust.

Consider the case of a new leader who was trying to resolve an ongoing dispute in her department regarding vacation scheduling. Although accepted in her role by the group, she was not fully trusted because of several previous incidents. She was also the most junior person in the group, having been in the department for only ten years. One group liked the current method of scheduling vacation, which was based solely on seniority. A second group perceived the seniority method to be inequitable, particularly in light of the fact that the least senior person had been in the department for ten years. With no retirements pending, this group saw no opportunity to take vacation during the more preferable times of the year. These two positions appeared to be firmly entrenched, with no compromise in sight. To break the impasse, the new leader presented an alternative model to the group. However, instead of taking responsibility for the idea, she said that the option was developed by one of the more senior and respected members of the group who was not at the meeting. She presented this deception in order to counter what she rightly anticipated would be rejection of the idea if the group thought it came from her. Her deception initially worked, and the method was supported by a majority of the group. However, the deception was soon discovered and overall group relationships deteriorated to a new low—the group fell further into the Conflict Trap. With trust lost on all sides, little room existed for meaningful discussion and problem solving.

Leaders frequently attempt to manipulate outcomes, thinking that deceptions and omissions will not be noticed. We often use deception by giving misleading information or withholding relevant information because we do not know how to be honest and still achieve the desired outcome. We are worried that the truth will keep us from our goals. More specifically, we deceive in the misguided hope that we will avoid conflict.

This situation demonstrates the reality that it can be very challenging to be honest. The situation reflects our wider experience that deception rarely works, particularly in the long term.

Deception ultimately creates more conflict, not less.

We reviewed how deception is actually a form of our internal defence system. We learn how to be dishonest at a very early age. We learn to lie so that we do not hurt someone's feelings, to lie in order to self-protect, and to lie in order to manipulate an outcome. And while we usually say that lying is wrong and most people dislike being lied to, most of us regularly lie for one of the reasons noted above, rationalizing the lie as a necessary step to support a larger good. In other words, the end justifies the lie.

The real problem with lying is functional, not just ethical. Lies create four functional problems. First, lies deny others insight into their own behaviour and choices. Lies actually reinforce the behaviour we would like to extinguish. If we lie by saying that we like a gift, we might get more of the same. If we lie by saying that we were not offended by a joke, we will hear more of the same. If we lie by saying that we know how to do a task when we do not, we will not receive the help and instruction we need to do the task properly.

Second, lies impair trust. Once we are lied to, we will be far more likely to question the validity of anything that the lying person says or does in the future. A strong perceptual filter will have formed in our minds and will bias everything we hear from that person through that lens. If a relationship is irrelevant, then trust is unnecessary. However, if a relationship needs to endure, then remaining mistrustful will only serve to reinforce the Conflict Trap.

Third, lies hide interests. Interests are exactly what need to come to the surface in order to keep us on the Profit Track. Lying stuffs interests deep beneath the surface as we rationalize and fabricate reasons—other than the real reasons—why things are happening as they are. The further buried our own and others' interests are, the more securely we are stuck in the Conflict Trap.

Finally, lies create process issues. Most of us recognize that often when we start with a lie, we have to develop further lies to keep the first lie from being exposed. If we are found out, as lies often are, the legitimate concerns and interests that we have can be dismissed because our credibility is lost as a result of how we acted. For example, a frustrated salesperson who had seen himself as suffering for years under the bullying behaviour of a co-worker finally turned to her one day and swore at her. She reported the behaviour and, when the salesperson was confronted, he denied swearing. Other witnesses reluctantly confirmed that he had sworn. However, they were worried management would be hard on him for swearing when they saw her bullying behaviour as the real problem. He was reprimanded for swearing and lying. His legitimate concern about her bullying behaviour was lost as the focus of management's attention centred on his inappropriate response and deception.

The real reason most of us lie is that we fumble for the words that allow us to be honest without jeopardizing other interests or damaging relationships. As a personal example, many people can relate to the quandary they face when a spouse asks, "Do I look fat in this?" If "yes" is the honest answer, should we say it? Probably not. We do not want to hurt our partner's feelings. We do not want to cause conflict. However, answering by saying "no" denies your partner a more objective assessment of how they look, and if how they look is important to him or her, or to you, the lack of honesty can grow to negatively influence the relationship. The skill that is relevant here in building honest, trusting relationships is framing with tact. Framing is the skill we use to say what we want to say. Tact is choosing words that convey interests in ways that minimize defensiveness. In other words, if you have a lump of coal to give someone, it is in your best interest to wrap it up in attractive paper so that neither you nor they get their hands dirty when they take it. One honest and tactful response to this dilemma might be, "Honey, I think you're gorgeous. I think that outfit doesn't flatter you as much as the other one." Honesty involves some risk taking, but it is crucial for developing trusting and productive relationships, particularly at work.

Another example involves giving and receiving feedback. Leaders who have the most success with their staff's acceptance of negative feedback from them have learned how to use tact. One strategy is to sandwich the negative message, such as expectations of greater timeliness, between two positive messages, such as how thorough the employee is and how their creativity is valued.

Consider for a moment the use of e-mail in communication. As previously mentioned, as much as 93 percent of a message can be conveyed by body language, tone, and volume. E-mail does not allow any of these to be expressed. The most we can hope for is to use capitalization and emoticons. While e-mail is very efficient for sharing information, e-mail is devoid of tone. Thus, one should never use e-mails to convey messages that might have significant negative emotional impacts. Even a notice about upcoming layoffs is more effectively conveyed in person. Emotional information can even be communicated more effectively on paper than by e-mail. If someone sends an angry or terse e-mail, picking up the phone keeps us on the Profit Track. Replying by e-mail takes us down deeper into the Conflict Trap. The lack of tone inherent in e-mail and the inability to clarify the message presents barriers to being tactful and conflict frequently escalates.

Some people seem not to worry at all about sparing the feelings of others and use very blunt and insulting language to convey their opinion. Many conflicts either begin with or escalate in response to people who see no place for tact and defend their blunt communication as "just being honest." One senior leader defended his regular use of sarcasm, insults, and condescending comments as necessary means to achieve profitable outcomes. He did not realize his behaviour was actually interfering in a dramatic way with group cohesion and individual performance; much of his staff members' time was spent dealing with the despair they felt that stemmed from his "honest" behaviour. In our view, true honesty must adhere to principles of respect and personal dignity. Productive relationships do not exist in the context of dishonesty or in the face of bluntness that disregards the dignity and self-worth of peers, managers, or employees.

Tact without honesty creates misunderstanding.
Honesty without tact creates conflict.

Trust involves one additional and critical component in addition to tactful honesty. To feel comfortable being honest, we have to hold an expectation that the people with whom we are honest will be receptive to our message; that they will not respond with aggression, hostility, or rejection. This is where courage is needed. Without courage, we are more likely to deceive and detach in order to maintain safety, even when honesty is crucial to achieving gains and profit. Therefore, it is often advisable to establish a foundation for honesty with co-workers by agreeing to principles and guidelines before engaging in difficult conversations.

Avoid a Veil of Secrecy

Another interpersonal dynamic that directly affects the development of trust is the use of secrecy. Withholding information and keeping secrets may not be considered dishonest, but these practices can result in the same negative consequences in terms of mistrust and damaged relationships. For example, hundreds of leaders we have worked with use secrecy as a strategy to avoid conflict by withholding information that others would find objectionable. This information is withheld until the last possible moment, when any opportunities the affected parties might have to resist and fight are limited. In one case, a senior leader who assigned tasks to employees on an annual basis typically withheld his decisions about who would receive which assignment until the final days before the next work cycle began. This approach left staff members living in uncertainty, but also with some hope that they would get their preferred assignments. However, the leader would also tell staff whom he liked and trusted what their assignments were ahead of time and would ask them to keep the news "confidential" until all the assignments were announced. By doing this, he placed his preferred staff in the uncomfortable position of having to deceive their co-workers and left the remaining staff stressed about the final assignments. When the staff members discovered this pattern—and rarely do secrets actually remain secrets—process type conflicts ensued in a number of directions.

Thus the strategy of keeping controversial information and decisions secret in order to avoid causing a stir usually backfires, resulting in a legacy of mistrust and conflict. Media training advises that a skilled spokesperson always keeps an interview running on their terms. Being approached by journalists about a cover up that has been exposed as a lie is far more damaging than it would be for the spokesperson to contact the media for an honest press conference about unpleasant news, without covering it up.

Cognitively we fill in uncertainty with our own impressions of what is likely happening. When secrets are thought to be kept, we assume the withheld information must not be in our interests, otherwise it would not be kept secret. This conclusion may be wrong, but it occurs naturally in situations of uncertainty when we believe information is being withheld or decisions have already been made. To avoid conflict, we advise avoiding secrecy and framing concerns, criticisms, or controversial decisions in a clear, respectful, tactful, and empathetic manner. Also, when you involve people in decision processes and they understand rationales and options, you can reduce resistance while you maintain trust and open dialogue.

Inclusion builds buy-in and erodes resistance.

Focus on Impact, Not Intentions

Human rights law has advanced a very important aspect of successful problem solving and relationship building while it also promotes fairness: it has established that the focus in cases of harassment should be on the *impact* of one's behaviour rather than on the *intentions* of the person who displays the given behaviour. *Impacts* are effects that behaviours produce, such as emotions, perceptions, physical sensations, and changes in circumstances. *Intent* is the effect the person meant to convey or cause by the behaviour, whether or not it had the impact the individual intended. For example, if I pinch a co-worker's behind, I might intend to be playful and fun. The action might be perceived as playful and fun if the other person decodes exactly what I encoded. More commonly, though, the impacts are humiliation, anger, confusion, strained work relationships, avoidance of future contact, and perhaps even litigation. What I intended to encode was not the impact experienced by the other person.

Prior to the emergence of human rights legislation, people had no legal impediment to mistreating others at work. They could make offensive comments, display offensive pictures, engage in abusive conduct, and the like and be absolved of wrongdoing by claiming they were just trying to be funny, to lighten up the place, or to get the best out of their employees. In other words, if you did not mean to harm or discriminate, then you had done nothing wrong.

Human rights have provided a legal basis for what relationship experts have known all along: we are responsible not only for what we do, but for what we cause. For relationships to work and for conflict to be handled well, there needs to be an acknowledgement and acceptance of mutuality in relationships that extends beyond what we intend.

Though discussing my intent can be useful when I seek to resolve conflict, it is not as useful as discussing impacts. When I upset someone and then explain my intent to that person, it often sounds like an excuse. When someone has upset me, I tend to develop distorted assumptions about his or her intent. These distortions seem very real to me but are distortions nonetheless.

Staying on the Profit Track involves focusing discussions on impacts and interests. Discuss what happened, how others were impacted and how you were impacted. By focusing on the impacts and not wasting time on making excuses or assumptions about intent, we build stronger relationships and remain on the Profit Track. Discussing impacts also leads us to understand interests—to feel respected and safe, to be productive, to enjoy time at work.

Respect in Action if Not in Thought

Respect is a common value cited by most organizations in their mission, vision, and values statements. Yet making respect visible is elusive for many people. For example, should you be respectful of people whom you do not respect? Keep in mind the previously noted finding, that Canadian workers rated "Being treated with respect" as the most important aspect of job satisfaction. Respect is a key interest that all of us seek and protect. The moment respect is threatened or lost the affected relationships will degrade and productivity will be compromised. Therefore, the demonstration of respect, even if you have lost actual respect for a person in terms of their knowledge, job performance, or even ethics, is essential to maintain effective workplace relationships. We do not have to like someone in order to show respect for him or her.

Engaging in respectful behaviour does not mean being dishonest. You can disagree, provide critical performance feedback, challenge viewpoints, and express frustration while you are respectful in language, tone, and expression. Remember that even if you do not *have* respect (as a noun) for an individual, respect is also a verb. From a leadership perspective, respect is demonstrated through five main practices:

a) Accept that there are individual differences, different values, and unique life circumstances, and that judgement or prejudice does not reflect this acceptance.

b) Listen to others in a manner that considers their interests and work experiences from their perspective, even if our perspective differs.

c) Involve others as active participants in determining their tasks and work goals.

d) Provide direction and support in a manner that does not take advantage of confidential knowledge or power over others.

e) Endeavour to appreciate and accommodate, whenever reasonable and fair, the needs and preferences of employees.

Managers have come to us with the dilemma of having two staff members in mutual conflict. One will report to the supervisor one day how the other person is bullying them. The next day, the other staff member approaches the manager reporting a list of harassing behaviours allegedly performed by the employee from the day before. Upon investigating, it is difficult to ascertain who is more mistreated since they both treat each other badly. We coach staff members in this type of situation about the value of *treating* someone respectfully, even when you do not *have* respect for them.

The #1 Rule of bringing attention to someone else's bad behaviour:
Make sure your own behaviour comes off smelling like a rose!

If you are reacting to disrespectful behaviour with respect, it makes it much easier for others to come to your aid and address the other person's bad behaviour. Otherwise, that individual's bad behaviour can become hidden behind yours.

By demonstrating respect, you take control of improving the quality of workplace relationships, which in turn establishes the strongest possible foundation for staying on the Profit Track.

Match Communication and Conflict Styles

As discussed in chapter 6, all of us have grown up in settings, families, and cultures that leave us with unique communication styles. Based on how our values have been shaped, some of us communicate more comfortably when in conflict than others do. Building relationships to stay on the Profit Track does not mean using a particular strategy, style, or skill all the time. This is the error that Julia, in the case study at the beginning of this chapter, was using. The key is to change your strategies and skills moment-to-moment, depending on what the other party has just done or said.

For example, a colleague of ours bought a truck recently and got an outrageously good deal. First, he did his homework. He established his strategy by clarifying exactly how much the dealer paid for the truck. He knew this would be the bottom line, since the dealer would not sell a new truck at a loss. As he and his spouse sat down with the car salesperson, everything was smiles. She seemed very eager to accommodate his needs. He responded by acknowledging that she also had needs—to make a profit! However, he was transparent about his goal: he wanted the best deal and was aiming to keep her profit margin low. As they negotiated about different features, he made an offer very near to the cost the dealer paid. He knew it would not insult her because it was still above the dealer cost. She responded competitively, with, "Oh, I don't know. That is way lower than this dealership has ever gone. I'll have to check with my manager." Prepared for this common tactic of running back and forth with the manager, he matched her competitive move with a respectful, but equally competitive, strategy.

"Okay," he said, and she left. When she returned she saw him studying a brochure with his spouse about a similar car from a different dealer across the street. They seemed enthusiastic about getting this over with so they could head over to the other dealer. Though the salesperson had returned with a frown, she immediately brightened and said, "Oh heavens, you don't want to go for that car! We can work something out I'm sure." They continued like this—one moment mutually accommodating, the next moment each being respectfully competitive—and ultimately they reached a collaborative outcome. Not only did our friend get the car at the price he named, he also got several options thrown in. The dealership got to make a deal on an otherwise slow day.

When we are being triggered, we are not being strategic enough to match the other's approach.

Generally, never be haughty with the humble or humble with the haughty.

If we are competitive with those who are being accommodating or collaborative, we will anger them and they will resist us. If we are being accommodating or collaborative with someone who is competitive, we will end up feeling like a doormat. Building relationships involves learning when to match tenderness and when to match toughness, always respectfully.

Keep Expectations Clear

Managing expectations can be an effective strategy because events or behaviours that run contrary to what people expect are common sources of conflict. Building relationships and maintaining our course on the Profit Track involves transparency about what people can expect. Even if leaders choose not to release all their information for strategic reasons, effective leaders communicate this practice. They clarify that not all information is being released and why. They do communicate whether or not it will be released and when. If the withheld information is bad news, they request that people prepare for bad news. People who have mastered the Profit Track communicate clear information about what to expect and, if expectations change, they offer updated information. Consider for a moment how you reacted to bad news that you had time to prepare for and bad news that surprised you. Typically, having preparation time equips us with extra tools to handle the bad news.

Be Descriptive and Specific

Finally, part of building relationships on the Profit Track requires one to be honest and manage expectations well by communicating clearly, and with as little emotional reactivity as possible. Two of the ways that negative emotions like frustration, anger, and fear creep into the driver's seat include exaggeration and the use intensifiers. As mentioned in Part 1, when we are reacting emotionally to a conflict, the subtleties of communication, which are so critical in conflict, are easily forgotten. Imagine, for example, that we spoke last week—you raised your voice at me and now, indignant and fed up, I approach you to tell you how I did not appreciate you "screaming" at me. I may not see "screaming" as an exaggeration, but remember that people need to see themselves as generally good people. If you perceived that you had raised your voice but under no circumstances would you consider it "screaming," you will perceive me to be exaggerating. I do not need to use a word like *screaming* when "your voice sounded raised to me" is more descriptive and specific. I do not need to exaggerate to be effective.

Similarly, when upset, we tend to use intensifiers or words that add weight to our experience, such as *always, never, very, all, none, extremely, completely*, and so on. "You're always screaming at me in front of everyone and I'm extremely mad at your completely unprovoked attacks," is vague, intense, and unnecessarily provocative. Instead, it would be more descriptive—and a means to problem solving and relationship building to frame the statement this way: "On Tuesday when we were talking, your voice sounded raised. I wondered about what others in the area might have been thinking. When it happened again on Wednesday, I thought we better talk about it."

This approach leans into the conflict and opens dialogue. In contrast, exaggeration and intensifiers promote defensiveness, damage relationships, and get people stuck in the Conflict Trap.

Building Relationships at a Glance

- Conflict is about relationships.
- The more we blame, the more control we give away. Framing responsibility as "control" stops blaming.
- Reject stereotypes.
- Be transparent, honest, and tactful.
- Focus on impacts, not intent.
- Do not be haughty with the humble or humble with the haughty.
- It is in your best interest to prevent others' bad behaviours from triggering you to act disrespectfully—take the higher ground.
- Match your communication to the other person's style.
- Manage expectations by being clear, descriptive, and specific.

12

Step 4
CULTIVATE INNOVATION

A small consumer products firm was experiencing stagnation and diminishing profitability. Just two years earlier they were named one of the "companies to watch" by a leading trade magazine. At that time they hired a new president to manage company operations and inspire growth. The new president assumed full control of every aspect of the company. He hired new staff in research, sales, and marketing to prompt the growth that they all envisioned. Yet the growth never came. The president, consumed by his own self-importance and his desire to achieve, regularly rejected his staff's ideas and opinions in favour of his own. He approached brainstorming exercises as debates, and his adeptness at arguing often left his staff feeling demeaned and fatigued. He micro-managed his management group to the extent that every decision they made focused on how not to stir up the boss. In this adversarial and intimidating culture, creativity was suppressed, concentration impeded, and ingenuity stifled. There was little safety for expressing new ideas that might meet with condemnation from the president. Conflict was the norm and profitability decayed in terms of personal well-being and company growth.

AS WE HAVE OUTLINED, conflict comes from the clashing of interests. You want credit for quality work, as do those around you. You want to be treated with respect, as do those around you. You want others to do their fair share, as do those around you. You want to come up with new and better ways to do things, as do those around you. Conflict can arise when you are blocked from doing quality work, when you are not treated with respect, when you are expected to do more than your fair share, or when you are denied the opportunity to contribute ideas and suggestions. These types of conflicts directly undermine our ability to innovate—for the purpose of our own development and for the growth of our organizations.

Conflict also arises from our diversity. We perceive, pursue, and value things differently from each other. We think differently. For example, some people think more in pictures, others more in stories, others in dialogue or debate, and so forth. These differences can add to the conflicts we encounter and distract us from pursuing our objectives. Yet difference is also what sparks innovation. By definition, to *innovate* is to "bring in new methods, ideas, etc." Conflict is therefore a key driver of innovation. Author Ronald Heifetz conceptualizes conflict this way:

> *"...conflict is the engine of creativity and innovation."*[80]

Innovation involves thinking in novel and different ways. Yet innovation remains constricted in many organizations because conflict and difference are mishandled and suppressed. In the above case, the company president believed he was the bastion of creativity and intelligence. He came to the company as its saviour and needed everyone in the company to know it. Impression management was so important to him that it overwhelmed his ability to objectively perceive what he was doing to his staff and the company. He brought with him a personal style consistent with the organizational cultures of individualism, adversarialism, and intimidation, and he imbued the company with that culture. He used power and threat as tools to motivate. He believed innovation was a product of effort and that effort needed to be closely managed. Unfortunately for him and his staff, his approach had the opposite effects. Difference can prompt innovation, but only if individual practices and organizational leadership enable it, safeguard it, and reward it.

Metaphorically, a container must first be constructed into which difference can be poured. Without the container, differences spill all over the floor and make a mess. Conflict that causes denial, despair, and detachment interferes with innovation and productivity. Conflict that sparks learning and new ideas inspires innovation. In this chapter we highlight several practices that enable workplace conflict to spark innovation, growth, and profitability.

Enabling Innovation

Get Lost

Being in conflict is a bit like being lost. Both involve a level of uncertainty, a lack of complete control over one's environment, and interdependence with the environment. It is uncomfortable to be lost, yet many interesting things happen when lost. Mazes and ancient labyrinths were ways of becoming "intentionally lost," they were means to inspire fresh ideas and new thinking. Today we enjoy the challenge of mazes, puzzles, and the like because they test our capacity for thought and inspire us to discover new ways of thinking. Conflict can do the same. It can inspire us to tap into our own depths and open up to the needs and ideas of others, to search for solutions that escaped us up to that point. And just like dealing with mazes, if we try a path and hit a dead-end, we need to try a different path. Yet it is amazing how often people in conflict keep using the same approaches, and then act surprised when they do not work again. As the popular saying goes, "Insanity is doing things over and over again and expecting different results."

When you find yourself stuck in conflict, at a loss for what else to do, it is important to recognize that the only effective strategy is to try something new, something different. It may be a simple difference in execution. For example, if you tend to speak first and then listen, you may find listening to the thoughts, opinions, and experiences of others first, before forming your own opinion, will help to reduce the feelings of conflict. In contrast, if you tend to listen first and then find yourself feeling run over by more dominant co-workers, you may want to assert yourself more at the start of an interaction. Remember that acting in the same ways and expecting a different outcome is unrealistic.

Alternatively, rather than change your approach, your change can involve seeking an entirely different outcome. For example, many of us in conflict tend to lobby initially for our solution—a win–lose strategy—and, if stymied, pursue a compromise—a lose–lose strategy. Sometimes these approaches can be appropriate and beneficial. However, they both can undermine the achievement of outcomes that are more beneficial to all parties. The president of the above company approached every discussion as a debate about his leadership. He yielded to compromised outcomes at times when he observed that he was not going to win. For example, to avoid further conflict with one manager the two agreed to speak to each other only when necessary. This compromise solution to their interpersonal conflict caused both of them harm, even though they both felt at the time that it was the only solution. Competing over the attainment of interests both creates and perpetuates conflict. Moving to compromise too quickly also perpetuates conflict because the initial conflict is really not resolved and generates resentment and loss. Thus, if you anticipate or experience conflict, it is helpful to reconsider the outcomes you wish to pursue. Take into account a fuller range of interests, including the value of building relationships, reduced stress, and enabling innovation.

Consider these points:

- "It should work!" is the declaration of those who accept an ineffective status quo and fail to innovate.
- "What else can I do?" is the question asked by those who innovate and profit.
- "It will never work!" is the declaration of the sceptic who blocks creativity.
- "How will we overcome the barriers?" Ask those who innovate and you will profit.

The president of the consumer products firm was sure his approach would elevate the company to new heights. When internal strife blocked growth, he thought it must be someone else's fault because his management style and intellectual strength should work. He left little room for the reality of individual differences and alternative modes of operating. He leaned away from and avoided certain issues; others he charged into. In either case, his conflict strategies were counterproductive. His approaches may have achieved some immediate reduction of tension on the one hand—mostly his own—or induced compliance on the other hand, but they failed to achieve a meaningful resolution of workplace strife. They directly impeded the freedom of thought and expression required to cultivate innovation.

Leaning in is counter-intuitive for most of us. Yet leaning away from creativity leads to stagnation. Charging into it leads to unrealistic ideas. Leaning in supports creativity of thought and opens up the expression of ideas, even stupid ones. It just might be someone else's "stupid" idea that sparks your own thinking process and enables you to come up with the brilliant strategy that works. If ideas are not offered for fear of encountering ridicule, everyone loses.

Although cliché, the concept of thinking outside the box remains a key to innovation, especially when in conflict. Try solving the following puzzle.

FIGURE 12.1
Challenge—"Out of the Box Thinking"

Draw nine dots as presented below and—without lifting your pencil off the page—connect all the dots using only four straight lines.

The solution necessitates that you extend your lines outside the area of the dots. We find that solutions exist to most conflicts if those involved open themselves up to tap the energy of the conflict, learn from their differences, build interdependent relationships, and think in novel and creative ways.

FIGURE 12.2

Solution to "Out of the Box Thinking"

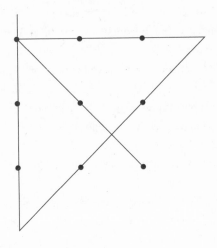

Everyone Can Innovate

Anyone can be innovative, given the right stimulus and opportunity. Again, everyone is different and each of us has our own sources of creativity. Enabling innovation involves inviting all involved people into the creative process and then minimizing barriers to creativity. Too often we have observed people, particularly leaders, attempt to resolve conflicts for others based on their own views of what is needed and what is right. This "self-assigned impossible task," as Anton Obholzer refers to it, sets leaders up for failure.[81] If a leader takes on too much responsibility for resolving the issue, she disempowers others who are involved in the conflict and sets up a rescue fantasy that "The manager will do it." Employees then back off from their own responsibilities and wait for management to fix it. Of course, if the conflict is then impossible to fix, management gets blamed.

We are not suggesting that management abdicate responsibility. This *leaning away from* approach gives too much control away. We are suggesting that using curiosity and courage in our roles as leaders will assist others to pass through the Narrow Place and on to the Profit Track, into innovative thinking. It is surprising how often leaders fail to ask conflicted parties the simple questions about what would resolve the conflict for them. It is as if leaders are afraid to ask those in conflict what they want because they might make unrealistic demands. So what? Even the most unrealistic demands can reveal legitimate and realistic interests. For example, if the CEO of the aforementioned firm had asked the staff what they wanted, they might reply: "Fire the president!" The CEO might see this response as punitive and unrealistic, but by not reacting and staying curious the CEO could ask, "So, if he was fired, what would that do for you?" As the discussion continued, it would likely end with the CEO summarizing employees' interests by saying, "Okay, so you want his behaviour to stop and for your ideas to be taken seriously. Let's generate some options about how to make that happen, whether or not he gets fired."

Many leaders also move to more complex processes and outcomes before considering straightforward strategies that may address the interests of all involved. This is partly due to our tendency to encourage the taking of positions prior to a full exploration of the relevant interests. Once a position is adopted we tend to defend the position rather than search for alternative ideas. The goal of innovation on the Profit Track is to move everyone, including us, away from our positions and onto our interests.

You also need to enable yourself to innovate. Many of us have become cynical and apathetic after living through years of experience that we believe have taught us we are not creative or that our creativity is just not appreciated. Rather than risk further rejection, we clam up and even stop thinking. We are stuck in detachment. This approach, however under-standable, keeps us trapped in conflict. We stay in conflict with those whom we perceive as devaluing us; we stay in conflict with ourselves for accepting this "'fate." However, by developing awareness, paying attention, and acknowledging that the situation is a problem, we can move away from detachment and out of the Conflict Trap. With curiosity and courage we move onto the Profit Track. Developing insight by tapping the energy of conflict and building relationships begins to inspire us to be more innovative. The optimism that comes with inspiration is critical to the process of innovation and discovery.

Safeguarding Innovation

Allow Room for Innovation to Grow

Innovation is a growth process. Ideas, like seeds, need an environment that supports growth, allows time, enables relationships to be developed and safeguards the integrity of the creative system. Ideas, like seeds, need to be fed and nurtured. These seeds of thought come from the totality of our life's experience. We can harvest our history, our experience, our knowledge, our relationships, and the experiences of others to stimulate our own creative process. We get stuck in the Conflict Trap and revert to basic modes of cognitive processing rather than use our higher order cognitive abilities.

> *Under stress, we all regress to more primitive ways of functioning.*

If we are not creating room for innovation to grow, if we are leaning away from or charging into conflicts, the stress of this environment pushes us further down Maslow's Hierarchy of Needs. We cannot create innovative strategies to increase our own or our organization's return on investment when we are struggling to just get through the day with our heads down and avoid our colleagues. Creating room for creativity means leaning into stress and conflict.

To allow the seeds of innovation to germinate and flourish, they need workplaces that show acceptance, tolerance, and openness. Specifically, to support others and ourselves on the Profit Track, we must avoid making reactive comments that embarrass, humiliate, or denigrate our co-workers and ourselves. Of course, we believe some ideas are "stupid," some people are oversensitive, and some requests seem ridiculous. Yet, if we respond to these ideas, sensitivities, and requests with brutal honesty, disrespectful frustration, or sarcasm, we risk suppressing future expressions that may be the one productive seed in the barren soil. We also risk missing the opportunity to let the seed of an idea spark our own creativity. There is a fine line between silly and smart or between crazy and creative. If we respond to silly or crazy with judgement or ridicule we miss an opportunity to use the seed to inspire our own innovation on the Profit Track.

Take chances, make mistakes.

Often, the most creative ideas come from those who have the least inhibitions. Children and people who work with children arguably offer the most fertile ground for the seeds of creativity and innovation. This statement, used by the teacher in "The Magic School Bus" series of books and television shows, reflects the key mindset in safeguarding creativity:

Innovation is dependent on failure.

Without failure, learning is blocked and discovery stymied. Support for failure is extremely under-appreciated in our organizational cultures. Richard Branson, the billionaire founder of the Virgin Group, attributes all of his successes to calculated risks and his biggest successes to his biggest failures. He says: If you want people to remember your face, you have to be prepared to fall on it. Often leaders will verbally encourage employees to take calculated risks, but if failure occurs the employee is not supported. Instead they get chastised for poor judgement and threatened if they fail again. Safeguarding innovation involves supporting risk-taking prior to and after failure in order to enable people to learn from mistakes and turn that learning into innovation.

An example of risk-taking can be seen in management decisions regarding the readiness of employees to take on new responsibilities. We have often heard managers limit opportunities for their staff with their assessment that the staff member is "just not ready." If the employee wants the added responsibilities and is prepared to assume the risks, the employee will experience conflict with his or her manager. They become disheartened and apathetic as a result of management blocking their growth. In contrast, the manager believes he or she is acting in the "best interest" of the person and the organization.

Leaning into the conflict would involve the parties discussing the interests at stake and generating a solution that allows the risk to be undertaken while also mitigating the potential consequences of the risk. Safeguarding innovation means allowing for risk while managing the risk within each person's sphere of influence. If, as a leader, I am attempting to manage staff members' risks, I will do this more effectively by influencing the staff members' management of their own risks within their sphere of influence, rather than by trying to manage them from my sphere of influence. *Leaning into* involves empowering and equipping staff to handle risk. *Charging into* involves trying to take care of the risks for them. *Leaning away from* creates foolhardy risks. Without risk and the possibility of making mistakes, innovation is lost and conflict remains a trap.

Rewarding Innovation

The Whole Is Greater than the Sum of the Parts

Separate the pieces that make up a car and lay them out on a driveway. What do you have? A collection of parts that do little on their own. Put them back together in a precise and integrated manner and they create an outcome greater than the sum of the parts. Use better parts and get greater outcomes. Innovation functions in a similar way. Put together a group of individuals, each with their own set of experiences, interests, and areas of knowledge, and ask them to solve a problem. Working on their own they will each come up with ideas based only on personal experiences, knowledge, and their individual capacities to think. This approach limits solutions to the best ideas generated individually. Put the group together in a strategic manner to solve a conflict or problem and they share ideas, experiences, and knowledge in a manner that sparks something greater than individual thought alone. For example, well-functioning groups of people can solve anagrams and other visual or word puzzles far more efficiently and productively than individuals working alone—even better than the smartest individual in the group. This is because the creative process benefits from diversity of input.

However, group effort will not be more efficient than individual production if the natural conflict that arises from group interaction is not managed in a manner that rewards the pursuit of group-interest over self-interest. In other words, rewards for achievement need to be linked to group outcomes rather than individual contributions. If competition is the group norm, each individual will essentially want to work alone so that he or she will receive credit for coming up with solutions. If being adversarial is the group norm, individuals may engage in activities to distract others and make themselves look better. If intimidation is the group norm, less powerful group members will be reluctant to contribute for fear of being ridiculed, demeaned, or having their ideas stolen by other group members.

Consider the car again. A certain amount of friction is necessary for the parts to come together and produce the greater outcome. This friction is managed by the use of oil that reduces friction and enables the parts to perform optimally. Too much friction will eventually disable the functionality of the car and will possibly destroy individual parts along the way. Conflict affects groups similarly. A little bit of conflict is natural and, when managed effectively, can spur healthy competition and overall group achievement. Too much friction and individuals get worn down and become fatigued and dysfunctional. As a result, the creative process is blocked and innovation suffers. Whether trying to discover solutions to ongoing conflicts or simply trying to spark innovation in situations of interdependence, collective effort needs to be rewarded rather than individual achievement.

Reward Effort Not Just Outcome

At times, the best efforts may not pay off. If all we do is reward outcome, we neglect the reality that outcomes are affected by many determinants, some of which are beyond our control. Clearly, we need to reward achievement; however, if we neglect effort then we generate apathy and discourage future effort. In our previous case involving the nurse who tried to convince the patient to stay in hospital, she was condemned for an outcome that was not fully under her control. Her best effort went unnoticed and unrewarded. If this pattern is repeated, she will feel heightened despair and hopelessness; she will likely detach and become apathetic. Most of us have encountered times when we have asked ourselves, "If giving my best is not recognized or rewarded, why should I continue to give it?" The rational answer is that we should always do our best. The realistic answer is that to sustain our desire, our inspiration, and our investment we all benefit from positive reinforcement—from being recognized and rewarded for giving our all—even if we do not succeed.

Staying on the Profit Track means managing conflict by rewarding ourselves for approaching conflict in more productive and supportive ways. Resolution feels good. Resolution lowers stress, lowers anxiety, lowers anger, and lowers fear. Achieving resolution brings its own palpable rewards. Even when the conflict is not immediately resolved, paying attention to it and acknowledging it reduces its negative consequences. It is just as important to reward others for change, for growth, and for attempts to find resolution—even if they are minor or disingenuous, or if the conflict is not neatly resolved. By rewarding the efforts of others who are trying to be more considerate, more thoughtful, and more respectful, we reinforce their investment in the goal of resolution so that they continue with their efforts.

For example, consider this situation: someone apologizes to you but qualifies his comments so that he seems to undermine the apology. He might say, "Well, I'm sorry if you got so upset because you're so sensitive." First, you may recall times when you offered this type of apology, and thus may understand that at some level the apology is genuine, even if poorly expressed. Second, even though you may perceive the apology as condescending and want to respond with increased outrage, this response would only increase and solidify the conflict. Alternatively, you could seize the opportunity by accepting the imperfect apology and expressing how much you value the other person's recognition that he did something hurtful. You might say, "Yeah, it was an upsetting discussion and didn't sound very sensitive to me." The second approach leaves you feeling more in control, essentially addresses the conflict, and leaves the other person understanding that he really did apologize to you. Even if he was not truly genuine when he expressed the apology, once he expresses it he can become committed to it because of the power of cognitive dissonance. Your acceptance of the apology is what stimulates the feeling of dissonance, which in turn prompts his full acceptance of the apology. This approach restores the ability to work together in situations of interdependence and helps to build a more functional relationship in the future. In fact, the other person will be dissuaded from engaging in the same kind of event that caused the conflict in the first place because he will have no desire to experience the resolution process again. You have won, but in some ways he has won as well. Rubbing his face in his misdeeds will always undermine your own goals of resolution and achievement, and this is a sure way to stay stuck in the Conflict Trap.

A final word about apologies and innovation: we have seen many conflicts where resolution was evasive because either one or both parties remained so attached to their positions that they would not be satisfied unless the other apologized. Our experience has been that seeking an apology is often a position. Generally, the position of an apology represents three interests:

- An acknowledgement of the negative impacts
- A recognition that that the other party could have acted more respectfully
- A commitment that it will not happen again.

In conflicts where resolution hinges on apologies, being innovative and mastering the Profit Track means ensuring that these three interests are addressed, whether or not an apology is forthcoming.

Cultivating Innovation at a Glance

- "Conflict is the engine of creativity and innovation."
- Although getting lost is unpleasant, interesting and creative things happen when you are lost—you find things you were not looking for.
- Everyone is innovative—when encouraged.
- Innovation needs space to grow.
- Innovation involves taking risks and making mistakes.
- Group efforts generate more innovation and creativity than do individual efforts when leaning in strategies like acknowledging, questioning, and framing are used.
- Key skills for cultivating innovation in conflict include acknowledging in questioning, and the framing and reframing of positions into interests.

13

Step 5
MAKE BETTER DECISIONS

The profitability of a large unionized organization was being compromised due to the costs associated with trying to resolve frequent complaints of harassment and abuse. Its administration and human resources department had developed and imposed a harassment policy, but several employee groups had rejected the policy and said that as a group they would not accept its authority. Complaints continued to be made, prompting expensive investigations or arbitration procedures that rarely resolved the complaints to anyone's satisfaction. More importantly, these formal procedures did nothing to resolve the actual conflict situation. They typically left the involved staff contemptuous of the resolution procedures, the organization, and each other.

Recognizing that their approach was not working, the administration researched what alternative models might be more successful. Following a model used by another organization, they established a working committee and delegated the responsibility to the committee to develop a policy and procedure that would be effective and acceptable to all the different stakeholders. The committee included representatives from management, the professional staff, and the unions. An expert in workplace human rights, facilitation, and dispute resolution was hired to facilitate the development process and manage naturally occurring conflicts in order to come up with a policy and procedure that satisfied the interests of all stakeholders. This was accomplished within several months, and all groups felt positive about the standards of conduct and procedural safeguards put in place by the policy. With the new policy in place and a new procedure that offered all staff access to an impartial dispute resolution specialist, the organization saw complaints costs decrease and staff cooperation and productivity increase.

Two years later, a human rights tribunal member heard about the organization's new approach and commented, "I wondered where all those complaints had gone!"

ULTIMATELY, THE EFFECTIVE MANAGEMENT OF CONFLICT involves individuals and organizations making better decisions. The decision-makers at the organization mentioned above had the awareness and courage to acknowledge that what they were doing was not working, that their approach was just causing more conflict, and that alternative approaches might exist. With a little attention, they were able to squeeze through the Narrow Place and, with a little insight, inspiration, and investment, get onto the Profit Track.

In the end, we do not have to be trapped by conflict. We do not fall into the Conflict Trap because we are not smart or capable or knowledgeable. We become trapped because we are trained to think in ways that limit our choices and complexity of thought. We become trapped because we fall subject to group pressures that limit the productive exchange of ideas and needs.

Individuals and organizations do not fail because they are focused. They fail because of what they focus on. In being focused, they can lose perspective about the clashing interests. Successful individuals and organizations on the Profit Track succeed because they are focused and they effectively consider, weigh, and balance interests in decision-making.

More specifically, people fail to make good decisions in conflict because we focus too much on *either* the people we are in conflict with or the bottom line—to the exclusion of the other. We fail because we focus too much on our positions and the positions of others rather than on our differing and mutual interests. We fail because we focus too much on maintaining control rather than sharing control. We fail because we *deny* the signs of trouble, *despair* when things are going wrong, and *detach* from accepting responsibility for pursuing convergence. We fail because we get caught up in the emotion of the conflict and pursue our biased view of what is right—at the expense of resolution and profit.

Pitfalls en route to the Profit Track

The decision to lean into conflict rather than charge in or lean away will put you squarely on the Profit Track. The inspiration generated by innovation and the investment in balancing interests enable you to make better decisions, to resolve conflicts, and to prevent conflicts from undermining growth. We succeed at turning conflict into profit when we make decisions that support collective goals, interests, and interdependent relationships. In this chapter we discuss a variety of practices that help us to improve decision-making and to appreciate the vital role conflict plays in the process.

Avoid Groupthink

Groupthink, first postulated by psychologist Irving Janis, occurs when a group focuses too much on convergence, with the goal of preventing conflict from occurring, and makes bad decisions with minimal individual responsibility. Groupthink can be thought of as the suppression of conflict. It occurs when groups place a higher priority on efficiency and impression management than on outcomes, without realizing that this is what they are doing. It often occurs within groups of individuals who have worked together for a long time, who have similar backgrounds, and who have come to see problems from a shared and limited view. Thus, groups that fall subject to groupthink replace the goal of effective decision-making with the goal of conflict suppression at all costs. Groupthink is the opposite of innovation. Groupthink compels group members to sublimate different views and competing interests in order to ensure a smooth and efficient decision-making process. In other words, groupthink causes group members to lean away, en mass, from conflict within the group. When it comes to a group generating the best decisions, it can be just as debilitating as the charging into approach of over-heated conflict.

Two historic examples involving disastrous decisions demonstrate this phenomenon. The first involved the decision by then-U.S. President John F. Kennedy and his administration to invade Cuba in 1961, referred to as the Bay of Pigs Invasion. Janis, who described this decision as one of the "worst fiascos ever perpetrated by a responsible government," did not attribute the mistake to the deficiencies of the decision-makers.[82] His study of the decision-making process suggested that blame could not be placed on the shortcomings of the individuals, all of whom were very intelligent and knowledgeable, but on the management of the decision-making process. He observed that Kennedy's tight control over the discussion and the manner of input open to his cabinet resulted in the sublimation of expressions that could have prevented this ill-conceived decision from being made.

The second example, involving NASA, was the administration's decision to launch the Challenger space shuttle in January 1986, which resulted in the death of all seven people on board. Research into this disaster suggested that although there were ample warning signs that the disaster could happen, the signs were ignored by the NASA leadership group.[83] This decision was influenced by the phenomenon of groupthink in which the pursuit of effective problem resolution takes a back seat to the goal of suppressing conflict at all costs.

As we stated in the first chapter, we should not mistakenly perceive difference of opinion and dissent as conflict. Yes, difference and dissent may increase tension, but actual conflict will only result if these differences threaten the practical or psychological interests of group members. If there is not a clash of opposing interests, there is no threat. If threat is not an issue, than difference serves a critically constructive purpose. In the Bay of Pigs situation, Kennedy's interest was to select the best option to address a complex and difficult external threat, as well as to appear strong and in control early in his presidency. In contrast, each of Kennedy's advisors' main interest appeared to be to demonstrate respect for and loyalty to the President and to achieve concurrence as smoothly as possible. These interests were, in part, the result of Kennedy's leadership style at that time, a style that served to squelch criticism and induce group pressure to comply with this norm. Kennedy would make his opinion known at the start of a discussion, almost daring his advisors to disagree, which they were reluctant to do. In this case, the different and unacknowledged interests that Kennedy held, in conjunction with those of his advisory team, produced the debilitating conflict. Moreover, once each advisor stated his support for the plan and suppressed his individual concerns—an act that was consistent with the motivational pressure of cognitive dissonance—each group member felt an internal need to maintain his support as further discussion ensued, even in the face of contradictory information. By suppressing their true individual interests, they formed a group position. They had to believe what they were doing was right and moral and that it would succeed. Sadly, history demonstrated that the decision was ill conceived and, as with the Challenger disaster, there was ample evidence to predict the failure right from the start.

Yet Kennedy appeared to learn quickly from the Bay of Pigs debacle. Drawing on his study of Kennedy's approach before and after the Bay of Pigs decision, Janis postulated three factors inherent in guiding a more effective approach to decision-making:

(A) AVOID PREMATURE CONSENSUS SEEKING
This is accomplished by the following tactics:

- Encourage open inquiry
- Delay the presentation of the leader's opinion to mitigate social influence and impression management
- Allow dialogue to occur in sub-groups without the leader present
- Ensure that someone in the group play the role of "devil's advocate"

By avoiding premature consensus seeking, problem solving is kept interest-focused and positions are avoided.

(B) CORRECT MISPERCEPTIONS AND MANAGE EMOTIONS
People must recognize that their own biases and emotions have the potential to cloud their objectivity and impair their decision-making competence. The Profit Track requires us to take these steps:

- Acknowledge our limitations
- Seek expert information when potentially helpful

- Translate emotional responses to threats into empathetic consideration of why the other party is threatening

By rationally exploring the perspective of the other party and not simply demonizing it, we end up with a more comprehensive appreciation of the threat itself and can construct more effective responses.

(c) CONSIDER ALL POSSIBLE OPTIONS

Good decision-making involves developing and evaluating all possible options to resolve a problem, even those that seem worthy of immediate rejection. By comparing and contrasting options, particularly as they relate to satisfying the interests at stake, you are more likely to identify the best of the alternatives. Too often, when we stampede to a resolution, critical interests are overlooked and only become clear later, to our regret.

Although these strategies appear reasonable, many groups continue to fall subject to groupthink. NASA has suffered two more avoidable disasters (i.e., the "blindness" of the Hubble telescope, and the explosion of the space shuttle Columbia); both were influenced by the phenomenon of groupthink. We have seen numerous leadership groups select ill-conceived ideas to address complex problems because the groups failed to implement one or any of the above strategies.

For example, a major hospital in Vancouver decided to combat the rising costs of absenteeism by offering staff members who did not call in sick for six months the chance to win a gift certificate worth $300. Absenteeism was a major problem for the organization, yet this decision became the subject of ridicule by the organization's staff and the local media. Interests and outcomes related to this decision, which were apparently not considered or were dismissed as insignificant by the leadership group, included these elements: (a) the low likelihood that staff currently abusing sick leave benefits would stop doing so in response to the chance to win a small gift certificate, (b) the likelihood that highly conscientious staff may report to work when they are in fact sick and thereby endanger co-workers and patients, and (c) research that demonstrates that absenteeism is related far more to hostile, unpleasant work environments than it is to the unethical abuse of sick leave benefits. One would suspect that groupthink might have contributed to the implementation of this ridiculed and conflict-creating decision.

Leaning into conflict acknowledges the benefits of allowing healthy conflict to occur and manages it in ways that translate foolhardy reactivity into constructive, meaningful, and creative decision-making.

Discuss Interests before Positions

As discussed above, the Profit Track requires that a logical sequence occur in decision-making processes. The sequence is consistent with psychological and sociological factors that support decisions. The Profit Track sequence of decision-making minimizes resistance, prevents groupthink, and promotes better decision-making. Simply put: keep discussion focused on interests and away from positions. If we stampede to a solution too quickly, the solution becomes a position and blocks interests from providing more information. When you or others arrive at a solution or a position, ask yourself and them, "If we did this, what would it do for us?" This will head you back into interests.

Also, by identifying and discussing interests prior to positions we can avoid the negative influence of cognitive dissonance. We know that once we state a position we become internally committed to that position, even in the face of contradictory evidence or persuasive counter-argument. Discussion of interests goes against the grain of our training so it takes extra insight and focus to resist the urge to engage in arguments. Some believe that discussing interests prior to making a decision may be inefficient because it will lengthen the duration of decision-making processes. Although this can be true, it is more likely to save time in the end because it will circumvent position-based arguments that typically occur when others protest a decision. Return for a moment to the team-based patient discharge example: when team members discuss interests and options first, and make decisions after, those decisions will be based on a more complete and shared understanding of the interests at stake. The decisions will be better decisions and will endure. Team members thus have the chance to change their minds prior to the decision being made without groupthink or the pressures of cognitive dissonance forcing them to adhere to a previously stated opinion.

The influence of cognitive dissonance can also be very useful in attempts to overcome resistance. If you have followed the first two steps of the Profit Track, you will have used inquiry and reason to manage the emotion generated when conflict has arisen, and you will have learned something about the interests and perspectives of the other parties. Once other individuals have stated their interests—agreeing, for example, that good communication is valuable or that maintaining a certain standard is important—they have provided you with an avenue to pursue resolution.

For example, an organization's financial manager approached a leader in the company with a problem: they had been paying a new contract researcher a higher monthly fee than was agreed to at the start of the contract. The mistake was a simple calculation error made by someone in the financial department. The financial manager proposed to correct the problem by informing the researcher of the mistake and reducing his pay over the remaining contract period to compensate for the overpayment. The leader vehemently objected to the proposal, stating that it would be against his "principles" to do so. The leader proposed that they continue to pay the researcher at the higher rate and absorb the overpayment. He added that he could not believe the financial manager would even think of doing something so unprincipled. At this point in the dispute, one's response might be frustration with the rigidity of the leader's position and offence at the condemnation. One will want to argue that the leader is wrong, that his approach does not practice sound financial management, and that his plan is no more principled than the alternative. However, rather than argue about the different positions, the financial manager can use inquiry at this point to open the door to a more informative and collaborative discussion. For example, the financial manger could respond by asking the leader to clarify the principle is he referring to and explain how it applies to this situation. The financial manager could then ask if there are other principles, as well as interests, that should also be considered. By using inquiry and learning more about the leader's perspectives, the financial manager will be in a better position to point out that his own principles are actually aligned more with admitting the mistake and respecting the original terms of the contract, rather than with covering up the mistake and eating the loss. The financial manager could also suggest they may want to look at this problem and its potential solutions from the perspective of board members, employees, and other stakeholders.

By exploring the interests, and in this case the principles, of the people with whom we have a dispute, we arm ourselves with valuable information that can be used to demonstrate how our solution is actually better aligned with their stated interests and goals. Subject to the influence of cognitive dissonance, they will want to remain consistent with their stated interests and will therefore be more open to participating in finding a collaborative decision.

Include All Relevant Parties

Effective decision-making involves acquiring the most information possible. The more information we have, the better we understand the dilemma that requires a decision be made and the implications of it. Surprisingly, particularly in large organizations, decisions are made without consulting parties who will be impacted by the decisions. Presumably there is a belief that because so many parties experience impacts, a consultation process would be neither practical nor cost-effective. If the anticipated impacts are minimal, this approach can be logical. However, the minute that significant negative impacts are either likely to occur or begin to occur, then consultation with relevant parties is far more effective than trying to push a decision through.

Consultation is information gathering. A lack of consultation means a lack of information. You may believe you have all the information and therefore do not need to consult others. But consider this: how would you know what you do not know? How could you know that after months and countless hours of implementation time others would resist your plan because they see your solution as a threat, or that they do not see it meeting their needs? Like the organization at the beginning of this chapter, failing to consult the primary parties involved cost it far more in the long run than investing a little in consultation. A successful consultation strategy would not involve every member of the organization. It would involve a representative stakeholder from each area of the organization. Rather than invest time, energy, and money in a decision that may be challenged, resisted, and blocked later, consulting requires the investment of less time, energy, and money at the interest exploration stage of decision-making; consulting leads to more effective and workable decisions. If there is any resistance, it will come from those who were impacted by the decision but were left out of the process. So do not leave anyone out.

Stay Focused on the Goal

Finally, we return to this question: would you rather be right or happy? When dealing with conflict, would you rather be right—and stay in conflict—or be neither right nor wrong but achieve a satisfying resolution? There may be times when being right is more important than finding resolution. There are times when detaching from a conflict is the safer and more reasonable option, especially when the relationship in question is not worthy of the effort to maintain it. However, if your real goal is to resolve a conflict in a manner that keeps you on the Profit Track, then it is imperative that you avoid the psychological, emotional, and cognitive pitfalls associated with the Conflict Trap. It is crucial that you focus on solving the problem rather than deny a problem exists, detach by blaming those you believe created the problem, or despair at the unfairness of it all.

It is true that many of us end up in conflicts that are not of our making, and this is unfair. It is unfair when we have to work for supervisors who threaten us and block our development and growth. It is unfair when we work with people who do not contribute their fair share. It is unfair when we do nothing wrong but are blamed because a co-worker has lied about something that happened. It is unfair when we have to supervise people who constantly complain and make our work lives miserable. It is unfair and fatiguing that we must spend time and energy to deal with a problem we did not create. Some may think it is even unfair that we must manage our anger, use tact, and be respectful when we get upset or frustrated by the perceived stupidity of others.

But consider the alternatives. We outline, here, the consequences of staying trapped in conflict:

- The erosion of productivity, growth, self-esteem, and relationships
- The potential for erosion to lead to more devastating consequences that are associated with implosion or explosion

- The poor choices made when in denial, when in despair over a problem, and when detached from the reality of the situation

In the long run, you will spend more time and more energy, and become more fatigued and despairing, the more you lean away from or charge into the conflicts that will inevitably arise in your working life. Invest your time and energy by leaning into conflict. When conflict arises, keep your focus on your true goals and on the value of strong and solid, interdependent relationships that enable you to achieve those goals. Stay insightful, inspired, and invested.

Making Better Decisions at a Glance

- Groupthink is a disastrous process of decision-making in which otherwise bright individuals approve foolhardy outcomes because they need to see themselves as being in agreement.
- Avoid premature consensus. Learn about all the relevant interests before you make a decision.
- Keep decision-making rooted in interests, not in positions.
- Involve all parties that will experience impacts in decision-making, either personally or through representative stakeholders—or expect resistance.
- By investing in involving parties who experience impacts, those who make decisions gather far more information than they would when making decisions without consultation.
- Consultation takes time, energy, and resources up front, but it saves a greater amount of time, energy, and resources later on.
- Focus on addressing the real goals of resolution and maintaining productive and effective relationships, even if you did not create the conflict at hand.

14

Putting It All Together

SO, WE HAVE DISCUSSED the definitions of conflict and how conflict can become a trap of denial, despair, and detachment. We have examined the psychological, interpersonal, and cultural implications of conflict. We have presented you with ideas about how to slip out of the Conflict Trap and move through the Narrow Place using curiosity and courage. We have described the Profit Track as requiring insight, inspiration, and investment, which are built by following these five steps: Tapping the Energy, Finding the Learning, Building Relationships, Cultivating Innovation, and Making Better Decisions. Now, to put it all together, let us look at one final case study that addresses a common workplace conflict.

Conflict Defined

"Good morning," you call out to Mark, one of your top employees, as you arrive. This is met with stony silence. Not again, you think. This time you're not going to avoid his silence and you decide to challenge him. You pause in the doorway to your office and turn toward him. "Good morning," you repeat more slowly and with unmistakable precision. "Good morning," he mutters without looking up. The obvious tension leaves you wondering, "What is going on *now?*"

At the initiation of potential conflict, consider these points:

- Conflict is typically created when there is a contradiction of interests, a perception of threat or loss, and interdependency between opposing parties.
- Conflict is about practical and, or, psychological interests. Practical interests must typically be addressed before psychological ones.
- Conflict is inevitable, ubiquitous, and natural.
- Conflict sources can be rooted in *processes*— *how* issues are addressed— or rooted in *outcomes*—*whether or not* interests are addressed.
- Our responses to conflict are nurtured and learned more than they are part of our instinctive nature. What is not yet learned can be trained, and what can be learned can be re-trained.
- A sense of entitlement, a competitive ideology, and prejudicial beliefs and values typically accelerate the intensity of conflict.
- Perception is reality.
- Conflict causes and is caused by our natural urge to either *lean away from* (flight) or *charge into* (fight) a situation that threatens our interests. The most effective response is neither of these, but is instead *leaning into* conflict.

The Conflict Trap

You have known that Mark has been pretty upset about Barb, another top performer in the unit. For years they just seemed as different as "chalk and cheese," and it appeared that they would never get along. Over the last few months each has come to you and vented their frustrations about the other. At first you hoped they would somehow work it out. Then it became clear to you and to them that they "just hated each other." You tried to avoid them as much as possible, and lately the work area has been pretty chilly and quiet.

As conflict intensifies, remember these points:

- Conflict, like bereavement, is a natural process that can quickly become an unhealthy trap in which we become entrenched.
- When we are stuck in this Conflict Trap, we experience denial, despair, and detachment, typically in that order.
- In denial, we attempt to defend against feelings of despair by pretending either that there is no problem or that it is not our problem.
- As denial breaks down we move into despair, where we develop a sense of hopelessness and helplessness about our ability to do anything about the conflict.
- The more we despair, the more we are driven to detach. Detachment represents the most dangerous threat to growth because in detachment we have "given up" on resolving the conflict and are just trying to cope as best we can.
- All three stages form the Conflict Trap, because the more we deny, the more we ultimately despair; the more we despair, the more we detach; and the more we detach the more we deny....
- The Conflict Trap affects us personally, it affects our work relationships and productivity, and it affects the people around us.

FIGURE 14.1

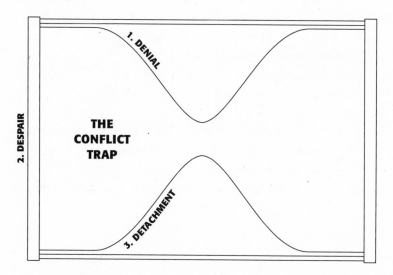

The Costs of Conflict

As you head into your office you can see that Mark is again the only one in today. You have noticed that Barb coincidentally gets sick on days when she would have to work with Mark. Though you have talked to her about the increased workload and the rising costs of her absenteeism, she is able to produce doctor's notes for her "stress leaves." A few really great staff members have recently resigned. You can feel a migraine nagging. As you sit down at your computer you see a note from Mark left on your desk that reads, "I thought you should see this." Paper-clipped to it is a small typed note that reads, "Mark—watch your back! You're not safe."

Now you know the conflict exists not just between Mark and Barb, it involves you and possibly the rest of the group. At this point in a conflict keep these elements in mind:

- Misunderstood and mishandled conflict impacts us personally and organizationally.
- On a personal level, we typically experience a range of negative impacts. As a result, our colleagues, family, and friends will also experience negative impacts.
- On an organizational level, our work teams and organizations experience negative impacts that trap us in conflict and become significant barriers to growth.
- As individuals, teams, and organizations descend into the Conflict Trap, they experience symptoms of several kinds:

  - Symptoms of erosion, like low morale and inefficiencies
  - Symptoms of implosion, like rising absenteeism and failing financial health
  - Symptoms of explosion, like threats, violence, and even death

FIGURE 14.2

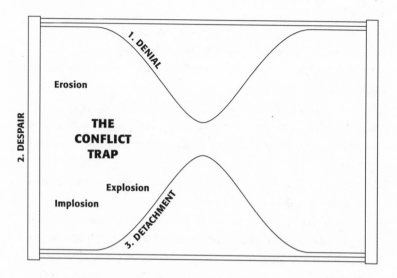

The Conflict Within Us

That's better. You now have a cup of hot coffee in your hand. Amazing how mornings like this make coffee seem somehow nutritious. You reflect on your attempts to nail the conflict between Barb and Mark. In talking with each of them, they refuse to accept any responsibility for what is going on and instead blame the other person. They are able to justify themselves fully and see themselves entirely as victims. Whenever you attempt to set expectations or monitor behaviour, they accuse the other person of lying to you about what has happened. It sometimes seems to you like they are really large children. After all, you say to yourself, you are a manager, not a babysitter. You ask yourself, "Why can they not just get along?" On their own, they are good people and strong members of the team.

As you begin to reflect on the dynamics of a conflict, consider the following:

- Conflict manifests within each of us psychologically.
- All behaviour makes sense, although finding the "sense" can demand substantial effort and patience.
- We are psychologically designed to protect ourselves against perceived threats through the use of defences that include denial, suppression, projection, displacement, reaction formation, identification, and rationalization.
- Though our defences are natural psychological protectors, they actually keep us stuck in the Conflict Trap.
- Deception is common, with ourselves and with others, and while deception is protective like armour, this type of shielding also desensitizes us and keeps us trapped in conflict.
- When in conflict, we tend to judge people and their motives rather than assess the situation with insight. We form attributions about ourselves and others to determine why we and others act in certain ways. These attributions are typically misguided.
- Believing is seeing insofar as our beliefs influence our interpretation of what we observe.
- Role theory, social influence, impression management, stereotyping, and cognitive dissonance are all psycho-sociological factors that drive how we experience and respond to conflict.
- All conflicts are "personality conflicts," and yet labels attached to personality and psychopathology are not usually helpful for understanding or resolving conflict. In fact, we move out of the Conflict Trap with even the most difficult individuals when we employ optimal skills and strategies.

If only they'd just get over it! Why won't one of them just quit? Perhaps you could get away with firing one of them. Yet they have both been strong contributors to your success in the past. You also fear complaints and lawsuits that may arise from firing one or both of them. Barb has said to you and others that she will not rest until Mark either "shapes up or ships out." Mark has taken the position that he got his job first, and if anyone is going to leave it will have to be Barb. It is clear that each of them is so focused on waiting for the other person to change that neither seems capable of looking at their own behaviours.

As you continue your reflection remember these considerations:

- When we are stuck in the Conflict Trap, manifestations of conflict with others can look more like an infestation.
- Conflict is heavily predicated on communication. When we communicate we encode our ideas, needs, and so on into words, tone, and body language, and then send our message to another party. That party then receives the message and decodes the words, tone, and body language to interpret the meaning of our ideas. *Filters*, such as context, gender, assumptions, biases, and culture, influence the message that is sent and the message received. This is particularly true when parties are in conflict, and it can result in *communication mishaps* that perpetuate the Conflict Trap.
- The *interests* at stake in conflict are frequently expressed as the *positions* we take on *issues* that lead us to dig in our heels and become further mired in the Conflict Trap. Moving others and ourselves off of these positions and into a discussion of interests is key to breaking free of the Conflict Trap.
- Resistance is always an unmet need—identify the need and discover the path to resolution and profit.
- The manifestation of conflict in organizations can be viewed as similar to an infestation by insect pests in agricultural settings. The most

effective strategies for managing insect pests, referred to as Integrated Pest Management (IPM), provides a metaphor for the successful strategy of *leaning into* conflict, and not the conflict-trapping approaches of *leaning away from* or *charging into* conflict.

- In dealing with conflict, we must identify what we have direct control over, what we can influence, and what we have no control over. Breaking free of the Conflict Trap involves focusing our energy on our sphere of control, broadening our sphere of influence, and letting go of the sphere of no control.

Conflict Across

As you reflect on the situation, you note that most of the issues that Mark and Barb fight over are relatively minor things. However, as you think about all the arguments, you begin to see a pattern in their behaviour. She usually talks in terms of the needs of the team, while he usually focuses on his own needs. She prides herself on being a person who will "tell it like it is," while Mark tends to be quiet around her and vents his frustration to you and others. Barb can be domineering and often boasts about her university education. Mark often reports feeling victimized and complains that Barb does not respect him. He prefers a more structured environment with clear rules, while she prefers flexibility. Finally, Barb describes Mark as cold and insensitive because he is less expressive than she is. On the other hand, Mark sees her as overly emotional and as "a flake." Will these two ever be able to work together productively?

As you ponder the differences that may be contributing to the conflict and preventing understanding and resolution, consider these elements:

- All communication is cross-cultural communication.
- Culture is the way in which a group of people perceives and responds to conflict.

- Cultures share similar values, although there will always be members of a culture who adopt different sets of values.
- These values can be arranged along the following continuums:

  a. Collectivist vs. Individualist
  b. Direct vs. Indirect Communication
  c. Internal vs. External Control
  d. Achieved vs. Ascribed Status
  e. Absolute Rules vs. Relative Relationships
  f. Neutral vs. Affective Interaction

- We must often make a choice when in conflict: "Do I want to be right, or do I want to be happy (i.e., profitable)?" Quite often, we will not be able to be both.
- The more there is *otherness*—the more different the other party is from us—the more likely we are to misinterpret what others communicate when in conflict. Yet we typically see our own misinterpretations as the truth.
- We become stuck in the Conflict Trap by ignoring the need that many of us have to "save face." Rather than "saving the other's face," we tend to want to "rub the other's nose in it."
- Western organizational culture tends to be individualistic, adversarial, and intimidating. These traits contribute to the denial, despair, and detachment that keeps us stuck in the Conflict Trap. Turning conflict into profit requires that we adopt new approaches to deal with each other and with the conflicts that are bound to arise in our working lives.

Into the Narrow Place

Your hand lingers over the telephone. Is it time to get some help? What would Human Resources offer that you have not already tried? You figure, "If I knew that, I would have already tried it!" You decide to check out your options, to spend some time just sitting in the conflict and listening to other perspectives. It is not that you cannot handle it; it is that you would like to handle it well. Now that you have become aware of how bad it is you plan to pay attention to what is really going on and what might help. You have acknowledged that you are ready to turn this conflict around.

As you move from your own sense of despair towards more productive action, remember these elements:

- There is a path out of the Conflict Trap and into profit, but it is a path less travelled through—a metaphorical Narrow Place.
- Moving away from the Conflict Trap towards the aperture of the Narrow Place requires *curiosity*—that is, making a conscious choice to employ a spirit of inquiry.
- Curiosity involves three key aspects: Developing *awareness* that there is a problem, paying *attention* to what the problem is, and *acknowledging* that it is a problem worth addressing.
- Pulling ourselves through the Narrow Place and onto the Profit Track involves courage. The Profit Track involves refusing to deny issues, refusing to collude with others' despair and hopelessness, and resisting the urge to detach, avoid, and lean away from problems. It also involves resisting the urge to tell all the parties why they are wrong and how they should change—resolution just doesn't work this way.
- To convert the Conflict Trap into the Profit Track requires that we use curiosity and courage to lean into the conflict.

FIGURE 14.3

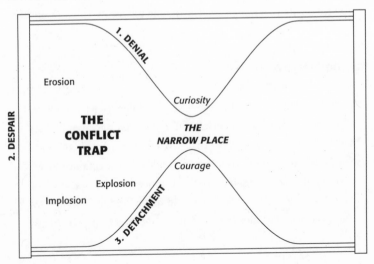

Turning Conflict into Profit

Onto the Profit Track

After consulting with Human Resources and following up with some reading, you recognize that there is much to do here. Already you can see choices that you wish you had made differently with Barb and Mark months, even years ago. However, you are beginning to feel excited about the future and refuse to beat yourself up about the past. You have started having more conversations with staff in the area, making efforts to go for coffee with people you have not done so with before. You ask them questions about what they would like the workplace to look like and about what they want. You hear some pretty unreasonable ideas, but rather than scoff at them you delve deeper asking, "So, if that happened, what would it do for you, for us, for the group?" You have decided to invest some resources now on the odds that it will save you a lot of resources down the road.

Remember these points as you head down the Profit Track:

- The Profit Track involves three stages: insight, inspiration, and investment.
- Insight arises from leaning into conflict with relentless curiosity. Just showing up and listening, even if only for a minute, yields insights.
- As insight builds, we begin to feel inspired, which brings back passion, a sense of the positive, creativity, and innovation.
- As we become more inspired, we invest resources. We make decisions to commit to what has become important to us and in doing so we are no longer detached.
- If we do not pursue insight and inspiration in our decision-making, we will not make a meaningful investment. When we respond to conflict by spending money on projects that do not build insight and inspiration, we can only expect a return on tucking (R.O.T.) that typically generates little.
- The Profit Track becomes a cycle of enduring learning, achievement, and growth—of personal and organizational profit. The more insight we develop, the more inspired we become. The more inspired we

become, the more we invest and are invested. The more we invest and are invested, the more insight we develop....

FIGURE 14.4

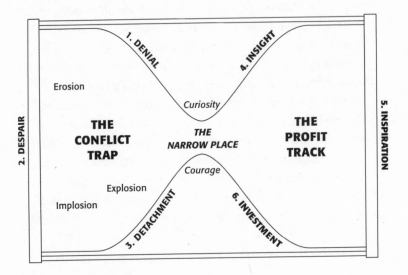

The Five Steps on the Profit Track

Having assessed the conflict and prepared yourself to lean in, you are now ready to engage the five steps on the track to resolution.

Tap the Energy

A few days later you enter the workplace. Mark is at his desk but Barb is nowhere in sight. "Good morning," you say as you head to your office. Again, Mark responds with silence. Rather than leaning away by pretending you did not notice, or charging into by trying to make him say "Good morning," you pause and say, "Mark, I've noticed lately that when I say 'Good morning' you don't often respond." Mark does not look up. You let a few seconds of silence hang in the air before saying, "and now you're silent again." Still no response. "Obviously, there is a problem, but frankly I'm confused. Let's go for coffee at 10—I'd like to hear what's going on from your perspective." He nods reluctantly as you head into your office.

As you tap the energy inherent in any conflict, remember the following:

- Negative impacts such as anger, frustration, and anxiety create energy that can be harnessed and utilized to generate resolution and profit.
- The more we allow ourselves to be anxious and reactive, the further away we move from our real goals.
- Anxiety is a physiological response in the body to complex situations that create complicated emotions in us.
- Techniques to reduce anxiety (or anger) involve physically taking deep breaths, which short-circuits the physiological response, and keeping the conflict in perspective using some type of cognitive intervention (e.g., reality testing).
- Techniques to reduce others' anxiety involve acknowledging that what they are saying is important to them.
- Acknowledging is not the same as agreeing.
- Tapping the energy of conflict involves leaning into conflict by resisting the urge to avoid, dismiss, minimize, or judge. Show up, ask questions, and listen.

Find the Learning

You are wondering if going for coffee together was the right thing after all. You have not touched your coffee and Mark has been venting his frustration about Barb for 20 minutes now, without showing signs of stopping. His face is getting redder and his voice is getting louder. You are starting to get worried about what other people at the coffee shop will think. You act as a role model to demonstrate how to separate the outcome issues about Barb from the process issues that have arisen because of how Mark is talking.

You say, "Mark, Mark—clearly this is really frustrating. We definitely need to work this out. I'm concerned about the way we're talking here in the cafeteria. I want us to talk about options for how we can make things better. Please, let's keep our voices at a conversational tone and volume."

You acknowledged how important the concerns are to him before you described what you see happening. Then you told him specifically how you would like the process to continue. He pauses, and then resumes his perspective in a lowered tone. It worked!

As you pursue learning, remember these components:

- Assumptions and defensiveness inhibit learning.
- In order to learn and grow, it takes humility and insight to recognize that what we know is likely incomplete—there is always more information to gather.
- What we are in conflict about are generally *outcome* issues. How outcomes are addressed (or not) are generally *process* issues. Separate the outcome issues from the process issues in discussions and seek what can be learned about both.
- The Platinum Rule of treating others as they wish to be treated trumps The Golden Rule of treating others as you like to be treated. The Platinum Rule encourages learning and growth along the Profit Track.
- Finding information involves asking open-ended questions and acknowledging perspectives, even those—and perhaps especially those—with which we disagree.

Build Relationships

You summarize with Mark what you heard him say by restating his positions in terms of the interests he considers important and at risk. By doing so you demonstrate your interest in supporting him and building a trusting relationship. You also try to shift him away from identifying himself as the victim by shifting the focus to the problem and its impacts, rather than the people involved.

"Okay, Mark. Clearly, this has been really upsetting. You want to be able to come to work and experience respect from your co-workers. A certain measure of structure is important to you because then you know what to expect and you don't like surprises. You also think Barb is the source of the problems you've described. So, you've said you'd like me to follow up with her to address her role in this. I'm a little worried about how much control we're giving her here. I appreciate that she has a role to play, but I'd like to talk again with you on Friday to discuss what you might be able to contribute to resolving your conflict with Barb. In the meantime, I'll meet with Barb."

As you start to rebuild relationships in order to stay on the Profit Track, keep these points in mind:

- Conflict is about relationships.
- The more we blame, the more control we give away. Framing responsibility as "control" stops blaming.
- Reject stereotypes.
- Be transparent, honest, and tactful.
- Focus on impacts and interests, not on intent.
- Do not be haughty with the humble or humble with the haughty.
- It is in your best interest to prevent others' bad behaviours from triggering you to act disrespectfully—you will only undermine your own success.
- Match your communication to the other person's style to keep balance in the dialogue.
- Manage expectations by being clear, descriptive, and specific; this keeps outcomes in perspective and the process clear.

Cultivate Innovation

The next day you are having coffee with Barb. You have described the need to keep the discussion between you confidential and mentioned how venting to others will only make things worse. You have presented to her an overview of Mark's perspective, framed in a neutral and constructive manner, and you have heard a lot about her perspective. Their views are so different you wonder if they have been on the same planet. Yet you observe that much of their conflict comes from perceptions they have about each other's intentions, and that both describe wanting only to do the best job they can and advance in the organization. Barb says to you that she wants you to fix it. You've told her that there is a role you can play to assist in resolving the issues and you would like to hear her ideas first. You ask her to describe the barriers that have kept the situation from being resolved. Later, you say, "I wonder what would be involved in overcoming those barriers," and you generate a list of options together.

In trying to discover new ideas and approaches to resolve issues and meet interests, yours and others', remember the following:

- Conflict is the engine of creativity and innovation if channelled effectively.
- Though getting lost is unpleasant, interesting and creative things happen when you are lost—you find things you were not looking for.
- Everyone is innovative—when encouraged.
- Innovation needs space to grow.
- Innovation involves taking risks and making mistakes, and not holding grudges against others for mistakes they may have made that harmed or threatened you.
- Group efforts can generate more innovation and creativity than individual efforts.
- Key skills for boosting innovation and becoming inspired include acknowledging, open questioning, and framing, and then reframing positions as interests.

Make Better Decisions

You have now had a few meetings with Barb and Mark together. It definitely felt like a few steps forward and some big ones back. Though there were moments of frustration, you stayed the course, you leaned into their conflict with each other and with you, and you refused to stampede to a premature resolution. The distortions seem to be decreasing. They actually seem to recognize each other as humans and have stopped referring to each other as monsters. As communication has improved, they have both identified concerns with colleagues. Based on your discussions with them, you have asked a consultant to facilitate a team discussion about how the group can work together more productively and efficiently. Absenteeism is dropping. Work performance is improving. Mark even says "Good morning" to you first now...and even to Barb.

Remember these elements as you make decisions when in conflict:

- Groupthink is a disastrous process of decision-making wherein otherwise bright individuals agree on foolhardy outcomes because of their need to see each other as being in agreement.
- Avoid a premature consensus. Learn about all the relevant interests before a decision is made.
- Keep decision-making rooted in interests and not in positions, because this is best path towards developing solutions.
- Involve all parties that experience impacts in making decisions, either personally or through representative stakeholders, in order to minimize resistance.
- By investing in and involving parties who experience impacts, decision-makers get much more information than they would by making decisions without consultation.
- Consultation takes time, energy, and resources up front, but it saves more time, energy, and resources later on.
- Focus on addressing the real goals of resolution and on maintaining productive and effective working relationships, even if you did not create the conflict yourself.

FIGURE 14.5

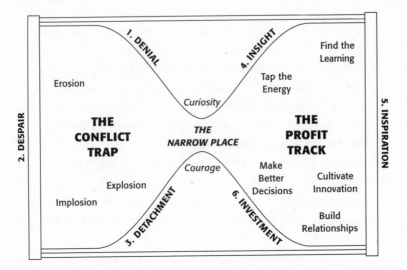

A final word...

By leaning into conflict, we can invert the hourglass and turn the Conflict Trap into a Profit Track. With the persistent and thoughtful use of the strategies and skills described in this book, you can draw on naturally occurring conflicts to feed vital energy, effective learning, stronger relationships, brilliant innovation, and sound decision-making. Previously overwhelming conflicts that eroded an organization's functioning, and that threatened to implode or even explode into financial, organizational, and personal losses, can now become sources of insight, inspiration, and investment. Resist the urge to lean away from conflict or to charge into it. Lean into conflict and you will release your full potential at work and in life!

FIGURE 14.6

The 6 Stages of the "Conflict to Profit" Model

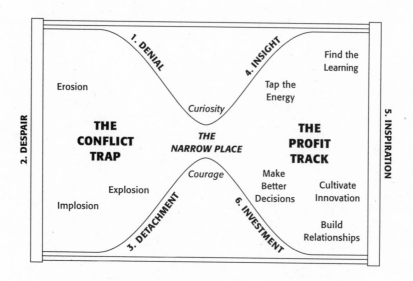

1. DENIAL
- Confusion
- Frustration

2. DESPAIR
- Anger
- Gossip
- Hostility
- Low morale
- Distraction
- Hopelessness
- Deficits
- Absenteeism
- Blaming

3. DETACHMENT
- Helplessness
- Bankruptcy
- Isolation
- Apathy
- Violence

4. INSIGHT
- Be aware
- Pay attention
- Acknowledge
- Show up
- Manage anxiety & anger
- Ask questions
- Listen
- Learn
- Hope

5. INSPIRATION
- Adopt The Platinum Rule
- Separate process from content
- Separate the person from the problem
- Empower
- Reject stereotypes
- Be honest, open and respectful
- Focus on impacts

6. INVESTMENT
- Stay focused
- Consult
- Interests first
- Avoid groupthink
- Reward efforts
- Take chances
- Allow room
- Lose yourself

References

1   Joyce Hocker and William Wilmot, *Interpersonal Conflict* (Iowa: William C. Brown
    Publishers, 1985), 23.

2   Dr. R. Forsyth, *Group Dynamics*, 2nd ed. (Pacific Grove, CA: Brooks/Cole Publishing,
    1990).

3   Abraham H. Maslow, *Motivation and Personality* (New York: Harper & Row, 1954).

4   K. Jaspers, *General Psychopathology* (Chicago: University of Chicago Press, 1963), 226–27.

5   K.W. Thomas, and R.H. Kilmann, *Thomas-Kilmann Conflict Mode Instrument*.
    (Published by XICOM, 1974).

6   P.J. Carneyale, and T.M. Probst, "Good News About Competitive People," in
    Using Conflict in Organizations, eds. C.K.W. De Dreu and E.V. de Vliert, (London:
    Sage Publications, 1997), 129–46.

7   Derrick Jensen, *The Culture of Make Believe* (New York: Context Books, 2002), 323–24.

8   R.A. Baron, "Positive Effects of Conflict: Insights from Social Cognition," in
    Using Conflict in Organizations, eds. C.K.W De Dreu and E.Van de Vliert, (London:
    Sage publications, 1997), 177–91.

9   K.A. Slaikeu, and R.H. Hasson, *Controlling the Costs of Conflict: How to Design a System
    for Your Organization* (San Francisco: Jossey-Bass Inc., 1998), 4.

10 Elizabeth Kubler-Ross, M.D., *On Death and Dying* (New York: Touchstone, 1969);
    William Lamers, cited in Mary Conner, "Understanding the Cycle of Normal Grief in
    Adult Patients," in *Behavioral Medicine Briefs* 3 (Department of Family Practice and
    Community Health, University of Minnesota, March 1999), website:
    http://www.med.umn.edu/fp/bmb/bmb3.pdf.

11 Niels Bohr, cited in K.C. Cole, *The Universe and the Teacup* (Orland, FL: Harcourt Brace,
    1997), 202.

12 R.A. Friedman, S.T. Tidd, S.C. Currall, and J.C. Tsai, "What Goes Around Comes
    Around: The Impact of Personal Conflict Style on Work Conflict and Stress," in
    The International Journal of Conflict Management 11, no. 1 (2000): 32–55.

13 Academy of Management Executive (1998).

14 Joint Commission Journal on Quality Improvement (2001).

15 Canadian Policy Research Networks, Changing Employment Relationships Survey,
    Canada (2002).

16   Safety Council of Canada, under "Bullying in the Workplace" (2002), website:
      http://www.safety-council.org/info/OSH/bullies.html.

17   Sloan Management Review (2001).

18   B. Spector, "The Unindicted Co-conspirator," in *Organizational Dynamics* 32, no. 2 (2003):
      207–20.

19   L. Duxbury, and C. Higgins, "Work-Life Balance in the New Millenium: Where Are We?
      Where Do We Need to Go?" CPRN Discussion Paper, no. 1/12 (Ottawa, ON: Canadian
      Policy Research Networks, October 2001), website: http://www.cprn.org.

20   Moffat v. Kinark C&FS, 99-05, Ontario Board of Inquiry.

21   Canadian Policy Research Networks, Quality of Employment Indicators Project (2000),
      website: http://www.jobquality.ca.

22   Office of the Chief Coroner, Ontario, Canada (May 2001), OC Transport Inquest.

23   K.A. Slaikeu, and R.H. Hasson, *Controlling the Costs of Conflict: How to Design a System
      for Your Organization* (San Francisco: Jossey-Bass, 1998).

24   Sherron Watkins, quoted by Lesley Curwen, "The Corporate Conscience," in *The
      Guardian* (June 21, 2003), website: http://www.guardian.co.uk/business/story/
      0,3604,982216,00.html.

25   Columbia Accident Investigation Board (August 2003), CAIB Report, vol. 1; M.E.
      Turner, and A.R. Pratkanis, "Mitigating Groupthink by Stimulating Constructive
      Conflict," in *Using Conflict in Organizations*, eds. C.K.W. De Dreu and E. Van de Vliert
      (London: Sage Publications, 1997), 53–71.

26   Workers' Compensation Board of British Columbia, Accident Investigation, File No.
      2002100391; Coroner's Court of British Columbia, Verdict at Coroner's Inquest
      May 30, 2003.

27   Abraham H. Maslow, *The Farther Reaches of Human Nature* (New York: Viking Press, 1971), 34.

28   Robert Bly, *A Little Book on the Human Shadow* (New York: HarperCollins, 1988), 15.

29   G.L. Clore, N. Schwarz, and M. Conway, "Affective Causes and Consequences of Social
      Information Processing," in *Handbook of Social Cognition*, 2nd ed., vol. 1, eds. R.S. Wyer,
      and T.K. Srull (Hillsdale, N.J.: Lawrence Earlbaum Associates, 1994), 323–417.

30   Daniel Goleman, *Emotional Intelligence* (New York: Bantam Books, 1995).

31   H.H. Kelley et al., *Attribution: Perceiving the Causes of Behaviour* (Morristown, N.J.:
      General Learning Press, 1972).

32   K.G. Allred, "Realizing the Advantages of Organizational Interdependencies:
      The Role of Attributionally Mediated Emotions," in *Attribution Theory: An Organizational
      Perspective* (Florida: St. Lucie Press, 1995), 253–71.

33   K.W. Thomas, and L.R. Pondy, "Toward an 'Intent' Model of Conflict Management
      Among Principal Parties," *Human Relations* 30 (1977): 1089–102.

34   P.G. Zimbardo, "Pathology of Imprisonment," *Transaction/Society* (April 1972): 4–8.

35   S. Asch, "Effects of Group Pressure on the Modification and Distortion of Judgments,"
      in *Readings in Social Psychology*, eds. E.E. Maccoby, T.M. Newcomb, and E.L. Hartley
      (New York: Holt, Rinehart, & Winston, 1958), 174–83.

36   E. Diener, "Deindividuation, Self-awareness and Disinhibition," *Journal of Personal &
      Social Psychology* 37 (1979): 1160–71.

37   P. Thomas, "Targets of the Cults," *Human Behaviour* 8 (1979): 58–59.

38 B.R. Schlenker, and B.A. Pontari, "The Strategic Control of Information: Impression Management and Self-presentation in Daily Life" in *Perspectives on Self and Identity*, eds. A. Tesser, R. Felson, and J. Suls (Washington, D.C.: American Psychological Association, 2000), 199–232.

39 Seijts, and Latham, "Creativity Through Applying Ideas from Fields Other than One's Own: Transferring Knowledge from Social Psychology to Industrial/Organizational Psychology," *Canadian Psychology* 44, no.3 (August 2003): 232–39.

40 "Eye of the Storm," *ABC News* (May 11, 1970).

41 Leon Festinger, *A Theory of Cognitive Dissonance* (Stanford, CA: Stanford University Press, 1957).

42 R. Goffee, and G. Jones, "Why Should Anyone Be Led by You?" *Harvard Business Review* (2000): 63–70.

43 M.H. Bazerman, T. Guiliano, and A. Appleman, "Escalation of Commitment in Individual and Group Decision Making," *Organizational Behaviour and Human Performance* 33 (1984): 141–52.

44 F.D. Schoorman, "Escalation Bias in Performance Appraisals: An Unintended Consequence of Supervisor Participation in Hiring Decisions," *Journal of Applied Psychology* 73 (1988): 58–62.

45 David C. Glass, "Changes in Linking as a Means of Reducing Cognitive Discrepancies Between Self-esteem and Aggression," *Journal of Personality* 32 (1964): 531–49.

46 D. Keirsey and M. Bates, *Please Understand Me: Character and Temperament Types*, (Del Mar CA: Prometheus Nemesis Book Co. 1984). Alan A. Cavaiola, and Neil J. Lavender, *Toxic Co-workers* (Oakland, CA: New Harbinger Publications, 2000).

47 K.A. Slaikeu, and R.H. Hasson, *Controlling the Costs of Conflict: How to Design a System for Your Organization* (San Francisco: Jossey-Bass, 1998).

48 Summarized in R.E. Nesbett, and L. Ross, *The Person and the Situation* (Cambridge: Harvard University Press, 1995), chaps. 6, 7.

49 Nancy J. Adler, *International Dimensions of Organizational Behaviour* (Cincinnati, OH: Thomas Publishing, 1999).

50 Michael Argyle, and others, "The Communication of Inferior and Superior Attitudes by Verbal and Non-verbal Signals," *British Journal of Social and Clinical Psychology* 9, pt. 3 (September 1970): 222–31; Albert Mehrabian, and Susan R. Ferris, "Inference of Attitudes from Nonverbal Communication in Two Channels," *Journal of Consulting Psychology* 31, no. 3 (June 1967): 248–58; Albert Mehrabian, and Morton Wiener, "Decoding of Inconsistent Communications," *Journal of Personality and Social Psychology* 6, no. 1 (May 1967): 109–14; Albert Mehrabian, *Nonverbal Communication* (Aldine Atherton, 1972); Albert Mehrabian, *Silent Messages* (Wadsworth Publishing Company, 1971), particularly 42–43.

51 Roger Fisher, and William Ury, *Getting to Yes* (New York: Penguin Books, 1981) ; The Program on Negotiation at Harvard Law School, website: http://www.pon.harvard.edu/ main/home/index.php3

52 Sandra Steingraber, *Living Downstream* (Toronto: Random House of Canada Limited, 1998); Mark. L. Winston, *Nature Wars* (Boston: Harvard University Press, 1997).

53 Peter J. Frost, *Toxic Emotions at Work* (Boston: Harvard Business School Publishing, 2003).

54   Adapted from Stephen R. Covey, *The 7 Habits of Highly Effective People* (New York: Fireside, 1999).

55   V.N. Redekop, "Speaking About Rights," *Canadian Human Rights Newsletter* XIV, no. 3 (1999).

56   F. Trompenaars, *Riding the Waves of Culture: Understanding Cultural Diversity in Business* (London: Economist Books, 1993), 7.

57   E. Shien, *Organizational Culture and Leadership* (San Francisco: Jossey-Bass, 1985).

58   Kluckhohn, and Strodtbeck, *Variations in Value Orientations* (Connecticut: Greenwood Press, 1961); G. Hofstede, *Culture's Consequences* (Beverly Hills, CA: Sage, 1980); F. Trompenaars, *Riding the waves of Culture: Understanding Cultural Diversity in Business* (London: Economist Books, 1993).

59   F. Trompenaars, *Riding the Waves of Culture: Understanding Cultural Diversity in Business* (London: Economist Books, 1993), 10.

60   Joseph Shannon, Ph.D., "Understanding Anger, Diagnosis and Treatment." Mind Matters Seminars (Spring 2000).

61   Related to Roy Johnson by a Ph.D. student at the University of Alberta.

62   D. Ho, "On the Concept of Face," *American Journal of Sociology* 81 (1976): 867–84; H.C. Hu, "The Chinese Concept of 'Face,'" *American Anthropologist* 46 (1944): 45–64; S. Morisaki, and W.B. Gudykunst, "Face in Japan and the U.S.," in *The Challenge of Facework: Cross-cultural and Interpersonal Issues*, ed. S. Ting-Toomey, (New York: State University of New York Press, 1994), 47–93.

63   Website: http://www.jcu.edu/philosophy/gensler/goldrule.htm.

64   Deborah Tannen, *The Argument Culture* (Toronto, ON: Random House of Canada Limited, 1998).

65   J.R.P. French, and B. Raven, "The Bases of Social Power," in *Studies in Social Power*, ed. D. Cartwright (Ann Arbor, MI: Institute for Social Research, 1959).

66   *Oxford Dictionary of Current English* (Oxford: Oxford University Press, 1992).

67   The Royal College of Physicians and Surgeons of Canada, "Report of the Working Group on Intimidation in Postgraduate Medical Education" in *The Culture of Make Believe*, ed. Derrick Jensen (New York: Context Books, 2002), 448.

68   Derrick Jensen, *The Culture of Make Believe* (New York: Context Books, 2002), 448.

69   See note 66 above.

70   William Bridges, *Managing Transitions: Making the Most of Change*, 2nd ed. (Cambridge, MA: The Perseus Books Group, 2003).

71   M. Scott Peck, *The Road Less Travelled* (New York: Touchstone, 180).

72   Matthew 7: 13–14

73   *The Vancouver Sun* (Vancouver, BC, Canada: Southam Pacific Press, January 9, 2004): C1.

74   Mihaly Csikzsentmihalyi, *Flow* (New York: HarperCollins, 1990).

75   Excerpted from *Conflict Mediation Across Cultures: Pathways and Patterns*, by David Augsburger, (Louisville, KY: John Knox Press, 1992).

76   See note 60 above.

77   Cameron Fincher, "Learning Theory and Research," in *Teaching and Learning in the College Classroom*, eds. Kenneth A. Feldman, and Michael Paulson, Ashe Reader Series, (Needham, MA: Ginn Press, 1994), 47–74.

78   Thomas S. Szasz, *The Second Sin* (London, UK: Routledge / Keegan Paul, 1973), 18.

79   Ronald Heifetz in William C. Taylor, "The Leader of the Future," *Fast Company Magazine* 25 (June 1999): 130.

80   See note 79 above.

81   Vega Zagier Roberts, "The Self-assigned Impossible Task," in *The Unconscious at Work*, eds. Anton Obholzer, and Vega Zagier Roberts (New York: Routledge, 1999), 110.

82   I. L. Janis, *Victims of Groupthink* (Boston: Houghton Mifflin, 1972), 14.

83   M. E. Turner, and A. R. Pratkanis, "Mitigating Groupthink by Stimulating Constructive Conflict," in *Conflict Management and Performance*, see note 25 above.

Index

Bold page numbers refer to charts and diagrams.

causal attribution, 67–70
  countering errors in, 196–99,
    207–8
  finding causes of behaviour in
    others, 67–70
  Fundamental Attribution Error
    (FAE), 83–86, 207–8
Challenger space shuttle launch
  as groupthink, 47, 238–40
challenges and skills
  relationship to happiness,
    167–69
charging into conflict
  as problematic, vii–ix, 49, 225,
    230
  as response to loss or threat of
    loss, 10, 24
  integrated pest management as
    model for, 101–5
  spheres of influence and, 110
  See also Conflict Trap;
    intimidation
cliques
  as erosion in Conflict Trap,
    44–45
cognitive dissonance, 78–82,
  241–43
cognitive intervention, 186
collectivist values
  benefits of collectivism, 142
  in culture, 114–15
  parable of feeding others in
    heaven and hell, 113
  values, collectivist *vs.* individualist
    values, 116–17, **126**

values continuum worksheet,
    115–16, **115–16**
  See also values
commitment. *See* investment
communication skills
  feedback, 212
  for framing the issue, 211–12,
    233
  for managing expectations,
    218–19
  for matching communication
    styles, 217–18
  for respecting difference,
    215–17
  open-ended questions, 195
  using exaggeration and
    intensifiers, 30, 219
  using in e-mail, 212
  using open-ended questions,
    195
  See also communication theory;
    communication values;
    verbal statements of
    individuals
communication theory, 90–94
  body language and voice tone,
    91–92
  conflict in, 112, 253
  cultural context for, 114–15
  filters as cultural values,
    127–28, 197–98
  filters in communication
    models, 92–93
  model of senders and receivers,
    90–94, **92**

overview of, 265, **265**

review of Conflict Trap, 248–55, **265**

review of Narrow Place, 255–56, **265**

review of Profit Track, 257–63, **265**

See also Conflict Trap; Narrow Place; Profit Track

Conflict Trap, 23–37

defined, 10–11

emotional response as fuel, 10–11, 23–24

impact of denial, 24–30

impact of despair, 30–33

impact of detachment, 34–35

impact of erosion, 44–45

impact of explosion, 47–50

impact of implosion, 45–47

importance of response to conflict, 41–42

opening and closing the Trap, 14, 55

overview in Conflict to Profit hourglass model, 248–55, **265**

overview of impacts, 36–37, **41**, 51, 236–37, 244–45, 249, **251**, 265

stages in, 23–24, 36–37, 44

studies of impacts on organizations, 42–44

verbal statements of individuals in, 168

See also Conflict to Profit hourglass model; denial in Conflict Trap; despair in Conflict Trap; detachment in Conflict Trap; erosion in Conflict Trap; explosion in Conflict Trap; implosion in Conflict Trap

confusion

as impact of denial, 265

See also denial in Conflict Trap

control

benefits of sharing control, 206

blame as loss of, 206

in culture, 114–15

in spheres of influence, 108–12, **109**

of information, 138–39, 141

values, internal *vs.* external control, 119, **126**

values continuum worksheet, 115–16, **115–16**

cooperation

in culture, 114–15

parable of feeding others in heaven and hell, 113

See also cultural roots of conflict

courage

in honest communication, 213

in Narrow Place, 155–56, 157, 256

Covey, Stephen, 111

cross-cultural communication
model. *See* communication
theory
Csikszentmihalyi, Mihaly, on
inspiration, 167, 168
Cuba, Bay of Pigs invasion
as groupthink, 237–39
cultural roots of conflict
adversarialism and argument,
134–35
benefits of difference, 230–31
cultural filters, 127–28, 197–98
difference as distinct from
conflict, 238
difference as potential conflict,
192, 199
Golden Rule and Platinum
Rule, 132–34, 260
impact on perception and
interests, 127–29
interpretations and
misinterpretations of
behaviour, 129–30
intimidation, 136–40
managing difference, 221–22
overview of, 114–15, 254–55
parable of feeding others in
heaven and hell, 113
pause time, 127–28
respecting difference, 215–17
saving face, 130–32, 143
See also values
curiosity
in Narrow Place, 150–52, 157,
195, 256

See also Profit Track: Step 2
(Find the Learning)

deception, 62–64
as intimidation, 138–39
causal attribution theory and,
68
cognitive dissonance and, 81
consequences of lying, 210–11
consequences of secrecy,
213–14
managing cognitive dissonance,
241–43
shielding, 64
short-term benefits of, 62–64
working with the lie, 198–99
See also honesty; Profit Track:
Step 3 (Build Relationships)
decision-making skills. *See*
Profit Track: Step 5 (Make
Better Decisions)
defence mechanisms, 54–61
denial, 55–57
displacement, 58–59
identification, 59–60
in psychology of conflict,
54–62
managing defensiveness,
194–96
projection, 58
rationalization, 59–60
reaction formation, 59
short-term benefits of, 54–55,
61
sublimation, 61

suppression, 57
See also Conflict Trap
denial in Conflict Trap, 24–30,
    55–57
as defence mechanism, 25–26,
    55–57
as first stage in Conflict Trap,
    23–25, 36–37, **265**
benefits of, 26
impact of, 265
types of denial, 25–30
verbal statements of
    individuals, 26, 28, 30, 55
dependency
in integrated pest management
    model of conflict, 105, 107
spheres of influence and, 110
despair in Conflict Trap, 30–33
as second stage in Conflict
    Trap, 23–24, 36–37, **265**
causal attribution and, 70
cycle of impacts of despair,
    31–33
impact of, 265
interpersonal and intra-
    personal despair, 32–33
theory of learned helplessness,
    30–33
verbal statements of
    individuals, 32
detachment in Conflict Trap,
    33–35
as final stage in Conflict Trap,
    23–24, 33–37, **265**
benefits of, 35

impact of, 265
investment as opposite of, 171
types of detachment, 34–35
verbal statements of individuals
    in, 34–35
See also investment
difference
as distinct from conflict, 238
as potential root of conflict,
    192, 199
benefits for creative process,
    230–31
respecting difference, 215–17
structuring difference, 221–22
See also cultural roots of conflict
direct *vs.* indirect communication
in culture, 114–15
managing expectations, 218–19
matching communication
    styles, 217–18
respect and dignity, 212
respecting difference, 215–17
values, direct *vs.* indirect as,
    117–19, **126**
values continuum worksheet,
    115–16, **115–16**
See also communication values
    and styles
dishonesty. *See* deception
displacement
as defence mechanism, 58–59
See also defence mechanisms
dissonance, cognitive
impact on conflict
    management, 78–82

face saving, 130–32, 143

FAE (Fundamental Attribution Error). *See* Fundamental Attribution Error

fairness issues
  acknowledgement of fairness issues in Narrow Place, 154
  impact of unfairness, 244
  impact of unmet interests on individual, **13**, 13–14
  in positions and interests, 95–96
  See also group issues; positions and interests

fatigue
  in integrated pest management model of conflict, 104, 107
  spheres of influence and, 110
  See also integrated pest management model of conflict

fear
  as consequence of unmet interests, **13**, 13–14

feedback
  and inspiration, 168–69
  as communication skill, 211–12
  as respecting difference, 215–17

feelings. *See* emotions

Festinger, Leon, cognitive dissonance, 79

fight response to conflict. See *charging into* conflict

filters
  in communication models, 92–93
  in cultural models, 127–28, 197–98

Fincher, Cameron, on learning, 193

Fisher, Roger, positions and interests, 96

flight response to conflict. See *leaning away* from conflict

folktales, parables, stories, and proverbs
  cobra with a temper, 113
  feeding others in heaven and hell, 113
  learning as telling, showing, doing, 202
  throwing sea stars, 147–48, 152

Forsyth, R., 4

framing the issue
  as communication skill, 211–12, 233

frustration
  as impact of denial, 265
  See also denial in Conflict Trap

Fundamental Attribution Error (FAE)
  as error in estimating character and context, 83–86
  managing FAE, 207–8

Glass, David, cognitive dissonance studies, 81–82

stages of insight, inspiration, and investment, 162

inspiration
 in Profit Track, **166**, 166–69, 173, 257–58, 265, **265**
 stages of insight, inspiration, and investment, 162

integrated pest management model of conflict
 as model for conflict management, 106–7, 110–11
 as system, 101–5, 107, 110, 253–54

intensifiers (*always, never,* etc.) in verbal statements, 30, 219

intentions of others. *See* causal attribution

interdependence and mutuality
 as essential part of conflict model, 5–6
 in organizations, 42
 See also collectivist values

interests in conflict, 94–100
 as essential part of conflict model, 5–6
 avoiding premature consensus seeking, 239
 deception and, 210–11
 definitions of *position, issue,* and *interest,* 96, 98
 giving and receiving apologies, 232–33
 impact of culture on, 127–29
 impact of unmet interests on individual, **13**, 13–14

in Maslow's hierarchy of needs, 6–9, **8**, 35–36, 228
 placing interests before positions, 241–43
 types of interests (practical, psychological), 6–9
 See also positions and interests

internal *vs.* external control.
 See control

interpersonal impacts of conflict.
 See Conflict Trap

interrupting in conversations (pause time), 127–28

intimidation
 as a root of conflict, 136–40, 143
 bullying and cognitive dissonance, 82
 bullying as workplace violence, 43
 definition of intimidation, 138
 dysfunctional behaviours, 138–39
 goals associated with, 140
 impact on innovation, 231
 managing cognitive dissonance, 241–43
 power as perception-based, 137–38
 social psychology of, 73–74
 verbal statements of individuals, **140**
 See also cultural roots of conflict

intra-personal impacts of
conflict. *See* Conflict Trap
investment
definition of, 170, 171
in Profit Track, **169**, 169–72,
173, 257–58, **265**
return on investment *vs.* return
on tucking, 171–72, 173,
257
stages of insight, inspiration,
and investment, 162
IPM (Integrated Pest
Management). *See* integrated
pest management model of
conflict
isolation. *See* detachment in
Conflict Trap

Jane (nurse) and Dr. Smith,
case study
in Profit Track: Step 1
(Tap the Energy), 175–88
Janis, Irving, groupthink, 237–38
Jaspers, Karl, on inevitability of
conflict, 10
Jensen, Derrick, on competition,
18–19
job security
studies of Canadian workers
rating of, 43
judgement
impact of mood on, 65–66
of causes of behaviour, 67–68

Kamloops Ministry shootings,
47–49
Kelley, H.H., on causal
attributions, 67–68
Kennedy, John F., Bay of Pigs
invasion as groupthink,
237–39
Kubler-Ross, Elizabeth, stage
theory of loss, 23–24

Lamers, William, stage theory
of loss, 23–24
leaning away from conflict
as problematic, vii–ix, 21, 49,
225, 226
as response to loss or threat of
loss, 10, 24
groupthink as, 237
in Profit Track: Step 4
(Cultivate Innovation), 230
integrated pest management as
model for, 101–5
spheres of influence and, 110
See also Conflict Trap
leaning into conflict
as preferable action, vii–ix, 21,
49, 225
integrated pest management as
model for, 101–5
See also Narrow Place; Profit
Track
learning
conflict styles as learned
responses, 14–16, 21